Hands-on help
for making your
novel stand out
and succeed

writing the
BREAKOUT
NOVEL
workbook

Donald Maass

WRITER'S DIGEST BOOKS

CINCINNATI, OHIO
www.writersdigest.com

Writing the Breakout Novel Workbook. Copyright © 2004 by Donald Maass. Manufactured in the United States of America. All rights reserved. No part of this book may be reproduced in any form or by any electronic or mechanical means including information storage and retrieval systems without permission in writing from the publisher, except by a reviewer, who may quote brief passages in a review. Published by Writer's Digest Books, an imprint of F+W Publications, Inc., 4700 East Galbraith Road, Cincinnati, Ohio 45236. (800) 289-0963. First edition.

Visit our Web site at www.writersdigest.com for information on more resources for writers.

To receive a free weekly e-mail newsletter delivering tips and updates about writing and about Writer's Digest products, register directly at our Web site at http://newsletters.fwpublications.com.

15 14 13 12 11   12 11 10 9 8

Library of Congress Cataloging-in-Publication Data

Maass, Donald
    Writing the breakout novel workbook / hands-on help for making your novel stand out and succeed / by Donald Maass.—1st ed.
        p.   cm.
    Includes index.
    ISBN-13: 978-1-58297-263-3 (pbk. : alk. paper)
    ISBN-10: 1-58297-263-X (pbk. : alk. paper)
    1. Fiction—Authorship. I. Title.

PN3365.M247   2004
808.3—dc22   2004044186
                                                                                                    CIP

Edited by Kelly Nickell
Designed by Barb Matulionis
Cover by Beckmeyer Design
Production coordinated by Robin Richie

Permissions

For Lorin Oberweger,
who made it happen.

About the Author

Donald Maass is president of the Donald Maass Literary Agency in New York, which he founded in 1980. He represents more than one hundred fiction writers and sells more than one hundred novels per year to top publishers in America and overseas. He is the author of fourteen pseudonymous novels and of the books *The Career Novelist* (Heineman) and *Writing the Breakout Novel* (Writers Digest Books). He is a past president of the Association of Authors' Representatives, Inc. (AAR).

Acknowledgments

Special thanks to the staff at the Donald Maass Literary Agency who held the fort and helped in innumerable ways during the writing of this book: Jennifer Jackson, Andrea Somberg, Rachel Vater, Soline McLain.

Thanks also to Lorin Oberweger's stalwart assistants in the organization and running of the Writing the Breakout Novel Workshops, Jason Sitzes, Roman White, and Katie Krienitz.

Thanks as well to Kelly Nickell, my supremely patient editor, for her excellent work and outstanding suggestions for the organization of this workbook; also to Scott Driscoll, Seattle writing instructor, who read an early draft of the exercises and made useful comments and suggestions.

Finally, thanks to the many participants in the Writing the Breakout Novel Workshops, whose feedback and enthusiasm have fueled me all the way.

For information about the Writing the Breakout Novel Workshops, visit www.free-expressions.com.

For information about the Donald Maass Literary Agency, visit www.maassagency.com.

Table of Contents

Part III: General Story Techniques

Appendixes

Introduction

For twenty-five years I have watched book publishing change. Conglomeration has narrowed the number of major North American publishing corporations to five. Best-seller syndrome and bottom-line thinking are more prevalent than ever. In most houses the marketing department reigns supreme, yet for all but a handful of novels promotional budgets are nil.

As profound as these changes have been, there have been even greater changes in bookselling. The number of independent bookstores has plunged. The chains have risen, only to surrender market share to online bookselling and wholesale clubs. The consolidation of mass-market paperback distributors has halved, and halved again, the typical sale of a rack-sized paperback. Backlist cedes ever more ground to frontlist.

As a literary agent who specializes in developing fiction careers, however, I believe there is one change that has more profoundly afflicted fiction writers than any other: computerized inventory tracking. By-the-numbers ordering by booksellers has turned recent sales history into the novelist's fate. But when you cannot ship more than the net sales on your last title, how can you grow? This catch-22 has thrown hundreds, possibly thousands, of fiction careers into crisis. An equal number have ended almost as soon as they were born.

Despite that gloomy picture, I am still in the business, happier, more hopeful, and more prosperous than I've ever been. Why? Because a few years ago I looked around and realized that many novelists are getting ahead—way ahead—even in this ugly publishing environment. Better still, an examination of their work showed me the reasons for their success; and these reasons are techniques that any novelist can use.

I published the results of my study in 2001 in *Writing the Breakout Novel*, a book that has been praised to me in person, on Web sites and in hundreds of e-mails and letters. Authors' groups have debated its principles. It is required reading in a number of fiction courses. I also have used what I learned in preparing that book in my developmental work with my own clients. The results have been dramatic. Stalled careers have been turned around, agency revenue is way up, and many clients tell me that they are writing with new joy.

Even better, I have found that the principles in *Writing the Breakout Novel* can be taught. My first workshop was created for the Pacific Northwest Writers Association's annual conference in the summer of 2000. I had just turned in the manuscript to my publisher. On the plane to Seattle I pulled out a yellow legal pad and worked up a dozen writing exercises that I thought would help writers see how to apply the techniques discussed in the book.

The positive feedback I received on that workshop was overwhelming. I began to lead the workshop at other conferences, expanded it, and eventually began to offer weekend-long Writing the Breakout Novel workshops in cities around the country. Participants are required to bring with them the manuscript of a novel or novel-in-progress. At the end of the workshop I ask how many participants will go home and devote months more effort to deepening their novels. Each time, every hand in the room goes up, often with rueful groans.

Writing a breakout novel is the hardest work you will ever do. But it can by done, and done by anyone with basic fiction writing skills and the patience and determination to take his fiction all the way to the highest level of achievement.

Writing the Breakout Novel Workbook includes all of the writing exercises that I lead in the Writing the Breakout Novel workshops. On the following pages you will learn how to read a novel like a writer, understanding the technique and motivation behind every choice an author makes. You will find help in making your characters more memorable, adding layers of plot and weaving them together, discovering the themes hidden in your work, using time and place more effectively, and much more. There is also a first-line brainstorming session, a pitch factory, and a tension tune up—probably the most difficult yet necessary section of the book. Do not skip that one.

In addition, before each exercise, I analyze breakout fiction that you can find on bookstore shelves right now. I draw examples of the application of breakout techniques not from the classics, but from current novels. The classics have much to teach us, as do books on writing, but I believe the "new fiction" section of the bookstore is better than any textbook. It's a university all by itself. See for yourself how contemporary authors cut through our industry's malaise and, sometimes with little help from their publishers, capture the imaginations—and dollars—of editors, critics, movie producers, prize committees, and, most important, consumers. (In order to analyze these novels, I do, at times, give away a great deal of the plot.)

Not every book I examine is a *New York Times* best-seller, but every one is a novel by an author who has broken out; that is, who has made a dramatic leap in sales over her peers or even ahead of her own previous work. As those who have heard me speak at writers conferences know, I believe that writing the breakout novel is not about creating a publishing event, but breaking *through* to new, more powerful ways of story construction.

In most cases the techniques of breakout fiction are not difficult to understand. Why, then, do not more authors use them? I believe it is because these principles generally are not yet taught in enough writing books and courses. Indeed, for me to grasp them I had to read one hundred breakout novels side by side to see what made them different. The exercises in this book will show you that once you see how to apply them, breakout fiction techniques can be utilized again and again in every novel that you write.

Before using this workbook, I recommend that you read the volume that started it all: *Writing the Breakout Novel*. Participants in my workshops find that they get more out of the experience when they are not hearing and digesting concepts like *inner conflict*, *personal stakes*, and *plot weaving* for the first time. I think you will find this to be true, too.

I also recommend that you really take the time to work through all the exercises in this book. A breakout novel cannot be written in a weekend. Talk to authors and you will find that their breakout novel probably took them three to five years to write; sometimes as long as ten. Each exercise that you do will change the novel that you are writing in multiple ways. For instance, the exercises that develop characters' personal stakes may well produce for you a list of new plot complications. Each one will require new scenes, even whole new narrative threads. Weave those together—that is, to find their *nodes of conjunction*—and you will find yourself shifting settings and the order of scenes.

At what stage of the writing process should you undertake these exercises? As I said before, in the live Writing the Breakout Novel workshops, I ask participants to bring the manuscript of a completed novel or novel-in-progress. It is useful to have a manuscript on which to focus, particularly in those exercises that deal with particular points in the story, like opening lines, a selected scene in which the motive will be reversed, and pages randomly chosen for a tension check.

Nevertheless, the exercises herein can be useful in earlier stages of novel construction, too. They will help you generate ideas as you flesh an idea into a premise, a premise into notes, notes into a rough outline, and a rough outline into the final outline for your novel. There is even an appendix at the back of this volume that will guide you through the outline process from beginning to end—whether you are at the planning stages or already have completed your manuscript.

It does not matter what type of novel you are writing: literary, mainstream, mystery, fantasy, romance, historical, or whatever. The techniques of breakout fiction are universal. They cross genre lines. They will tend to make a novel longer, though not necessarily. Stay open to what the exercises give you. If you feel overwhelmed, take a break.

You may wish to work through this book with your writing class or critique group. Discussion of the results can itself be productive. If nothing else, the work you do with this workbook will get your creative juices flowing. You will feel energized. Your unconscious will open, and story will flow. You will see new levels in your novel; make connections that you did not make before. Take lots of notes.

Then *write*. I do not care whether you work through all the exercises then revise, or whether you go back to work on your novel for a while after you complete each section. You will find the right pattern for you. I am concerned, though, about this: Do not rush. You are about to expand your mind and open up the possibilities in your current novel. Let them sink in, collide with each other, multiply, and dance. Enjoy the process. Writing fiction is supposed to be fun, remember?

Above all, aim high. Do not be satisfied with two or three positive changes for your novel; not even ten, twenty, or thirty. I expect that the exercises in this book will give you not just scores, but hundreds of new ideas. Use them all.

Do not be afraid. In the live Breakout Novel workshops, the part that produces the most resistance is the exercise I call "Tension on Every Page." Every experienced fiction writer knows that conflict is the essence of story; tension is necessary in all dialogue and in every scene. Well, everyone knows that in *theory*. Putting it into practice is something else.

As we pick pages at random and discover ways to create more tension in them, participants begin to get restless. Finding a change that puts more tension on one page that you thought was fine is a revelation. The second time, the discovery feels uncomfortable. The third time, panic can set in. It is around then that hands begin to shoot up. The question is always the same, "Can't there be *too* much tension in a novel?"

No, there can't. You think there can. You imagine you are exhausting your reader. (You certainly are exhausting yourself.) The novel can begin to feel to you over-laden, artificially juiced up, dumb. Nonstop *action* can make a novel feel pulpy, but if you closely examine the novels you most admire with a tension-sensitive eye, you will find that your favorite authors find subtle ways to infuse tension in every moment. Tension can be apprehension, a question, an inner need, uncertainty, contrasting desires, hostility hidden in humor—so many things.

When you get to this exercise, you will find that it asks you to make an improvement on every page of your novel. That's a lot of pages. That's a lot of work. Your heart will sink. I guarantee you will not want to go to all that trouble.

It is, however, utterly necessary. The big problem with 80 percent of the novels we reject at my agency is not too much tension; rather, it is too little. Indeed, not once in twenty-two years has the problem ever been too much tension. (The other 20 percent, in case you are wondering, lack truly sympathetic characters and, occasionally, have other problems.)

If you don't buy what I am saying, consider the manuscripts you read in your critique group. If you don't belong to a critique group, think about published novels. Next time you plow through a weak one, pay attention to the movement of your eyes. Watch how they skip down the page. Feel your inner impatience. *Nothing is happening*, you think. *C'mon, move it along!*

What you really mean is, *make that paragraph matter. And that one.* There is only one sure way to do that: to make it contribute to, deepen, or elaborate the conflict, problem, or complication at hand. When tension is present, the words matter. When tension is absent, our care diminishes on a curve.

I mention all this to advise you that at a certain point in working with this book you will want to put it down, work into your novel all the neat stuff you've come up with, and get it out the door to an agent. You will feel like you've done enough. You will feel proud and satisfied. After all, you have taken your fiction to levels it has never before achieved.

Resist the impulse to quit early. Do it all. Writing a breakout novel is a journey, an awakening, an education. Get the full benefit. You don't expect to get a B.A. after just one year of classes, do you? Here you're going for your Ph.D. Give yourself the space you need to achieve true mastery.

It takes time.

Once you have discovered what breakout techniques can do for your fiction, I believe that you will never want to go back to your old way of writing. Never again will you be satisfied with characters who have only one dimension. A single-layer plot will feel to you lightweight. You will put words together with a more demanding eye, pay attention to the effect of a setting on your characters' moods, think about how time has changed your characters' views of others and themselves, and more. You will be building the skills and honing the techniques that will make you more than a story hack.

In my observation, genre novelists may have the hardest time making the switch from straight ahead genre novels to breakout-level fiction. Romance writers who churn out three or more books a year, as well as book-a-year mystery novelists, often long for the freedom of the stand-alone novel. They feel frustrated: stuck at a level of sales and advances that is below their potential. I understand their frustration. This workbook is designed to reveal the techniques that will lift their writing, and sales, to new levels.

What about those embarking on their first manuscripts? They should not congratulate themselves prematurely. It takes time to master the fluid and complex art form called the novel, longer still to construct one on a breakout scale. Some have done so with their first efforts (Diana Gabaldon, Terry Brooks, and John Saul come to mind), but the fact is that writing at breakout level is demanding. It takes time, and not everyone has the necessary staying power.

Does three to five years, maybe ten, sound like a lot? If you depend on quickie advances for a living, it probably does. If that is your situation, what can you do? Keep writing your category romances, your series, or your work-for-hire novels, but set aside a disciplined period of time—a few hours a day or a few months per year—to develop your breakout novel. Get support. Make sure your agent is on your side. Let your critique group cheer you on. Keep your eye on the prize: The book that truly might make you a brand name.

If you are still early in your career, I hope that the principles in *Writing the Breakout Novel* and in *Writing the Breakout Novel Workbook* will inspire you to elevate your craft and not be satisfied with merely being good enough to get published. I hope that your measure of success will be not the gratification of getting an agent or seeing your name on a cover, but putting together a novel of real depth—of having something to say and saying it in a story with lasting power.

In fact, your prosperity as a writer may depend on it. Take a lesson from the story hacks: If you can churn out minimally acceptable fiction, you may get published but you will not become a brand name. In today's world of publishing, you may not even survive beyond your second, third, or fourth book.

I created *Writing the Breakout Novel* for many reasons. One was to show angry and frustrated midlist writers that the problems with their careers are only in small part due to corporate publishing and its dearth of support for anyone less than a best seller. The secret of success is dazzling readers—spinning them a story that they will never forget. Those readers will pretty much take care of the rest, spreading the word-of-mouth and coming back to buy each new title as soon as it comes out. You do that, don't you? It does not take a tour or a full-page ad in *The New York Times Book Review* to convince you to buy your favorite author's latest title.

Write on a breakout level and you will not feel dependent on capricious-looking promotional bucks, either. You will be secure in your fan base and in your confidence that you can keep your readers spellbound book after book.

Enjoy the journey. I have enjoyed bringing these exercises and observations to you. I hope you will enjoy using them as you create your breakout novel and all the wonderful novels that will follow it.

—Donald Maass

Part 1

CHARACTER DEVELOPMENT

From Protagonist to Hero

Why would we wish to read about characters whom we do not like? The fact is, we don't. We stick with characters we like, admire, and cheer for; we abandon characters we dislike, disapprove of, and don't care about. It's that simple. That is not to say that protagonists can't be flawed, troubled, torn, haunted, unhappy, hapless, or in any other condition that makes their situation ripe for drama and action.

But that is not the same as a protagonist who is downbeat, depressed, hopeless, bitter, stuck, or in other ways in a condition that makes us feel fed up. Have you ever known someone who couldn't shake off self-pity? How much tolerance did you have for that negativity? Not much, I bet. It is the same in novels. That is why lifting your hero above his circumstances—indeed, above himself—is so necessary.

How do you do that? It starts in your opening pages, when your protagonist gives us some reason to care; that is to say, identify with him or her. Why should we? Well, why do we feel sympathy for anyone? I believe it is because we see ourselves in them. Indeed, when we see in others ourselves *as we would like to be*, higher admiration sets in and with it deep concern and abiding hope. We want our heroes to win.

Quickly evoking that kind of identification with a protagonist is one of the secrets of breakout fiction. Most manuscripts do not manage it. It is as if authors are afraid to push too far too fast; they fear, perhaps, that if their protagonists immediately are strong they will not be credible.

Nonsense. Heroic qualities are highly desired. No one disbelieves in them. Everyone seeks them, and in their absence feels disappointed. Furthermore, it doesn't take much to endow a protagonist with qualities that we like and admire. A small show of gumption, a glimmer of humor, a dab of ironic self-regard can be enough for us to hang onto.

In Tess Gerritsen's thriller *The Surgeon*, ER surgeon Catherine Cordell has every reason to be fragile. Two years earlier she was the only victim to successfully fight off a brutal serial killer whose method involved tying women to a bed and performing surgery on them without anesthetic. But Catherine Cordell is strong. We first meet her in the emergency room:

> Dr. Catherine Cordell sprinted down the hospital corridor, the soles of her running shoes squeaking on the linoleum, and pushed through the double doors into the emergency room.
> A nurse called out: "They're in Trauma Two, Dr. Cordell!"
> "I'm there," said Catherine, moving like a guided missile straight for Trauma Two.

So far we know little of Catherine, yet we are drawn to her. Why? I think it is the strength inherent in the phrase "moving like a guided missile." This woman is focused. She knows what she is doing. That becomes even more evident a page later as she prepares to operate on a hit-and-run victim right in the ER rather than the more usual OR:

> "All rooms are in use. We can't wait." Someone tossed her a paper cap. Swiftly she tucked in her shoulder-length red hair and tied on a mask. A scrub nurse was already holding out a sterile surgical gown. Catherine slipped her arms into the sleeves and thrust her hands into gloves. She had no time to scrub, no time to hesitate. She was in charge, and John Doe was crashing on her . . .
> "Where's the blood?" she called out.
> "I'm checking with the lab now," said a nurse.
> "Ron, you're the first assist," Catherine said to Littman. She glanced around the room and focused on a pasty-faced young man standing by the door. His nametag read: Jeremy Barrows, Medical Student. "You," she said. "You're second assist!"
> Panic flushed in the young man's eyes. "But—I'm only in my second year. I'm just here to—"
> "Can we get another surgical resident in here?"
> Littman shook his head. "Everyone's spread thin. They've got a head injury in Trauma One and a code down the hall."
> "Okay." She looked back at the student. "Barrows, you're it. Nurse, get him a gown and gloves."
> "What do I have to do? Because I really don't know—"
> "Look, you want to be a doctor? Then *glove up!*"

Catherine's command of the situation is hard to resist. In a short time, Gerritsen has us cheering for this gutsy doctor. Catherine's bravura is a facade, though. We soon learn that the trauma of her brush with the serial killer known as The Surgeon has left her brittle and afraid. Indeed, when a new killer begins to imitate *modus operandi* of The Surgeon, so tightly controlled and anxious is her mental state that the police suspect Catherine herself. However, thanks to the strength with which Gerritsen already has invested her, we never doubt her sanity.

What about a protagonist who is not demonstrating heroism as we first meet her, but instead necessarily displays unattractive qualities? That is the challenge faced by Ann Packer at the beginning of her delicately observed literary novel *The Dive From Clausen's Pier*. The beginning of this story finds Packer's heroine, Carrie Bell, a year out of college and discontent with her familiar life and friends in Madison, Wisconsin. She is weary of her boyfriend of eight-and-a-half years, Mike, and quickly alerts the reader that an "unraveling" is looming between them.

All of this is perfectly human, yet Carrie's sullen mood in the opening scene, a Memorial Day picnic at Clausen's Reservoir, easily could make her difficult to like. This is an especially dangerous opening moment for Packer because in the novel's inciting event, Mike soon will dive from a pier into water unexpectedly shallow, break his neck, and wind up in the hospital in a coma. This circumstance guiltily ties Carrie to Madison when she would rather leave, a powerful inner conflict that infuses the novel with its driving tension. And yet in the novel's opening scene Carrie plainly is in a sour mood about her boyfriend:

> The parking lot was only half full, and we found a spot in the shade. From behind my seat I unloaded a grocery bag of chips and hamburger buns while he opened the hatch. He wore long madras shorts and a green polo shirt, and as I watched his movements, the quick, effortless way he lifted the beer-laden cooler, I thought about how that easy strength of his had thrilled me once, and how it didn't anymore.

Ouch! How are we to feel sympathy for this hard young woman? Especially later, after a tragedy incapacitates her, to all appearances, perfectly likeable and loving boyfriend? Packer is aware of this difficulty. She addresses it first by giving Carrie nothing bad to say about Mike. Theirs is just a relationship that has run its course. Carrie is a young woman yearning to spread her wings and fly away from her hometown. Who cannot understand that?

Next, Packer makes Carrie aware of her disaffection and its essential unfairness:

> I could feel everyone looking at me: Rooster, Stu, Bill, Christine—even Jamie. Looking and thinking, *Come on, Carrie, give the guy a break*.

Here is Packer's secret: It is Carrie's keen awareness that she is in an ill mood that rescues our opinion of her. She knows that her friends can see it. She has the honesty and grace to observe their looks of reproach and not to defend herself.

The words hero *and* heroine *sound impossibly grand, invoking wartime bravery and inhuman fortitude.*

In the hands of a less careful novelist, Carrie would be bitter about Mike, sarcastic toward him, ignore her friends, and indulge her dark feelings. We would find it impossible to sympathize with her. Packer takes a more balanced approach and leaves us with the feeling that Carrie is not mean-spirited, just a young woman who is trapped by her circumstances. That is a situation with which anyone can sympathize.

A still more subtle demonstration of opening strength can be found in one of Alan Furst's gripping World War II espionage novels, *The Polish Officer*. Furst's handling point of view in this novel borders on objective. At first his hero, Captain Alexander de Milja, is seen as if through the lens of a camera: from the outside only. It is September, 1939. As Germans invade Warsaw, de Milja supervises the burning of documents at the headquarters of Military Intelligence. One by one, de Milja watches the immolation of maps, plans, surveys, etc:

> Drawer 4088: Istanbul by street. Istanbul harbor with wharf warehouse numbers. Surveyor's elevations of Üsküdar with shore batteries in scale. Bosphorus with depths indicated. Black Sea coast: coves, inlets, bridges, roads. Sea of Marmara coast: cloves, inlets, bridges, roads.
>
> In the fire.
>
> Drawer 4098: Timber company surveys, 1935–1938, streams, logging paths, old and new growth trees, drainage, road access, river access. For forests in Poland, Byelorussia, and the Ukraine.
>
> "That series aside please," de Milja said.
>
> The clerk, startled, whirled and stared, then did as he was ordered. The timber surveys were stacked neatly atop maps, drawn in fine detail, of the Polish railway system.

De Milja's sparing a set of forest surveys from the flames may not seem particularly notable, but there is something calm, deliberate, and purposeful in de Milja's order to set them aside. We suspect that something is at work under the surface—something strong. As the action unfolds in the following pages we realize what it is. De Milja has grasped his country's essential situation: The Germans will conquer Poland. Maps, surveys, and plans will be needed for the resistance into which he is later recruited.

De Milja's intelligence, deliberate care, and ability to face a dawning reality set him apart. He has unusual strength. Even though Furst has not yet taken us inside his hero's head and heart, we already admire him for his actions.

How do you hint at the heroism of your protagonist in the opening pages of your current manuscript? How do you make us care? What about this character will we find admirable and attractive? More to the point, what is it that *you* find likable about this character *at this precise moment?* Figure that out, and you will be most of the way toward making us, your readers, care as much about your protagonist as you do.

Adding Heroic Qualities

Step 1: Who are your personal heroes? *Write down the name of one.*

_____

_____

_____

_____

_____

Step 2: What makes this person a hero or heroine to you? What is his or her greatest heroic quality? *Write that down.*

_____

_____

_____

_____

_____

Step 3: What was the moment in time in which you first became aware of this quality in your hero/heroine? *Write that down.*

_____

_____

Step 4: Assign that quality to your protagonist. Find a way for he or she actively to demonstrate that quality, even in a small way, in his or her first scene. *Make notes, starting now.*

_____

_____

> **!**
>
> ● **NOTE:**
> The words *hero* and *heroine* sound impossibly grand, invoking wartime bravery and inhuman fortitude. Actually, ask most people what heroic attributes they admire and you will get a list of qualities that any of us might have: belief in others, the ability to overcome one's own flaws, conviction in the face of opposition, acting in spite of misgivings, steadfast love, moral integrity, tenacity, generosity, a sense of plentitude, unconditional love, and so on.
>
> Such qualities are not seen every day, but they also are not found only on battlefields or in arctic wastes. The actions that reveal them can be quite small. Adding such an action to the introduction of your protagonist will have a huge impact on reader identification. Even if your protagonist's opening circumstances are ordinary or even awful, we need at least a small reason to like, to care about, and to hope for this character.

Follow-up work: Prior to the climactic sequence of your novel, find six more points at which your protagonist can demonstrate, even in a small way, some heroic quality.

_____

_____

_____

_____

_____

Conclusion: So many protagonists who I meet in manuscripts start out as ordinary Joe's or Jane's. Most stories build toward enormous heroic actions at the end, which is fine, but what about the beginning? What is there to make me care? Often, not enough. Demonstrate special qualities right away, and you will immediately turn your protagonist into a hero or heroine, a character whose outcome matters.

Multidimensional Characters

One-dimensional characters hold limited interest for us because they are limited as human beings. They lack the complexity that makes real-life people so fascinating. In well-constructed fiction, a multidimensional character will keep us guessing: *What is this person going to do, say, or think next?* Furthermore, we are more likely to identify with them—that is, to see ourselves in them. Why? Because there is more of them to see.

Eoin Colfer's young adult novel *Artremis Fowl* was billed as a "dark Harry Potter," a description that intrigued me. I grew even more interested when *Artemis Fowl* hit *The New York Times* best-seller list. The novel's twelve-year-old protagonist, I had read, was a criminal mastermind. How could a novel with such a dark protagonist be so popular?

Fatherless Artemis Fowl, the scion of a famous Irish criminal family, is indeed diabolically clever and bent on a wicked scheme: restoring the family fortunes by obtaining the gold that is set aside to ransom any fairy, should one ever fall into the hands of the Mud People; that is to say, humans.

If that was all there was to Artemis, he would indeed be difficult to like. But Colfer does not expect us to sympathize with a one-dimensional, amoral adolescent. Early in the novel Colfer begins dropping hints that there is more to Artemis than that; indeed, that he is a boy with a range of feelings like any other, as we are shown when Artemis visits his mentally frail and bedridden mother:

> He knocked gently on the arched double doors.
> "Mother? Are you awake?"
> Something smashed against the other side of the door. It sounded expensive.
> "Of course I'm awake! How can I sleep in this blinding glare?"

Artemis ventured inside. An antique four-poster bed threw shadowy spires in the darkness, and a pale sliver of light poked through a gap in the velvet curtains. Angeline Fowl sat hunched on the bed, her pale limbs glowing white in the gloom.

"Artemis, darling. Where have you been?"

Artemis sighed. She recognized him. That was a good sign.

"School trip, Mother. Skiing in Austria."

"Ah, skiing," crooned Angeline. "How I miss it. Maybe when your father returns."

Artemis felt a lump in his throat. Most uncharacteristic.

Artemis is trying to deny his longing for his father and his grief over his mother's condition, but Colfer makes sure that his readers do not miss them. Later on, Artemis succeeds in capturing a fairy, Holly Short, a high tech-equipped officer in LEPrecon, the elite branch of the Lower Elements Police. Artemis lays a deadly trap for Holly's superior officer, Commander Root, aboard a whaling boat, which blows up. Root is nearly killed; meanwhile, Holly suffers (or appears to) in captivity. Artemis gloats over his success, but mixed with his glee are other emotions:

Artemis leaned back in the study's leather swivel chair, smiling over steepled fingers. Perfect. That little explosion should cure those fairies of their cavalier attitude. Plus there was one less whaler in the world. Artemis Fowl did not like whalers. There were less objectionable ways to produce oil by-products. . . .

Artemis consulted the basement surveillance monitor. His captive was sitting on her cot now, head in hands. Artemis frowned. He hadn't expected the fairy to appear so . . . human. Until now, they had merely been quarry. Animals to be hunted. But now, seeing one like this, in obvious discomfort—it changed things.

Artemis Fowl believes himself to be single-mindedly focused on his goal of extorting fairy gold, but again and again his author shows us that Artemis has other, more human sides. These added dimensions make Colfer's hero a complex criminal mastermind—and one for whom we can feel sympathy.

Plot events themselves can provoke the emergence of a new side of a character. Ann B. Ross's fourth novel, *Miss Julia Speaks Her Mind*, scores a hit with its portrait of Julia Springer, a wealthy, sixty-ish lady in a small North Carolina town. Miss Julia is a proud, frugal, orderly banker's widow. She is well acquainted with the ways of a small town. When her dead husband's nine-year-old bastard son is dumped on her doorstep one day, Miss Julia is mortified—and knows that gossip about this development will ruin her life. She is terrified. What to do? After considering her options, Miss Julia makes a surprising choice:

Plot events themselves can provoke the emergence of a new side of a character.

"Here's what I'm going to do," I went on, feeling my way as I talked. "The first thing I'm *not* going to do is call any of those child welfare agencies. Keeping this child is my cross the bear, even thought I don't deserve it, and it's the only way to get back at Wesley Lloyd. He hid this child for a decade, but I'm not hiding him. And I'm not going to hide my face, either. None of this is my fault, so why should I act like it is? There's not a reason in the world. They're going to talk no matter what I do, so I'm going to give them something to talk about. I'm going to hold my head up if it kills me, and I'm not going to protect Wesley Lloyd Springer from the consequences. This is his son, and everybody's going to know it, without any guessing. I'm going to flaunt this child before the whole town, so let the cookies crumble!"

Miss Julia's suddenly stiff backbone becomes not only a reason for reader sympathy, but a plot spine as well. With a sharp eye, and sharper tongue, Miss Julia sets about transcending the town gossips and inheritance grabbers—mostly.

This new character dimension is not the first that Ross reveals. Although Miss Julia claims to be tenderhearted when it comes to children, there is little maternal warmth in evidence as she regards her husband's illegitimate son:

> Not hearing any movement behind me, I turned to see Lillian's arms around the little bastard, his head against her white nylon uniform. He turned loose the grocery sack long enough to wipe the sleeve of one arm across his running nose, smearing his glasses even more. It was enough to turn your stomach.

Later in the novel, after little Lloyd Jr., has been taken away by this televangelist uncle, Rev. Vernon Pucket, to be reunited, Miss Julia is told, with his mother, who is going to a hairdressing school in Raleigh, Ross reveals another side of Miss Julia:

> Oh, there were a lot of things I could've done and should've done, and now I had to live with it all. I got up sometime in the middle of the night and walked across the hall to little Lloyd's room. The empty bed made me realize how empty my house was, and maybe my life, as well.
>
> I was just a selfish old woman with nothing but a few million dollars to her name. No husband, no children, nothing to look forward to but more of the same. Even the thought of writing checks and buying things couldn't lift my spirits.
>
> I cried. Sitting there in Little Lloyd's room, not a light on in the house, an old, slightly blue-haired woman who'd thought of nothing but herself all her life. Yes, I cried.

Miss Julia's motivation changes from protecting herself to protecting little Lloyd Jr. Ross gives her a maternal side, after all.

How many sides of your current protagonist do you reveal? I know what you are thinking: *My hero is multidimensional. My hero is* complex! But let me ask you: Is he complex and multidimensional only in your mind, or actually on the page?

Take a careful look at your manuscript. On which pages, exactly, do you specifically unlock extra sides of your protagonist's personality? Can you highlight the passages? How many of them are there? List the pages numbers. No, really, don't just read this paragraph and congratulate yourself. Do it for real. Scroll through your manuscript, highlight, and count.

Come on now, did you really count? Okay. Now, how many extra dimensions of your protagonist do you actively show? If you cheated and avoided counting, I promise you, there are not as many as you think. If you really counted, now is the time to increase the number of dimensions that your hero has. The more extra work you do, the more involving your novel will be.

EXERCISE

Opening Extra Character Dimensions

Step 1: What is your protagonist's *defining quality*; that is, how would anyone describe your protagonist? What trait is most prominent in his personality? What kind of person is she? *Write that down.*

_____

_____

Step 2: Objectively speaking, what is the opposite of that quality? *Write that down.*

_____

_____

Step 3: Write a paragraph in which your protagonist actively demonstrates the *opposite* quality that you wrote down in step two. *Start writing now.*

_____

_____

_____

_____

_____

● **NOTE:**
Many workshop participants want to incorporate the resulting paragraph in their novel. Why? It shows a character's conflicting sides. Such a *multidimensional character* is more involving to read about. He is more realistic, more human, and, incidentally, gives your reader more opportunities for identification with him.

Follow-up work: Define a *secondary character quality*; write down its opposite; write a paragraph in which this character demonstrates the *opposite* secondary quality. In the same way, open third and fourth additional dimensions to your protagonist.

_____

_____

Conclusion: As I mentioned in the introduction, the second most common reason agents reject manuscripts (after low tension) is poorly developed protagonists. Now that you have opened extra dimensions to your hero, you will have an easier time building into this character a fundamental and full-blown *inner conflict*.

Inner Conflict

A step beyond the technique of adding character dimensions is investing your protagonist with two goals, needs, wants, longings, yearnings, or desires that are in direct opposition to each other. Wanting two things that are mutually exclusive means having inner conflict, being torn in two directions, and that is what makes a character truly memorable.

Inner conflict does not need to be limited to your protagonist. Any character can be conflicted. The prologue of Richard Russo's Pulitzer Prize-winning *Empire Falls* tells the story of C.B. Whiting, scion of the industrial dynasty that rules over the central Maine town of Empire Falls. As a young man, Charles longs to escape and indeed manages to linger in Mexico for almost a decade, but in the end a more powerful destiny tugs him back to Maine:

> For his part, Charles Beaumont Whiting, sent away from home as a boy when he would have preferred to stay, now had no more desire to return from Mexico than his mother had to return from Europe, but when summoned he sighed and did as he was told, much as he had always done. It wasn't as if he hadn't known that the end of his youth would arrive, taking with it his travels, his painting, and his poetry. There was never any question that Whiting and Sons Enterprises would one day devolve to him, and while it occurred to him that returning to Empire Falls and taking over the family business might be a violation of his personal destiny as an artist, there didn't seem to be any help for it.

In other words, C.B. is torn between bohemian freedom in Mexico and financial security at home in Maine, and he chooses the latter. But that is not the end of his inner conflict. Although he appears to accept this destiny, C.B. begins to build himself a hacienda (in Maine?) across the river from Empire Falls. Later, the arrival of a decomposed moose among the river trash that regularly washes ashore by his hacienda-in-progress provokes in C.B. a personal crisis:

Now, down by the river, his thoughts disturbed, perhaps, by the proximity of rotting moose, he began to doubt that building this new house was a good idea. The hacienda, with its adjacent artist's studio, was surely an invitation to his former self, the Charles Beaumont Whiting—Beau, his friends called him there— he'd abandoned in Mexico. Worse, it was for this younger, betrayed self that he was building the hacienda.

His inner conflict isn't over. C.B.'s conflicted spirit eventually seeks relief in an affair with a pretty young worker at his family's shirt factory—fragile Grace, the mother of the novel's protagonist, Miles Roby. This affair shadows Miles's childhood and leads C.B.'s iron-willed wife, Francine, the novel's antagonist, eventually to reel in and dominate not only Grace but Miles himself throughout his adult years.

Thus, the powerful inner conflict that Russo builds for C.B. Whiting spreads to affect generations beyond C.B.'s. Indeed, it nearly causes the destruction of Empire Falls itself.

Is there any character in contemporary fiction more conflicted than Laurell K. Hamilton's wildly successful series heroine Anita Blake? Anita is a St. Louis "animator," or raiser of the dead. (Why raise the dead, you ask? Among other reasons, to question them about the details of their wills.) She also works as a court-sanctioned vampire killer; vampires being, in Hamilton's alternate world, real and endowed with certain limited rights.

Anita Blake is tough, but in contrast has a soft spot for vampires and other were-creatures. Indeed, her series-long love interest is the French master vampire Jean-Claude. As the series progresses she becomes engaged, then unengaged, to a junior high school teacher and alpha werewolf of the local pack, Richard Zeeman. Indeed, it is Richard who draws Anita to Tennessee in *Blue Moon*, the novel that finally brought Hamilton to *The New York Times* paperback best-seller list. Richard has been arrested in the small town of Myerton, accused of rape. It is up to Anita to exonerate him before a rare "blue moon," only five days away, sends Richard on an uncontrollable feeding binge.

Anita's inner conflict—enforcing the law vs. sympathy (indeed, lust) for the creatures she is meant to hunt—would alone be enough, you would think, to energize this steamy and complex novel. But Hamilton does not stop there. Richard is her ex-fiancé at this point, but she still has strong feelings for him even though she has firmly chosen Jean-Claude for reasons we learn at the beginning of the novel:

Richard was an alpha werewolf. He was head of the local pack. It was his only serious flaw. We'd broken up after I'd seen him eat somebody. What I'd seen had sent me running to Jean-Claude's arms. I'd run from the werewolf to the vampire. Jean-Claude was Master of the City of Saint Louis. He was definitely not the more human of the two. I know there isn't a lot to choose from between a bloodsucker and a flesh-eater, but at least after Jean-Claude finished feeding, there weren't chunks between his fangs. A small distinction but a real one.

There you go: another example of how flossing might have saved a relationship. As I said, Anita is torn between two lovers, so much so that she thinks of them all as a triumvirate: master vampire, Ulfric (wolf king), and necromancer. For Anita, being torn in two directions is not just a romantic dilemma but a condition of life in her (well, Hamilton's) universe:

> But I wasn't riding to the rescue because Richard was our third. I could admit to myself, if to no one else, that I still loved Richard. Not the same way I loved Jean-Claude, but it was just as real. He was in trouble, and I would help him if I could. Simple. Complicated. Hurtful.
>
> I wondered what Jean-Claude would think of me dropping everything to go rescue Richard. It didn't really matter. I was going, and that was that. But I did spare a thought for how that might make my vampire lover feel. His heart didn't always beat, but it would still break.
>
> Love sucks. Sometimes it feels good. Sometimes it's just another way to bleed.

In addition to all that, Anita is conflicted about the very justice system that she serves, as Hamilton reminds us as Anita considers the news that idealistic Richard is relying on the truth alone to save him from the rape charge:

> It sounded like something Richard would say. There was more than one reason why we'd broken up. He clung to ideals that hadn't even worked when they were in vogue. Truth, justice and the American way certainly didn't work within the legal system. Money, power, and luck were what worked. Or having someone on your side that was part of the system.

Do you think that Anita has enough inner conflict? Hamilton does not. On top of everything else, Anita is a committed Christian. Each new adventure deepens her conflict between her beliefs and her actions, and *Blue Moon* is no exception. Anita's many inner conflicts are a primary reason that she is so memorable. That Hamilton continually deepens those conflicts almost guarantees that her readers will come back book after book. And so they do.

The narrator of Alice Sebold's literary best seller, *The Lovely Bones*, Susie Salmon, has a conflict that can never be reconciled. As the novel opens, fourteen-year-old Susie takes a shortcut through a cornfield on her way home from school. She is lured by a neighbor into an underground room, raped, and murdered. From heaven she looks down upon her family, her friends, and her murderer, observing their lives in the aftermath of her death.

Inner conflict is what makes a character truly memorable.

Susie's conflict? Sebold expresses it succinctly early in her novel as Susie describes her heaven (everyone has their own version), which is somewhat like her junior high school, but without teachers. Her textbooks are *Seventeen*, *Glamour*, and *Vogue*. She lives in a duplex with a roommate, but after a time the pleasures of paradise pall, as she explains to her intake counselor, Franny:

> Eventually I began to desire more. What I found strange was how much I desired to know what I had not known on Earth. I wanted to be allowed to grow up.
> "People grow up by living," I said to Franny. "I want to live."

Franny states, "That's out." Susie's desire to live despite being dead is a powerful inner conflict that infuses and informs the remainder of Sebold's luminous novel. Susie's hopeless yearning is felt again and again as she watches her father come apart with grief, her mother escape into an affair, her sister grow and eventually marry, and her baby brother struggle with the legacy of a sister whose absence is in itself an impossible-to-ignore presence. Susie misses her dog. She envies her younger sister's first kiss, her first sex, her first experiment with makeup.

Tasting the adolescence that for her was cut short only makes Susie restless in heaven:

> I did begin to wonder what the word *heaven* meant. I thought, if this were heaven, truly heaven, it would be where my grandparents lived. Where my father's father, my favorite of them all, would lift me up and dance with me. I would feel only joy and have no memory, no cornfield and no grave.
> "You can have that," Franny said to me. "Plenty of people do."
> "How do you make the switch?" I asked.
> "It's not as easy as you might think," she said. "You have to stop desiring certain answers."
> "I don't get it."
> "If you stop asking why you were killed instead of someone else, stop investigating the vacuum left by your loss, stop wondering what everyone left on Earth is feeling," she said, "you can be free. Simply put, you have to give up on Earth."
> This seemed impossible to me.

It would be easy for Sebold's novel to lose tension. Objectively speaking, little happens back on Earth. Her murderer is never caught. Her family comes apart, then back together, no more remarkably than any other family. Her father and the boy who loved her experience grief (see Turning Points in chapter eighteen), but how is that any different than most lives? Yet Sebold keeps Susie's longing powerful and ever-present. Susie's inner conflict is *the* central conflict of the novel: sweet, sad, and full of love of life and those lucky enough to live it out.

Sebold builds an entire story on nothing more than this simple yearning: to grow up and be alive. *The Lovely Bones* demonstrates the power of inner conflict not just to carry a novel, but to carry us deep into the sorrow and joy of human existence.

Is the protagonist of your current manuscript beset by an inner conflict? How clearly is that expressed? What actions does it result in? What about other characters in the novel? Use this exercise to help you develop this inner conflict, make it stronger, and give it expression—and to make your protagonist, and other characters, as memorable as they can be.

Creating Inner Conflict

Step 1: Thinking about your protagonist in the novel as a whole, what it is that your protagonist *most* wants? *Write that down.*

_____

_____

Step 2: Write down whatever is the opposite of that.

_____

_____

Step 3: How can your protagonist want both of those things simultaneously? What would cause your protagonist to want them both? What steps would he actively take to pursue those conflicting desires? *Make notes, starting now.*

_____

_____

> **! NOTE:**
> Genuine inner conflict will make your protagonist memorable. How? Look at it this way: When we say a character is memorable, what do we mean? Simply that we are thinking about that character after the story is over. What causes us to do that? Inner conflict. When it is powerfully portrayed, it lingers beyond the last page. Readers seek to resolve it. They will mentally talk to your heroine, trying to make her happy. They will imagine scenes in which things come out better for your poor protagonist. Trigger that response in your readers, and you will have succeeded in making your character memorable.

Follow-up work: Work on sharpening the contrast between these opposing desires. Make them mutually exclusive. How can you ensure that if your protagonist gets one, he cannot get the other? *Make notes.*

_____

_____

Conclusion: In creating genuine inner conflict, it is not enough simply to create inner turmoil. True inner conflict involves wanting two things that are mutually exclusive. It is most effective when it tears your protagonist, or any character, in two opposite directions.

Larger-Than-Life Character Qualities

Zingers: Oh, how I wish I could snap them off as needed! Unfortunately, they tend to pop into my mind about an hour after I need them. Happily, one of the pleasures of novel writing is that an hour later is not too late. Until the manuscript is turned in, there's plenty of time to slot those zingers in.

In Jodi Picoult's morality tale *Salem Falls*, Addie Peabody owns a diner in the small New Hampshire town that gives the novel its name. Addie is unwillingly wooed by the town sheriff, Wes Courtemanche. One evening Wes is pressing his attentions on her. He asks why she stays at the diner and if she could be anything in the world, what would she be? Addie answers: (1) She stays at the diner because she likes it; and (2) if she could be anything, she would be a mother. The last answer pleases Wes, and so he moves in for the kill:

> Wes slid his free arm around her waist and grinned, his teeth as white as the claw of moon above them. "You must be reading my mind, honey, since that brings me right to my third question." He pressed his lips over her ear, his words vibrating against her skin. "How do you like your eggs in the morning?"
>
> *He's too close*. Addie's breath knotted at the back of her throat and every inch of her skin broke out in a cold sweat. "Unfertilized!" she answered. . . .

Zing! Addie's barb does not entirely discourage Wes, but it does endow Addie with quick-wittedness and pluck. Addie says on short notice the kinds of things we wish we could say. Whether her author invents these darts with equal dispatch or after long mulling I cannot say. Whatever her method, Picoult uses the power of the out-of-bounds speech to build larger-than-life characters whom we cannot help but admire.

Another example—actually many examples—of verbal zingers revealing the pain and conflict in relationships can be found in Susan Wiggs's multi-layered contemporary romance *The You I Never Knew*. The novel's backstory reveals that Seattle graphic artist Michelle Turner left Crystal City, Montana, as well as her movie star father, Gavin Slade, under strained circumstances, as we see when she returns to Montana sixteen years later with her sixteen-year-old son:

> Her stomach constricted nervously as they walked along the front of the bleacher in search of Gavin Slade. She'd see him soon. Good grief, what would they say to each other?
> Their last face-to-face conversation had not been pleasant.
> *"I'm pregnant, Daddy."*
> Gavin had gone all stony-eyed. Then he'd said, "I'm not surprised. Your mother was careless, too."
> "My *father* was careless," she'd shot back.

Did you ever hold a grudge against a member of the opposite sex? You know, the creep who spent the night and never called again? The girl in high school who went all the way with some handsome bad boy but wouldn't let you, Mr. Nice Guy, lay a hand on her? (Nothing like that ever happened to me, nooooo.)

Did you ever wish that you could get back at the object of your grudge in some unforgettable way? Janet Evanovich's series protagonist, bounty hunter Stephanie Plum, does just that in the opening pages of her debut novel, *One for the Money*. The bad boy in this case is Joe Morelli, who took advantage of young Stephanie (who willingly accepted his advances, it must be said) on several occasions in their hometown of Trenton, New Jersey. As a sixteen-year-old, Stephanie, a virgin, is warned to stay away from Joe by her best friend, Mary Lou Molnar:

> "He specializes in virgins! The brush of his fingertips turns virgins into slobbering mush."
> Two weeks later, Joe Morelli came into the bakery where I worked every day after school, Tasty Pastry, on Hamilton. He bought a chocolate-chip cannoli, told me he'd joined the navy, and charmed the pants off me four minutes after closing, on the floor of Tasty Pastry, behind the case filled with chocolate éclairs.
> The next time I saw him, I was three years older. I was on my way to the mall, driving my father's Buick, when I spotted Morelli standing in front of Giovichinni's Meat Market. I gunned the big V-8 engine, jumped the curb, and clipped Morelli from behind, bouncing him off the front right fender. I stopped the car and got out to assess the damage. "Anything broken?"
> He was sprawled on the pavement, looking up my skirt. "My leg."

"Good," I said. Then I turned on my heel, got into the Buick, and drove to the mall.

How many times have *you* run over an ex-lover with your car? None? I thought so. How many times have you *wanted* to? Plenty? Yeah, I knew that too. What makes Stephanie Plum a larger-than-life character is that she does what the rest of us would never do.

A larger-than-life action can be even more effective when it is something that the character involved does not *want* to do. In the last chapter, I discussed Laurell K. Hamilton's series heroine, vampire hunter Anita Blake. Anita hunts and kills law-breaking vampires; despite that, her long-term lover is the Master vampire Jean-Claude. Anita has steamy sex with Jean-Claude, yet does not fulfill Jean-Claude's desire to truly go "all the way," as we see early in *Blue Moon*:

> He tried to turn my head to one side, nuzzling at my neck. I turned my face into his, blocking him. "No blood, Jean-Claude."
>
> He went almost limp on top of me, face buried in the rumpled sheets. "Please, *ma petite.*"
>
> I pushed at his shoulder. "Get off of me."
>
> He rolled onto his back, staring at the ceiling, carefully not looking at me. "I can enter every orifice of your body with every part of me, but you refuse me the last bit of yourself."
>
> I got off the bed carefully, not sure my knees were steady. "I am not food," I said.
>
> "It is so much more than feeding, *ma petite.* If only you would allow me to show you how very much more."
>
> I grabbed the pile of blouses and started taking them off the hanger and folding them in the suitcase. "No blood; that is the rule."

No means no to Anita Blake, obviously, particularly where it involves further blurring the lines between her mortal self and the vampires she both hates and loves. As Hamilton's series progresses Anita gains magical powers and authority over other creatures, but a girl has to have some limits, right?

But limits are made to be exceeded, and that is what happens toward the end of *Blue Moon* when one of Anita's vampire helpers, Jean-Claude's old friend and facially scarred second-in-command, Asher, is fatally wounded. There is only one thing that will save him: blood. Anita has vowed never to let a vampire feed on her, but Asher is near death. And so . . .

> I put my right wrist, encased in white bandages, in front of his mouth. "Take my blood."
>
> "To drink from you is to give you power over any of us. I do not want to be your slave any more than I already am."
>
> I was crying, tears so hot they burned. "Don't let Colin kill

you. Please, please!" I held him against me and whispered, "Don't leave us, Asher." I felt Jean-Claude all those miles away. I felt his panic at the thought of losing Asher. "Don't leave us, not now that we've found you again. *Tu es beau, mon amour. Tu me fais craquer.*"

He actually smiled. "I shatter your heart, eh?"

I kissed his cheek, kissed his face, and cried, hot tears against the harsh scars of his face. "*Je t'embrasse partout. Je t'embrasse partout.* I kiss you all over, *mon amour.*"

He stared up at me. "*Je te bois des yeux.*"

"Don't drink me with your eyes, damn it, drink me with your mouth." I tore the bandages away from my right wrist with my teeth and put my bare, warm flesh against his cold lips.

He whispered, "*Je t'adore.*" Fangs sank into my wrist.

Thus, in an act of self-sacrifice (see High Moments in chapter twenty), Anita does something that previously she would never, ever have done. Larger-than-life actions like these make Hamilton's Anita Blake the kind of heroine that readers return to again and again. She exceeds her boundaries in ever bigger ways.

Harshest of limits are those we impose upon ourselves in our heads. Our inner censors probably are more powerful than any censorship board any dictatorship could devise. Breaking through to new ways of thinking, however, is the foundation of growth. To change, we must first change our minds.

Karen Joy Fowler's short stories, teaching at the Clarion workshop, and general association with the science fiction community leaves many thinking that she is a writer only of speculative fiction. Fowler's subtle, finely-crafted novels are far more than that, however, as she proved with her third novel, *Sister Noon*, a study of character transformation set in turn-of-the-century San Francisco. A critical success, the book also was a finalist for the PEN/ Faulkner Award.

Sister Noon's heroine is conventional and colorless Lizzie Hayes, a forty-year-old spinster who is the treasurer of the Ladies Relief and Protection Society Home, an orphanage. With tiny, careful strokes, Fowler paints a picture of a woman whose world and personality constrain her as tightly as a Victorian corset. Passive and biddable as a child, Lizzie was prone to over-stimulation from books and sermons. Childish romanticism gave way to adolescent melancholia, expressed through diets and music. Even so, Lizzie abided by her mother's strictures, down to the last hated pea. A self-conscious adult, she gains strength from her religious faith and unswerving adherence to her chosen course.

Lizzie's life begins to change when an odd orphan girl, Jenny Ijub, is delivered to the Brown Arc (as the orphanage is nicknamed) by a colorful and scandalous San Francisco denizen named Mary Ellen Pleasant. Through Mrs. Pleasant, Lizzie is drawn into the orbit of the "House of Mystery" of Thomas and Teresa Bell, who puzzlingly "employ" Mrs. Pleasant as housekeeper, even though she clearly is wealthier than they are. Lizzie's first visit to the house hints at her inner longing for change:

> Sometime after Lizzie finished her tea [*See Low Tension Fixes Part I: The Problem With Tea in chapter twenty-two*], Mrs. Pleasant asked if she was happy with her life. She should have said yes. She rarely felt unhappy. Daily association with the downtrodden kept her keenly aware of her advantages. She knew the pleasure of doing good. She knew moments of great joy, often in church during the high notes of particular hymns. She would open her mouth to sing them, and her heart would leap with her voice up to where the sunlight filtered through the colored glass, igniting the motes of dust above her head. So many pleasures. The sight of red tulips. The little buzz of life in the grass. A letter with her name and foreign stamps. The smell of rain. The taste of pomegranate jelly. Reading novels in the afternoon, with no corset and her shoes off and her feet on a chair. . . . And yet she answered that she was not.

Through séances, drink, and exposure to the confusing mysteries of the Bell household, with its unnumbered brood of ill-matched children, of which Jenny Ijub apparently was one, Lizzie's granite foundation begins to shake. She begins to walk outdoors at unsafe hours, imbibe rose-hip wine, and care less for appearances. The news that Jenny was purchased (and may in fact be another child of Lizzie's own father), along with the effects of a diphtheria outbreak that quarantines the Brown Arc and takes six young lives, further shifts Lizzie's perception of herself. Lizzie notes the change:

> Are you happy with your life? Mrs. Pleasant had asked her on that first afternoon in the House of Mystery, and ever since the question, and only since the question, the answer had become no. How did she used to do it, take such pleasure in small things? How would she ever be able to do so again?

Looking backward, Lizzie reviews her limited experiences of sexual stimulation, and wonders at her resolution that she could do without. One evening she loses her way and finds herself on notorious Morton Street. As she walks past the houses where prostitutes display themselves in bay windows, she contemplates the small pleasures of the flesh with which she has satisfied herself, realizes that they are from God, and carries her thinking further:

> None of this belonged on Morton Street. Lizzie tried to imagine a looking-glass alley where men sat in windows and waited for women with money. She pretended she was entering a door, making a selection, demanding who and what she wanted. Money on the dressing table. The man like a puppet in her arms.

The fantasy was ludicrous. And upsetting. She didn't have a word for the combination of horror and thrill and buffoonery and sadness it gave her.

These are thoughts that the Lizzie Hayes of the novel's opening would never, ever have had. The change in Lizzie's thinking finally leads her to uncover the secrets of the House of Mystery.

How do you build a larger-than-life character in your current manuscript? What does your protagonist say, do, and think that he, or we, would never, ever venture? The following exercise will help you develop these qualities, but do not rely on that alone. Look for opportunities throughout your story to heighten these qualities.

To change, we must first change our minds.

Creating Larger-Than-life Qualities

Step 1: Write down the following:

What is the one thing that your protagonist would never, ever *say?*

_____

_____

_____

_____

What is the one thing that your protagonist would never, ever *do?*

_____

_____

_____

_____

What is the one thing that your protagonist would never, ever *think?*

_____

_____

_____

_____

Step 2: Find places in your story in which your protagonist must say, do, and think those very things. What are the circumstances? What are the consequences? *Make notes, starting now.*

_____

_____

_____

_____

NOTE:
What qualifies as a larger-than-life action? Winking at a stranger is easy for a flirt; to a shy person it is huge. Taking a swing at someone is no big deal for a boxer; for me it would be life changing. Whatever it is, it is a surprise. It feels big. It feels outrageous. It is satisfying because once in a while we would all like to let loose our inner devil—or angel. Here is your chance. Let your character do, say, or think something memorable.

Follow-up work 1: Find twelve more points in the story in which your protagonist can break through his boundaries.

_____

_____

_____

_____

_____

_____

_____

_____

Follow-up work 2: Find a single point in the story in which your protagonist pointedly _lets go_ an opportunity for a larger-than-life gesture.

_____

_____

Conclusion: A larger-than-life character is one who says, does, and thinks things that we would like to but never dare. This does not mean necessarily mean turning your characters into wise-crackers or pulp clichés. It does mean pushing them out of their own bounds, whatever those might be.

Heightening Larger-Than-Life Qualities

Sharpen larger-than-life qualities throughout your story. Fine advice, you may be thinking, but how do I know where to start? Larger-than-life opportunities can crop up anywhere; it only takes being alert to the possibility of sending your protagonist or point-of-view character beyond what is usual.

For instance, it is not uncommon in novels to find a character remembering a lost loved one, such as a wife who has died. Nothing special in that. Happens all the time. Does it require big treatment? Not necessarily. But it is an opportunity.

In Barbara Freethy's *Summer Secrets*, Duncan McKenna is a sailor who eight years before the action of the novel won a round-the-world race with his three teenaged daughters as his crew. Fifteen minutes of fame resulted, but even that fame and Duncan's fanatic love of sailboat racing cannot compete with his memory of his dead wife, Nora, as we discover when a reporter, Tyler Jamison, asks him about her:

> "What was she like?" he asked. "Your wife, Nora."
> Duncan lifted his face to the sun. "Close your eyes," he said.
> "What?"
> "Close your eyes," Duncan repeated.
> Tyler hesitated, then closed his eyes, wondering what was supposed to happen.
> "Feel that heat on your face?" Duncan asked.
> Now that he mentioned it, yes. "Sure." There was a warmth on his skin, a light behind his lids, the scent of summer in his nostrils. His senses were heightened with his eyes closed.
> "That's what she did for me," Duncan murmured. "She made me feel everything more intensely than I'd ever felt it before."

Where a lesser writer would simply use words to convey a nostalgic feeling, Freethy uses an active demonstration; one that is big, surprising, and larger than life—yet a perfectly natural way for a seafaring man to look at it. By heightening this moment, Freethy makes Duncan McKenna a larger-than-life figure—though not always an admirable one, as we later discover.

The second step in this chapter's exercise directs you to take a moment and make it smaller; that is, underplay it. In Dan Brown's best-selling thriller *The Da Vinci Code*, American symbologist Robert Langdon is asked to consult on the murder of an elderly curator, Jacques Saunière, who was shot in the Louvre after closing and, before he died, left behind highly cryptic clues.

What Langdon doesn't know is that the captain of Paris's homicide detectives, Bezu Fache, nicknamed "The Bull," thinks he is the killer. Langdon is warned by a beautiful young police cryptologist, Sophie Neveu, who is the murdered curator's niece. Sophie helps Langdon escape the Louvre—but not before they dispose of a GPS tracking chip planted in Langdon's pocket, misdirect the entire police force, solve several puzzling anagrams, and find two new clues.

All that in twenty minutes or so. Free of the Louvre, they zoom away in Sophie's miniature car, and a chase across the nighttime streets of Paris begins. As they careen onto the broad Champs-Elysées, Langdon looks out the rear window at the police cars massing behind them at the museum. His comment at this moment?

Let me ask you, what would you have Langdon say at a time like this? Something like, *Holy Sh—!*, perhaps? Maybe just, *Step on it!* Anything like that would certainly serve the purposes of the scene. Here is how Brown chooses to handle it:

> His heartbeat finally slowing, Langdon turned back around.
> "That was interesting."

Langdon's *sangfroid* at this tense moment is far more effective than an excited outburst. James Bond would be proud.

As you comb through your manuscript looking for ways to heighten anything your protagonist says, does, or thinks, look for ways to take things up in temperature, but also down. Play against the prevailing mood of a scene. A larger-than-life protagonist talks, acts, and reasons independently. Let your hero's speech, actions, and thoughts follow their own course, regardless of what is going on. Surprise us. That sounds hard, but it really is only a technique.

A larger-than-life protagonist talks, acts, and reasons independently.

Adjusting the Volume

Step 1: At random in the middle of your manuscript, pick anything at all that your protagonist thinks, says, or does. Heighten it. Make it bigger, funnier, more shocking, more vulgar, more out of bounds, more over the top, more violent, more insightful, more wildly romantic, more active, more *anything*. *Make the change in your manuscript.*

_____

_____

Step 2: Take that same action, thought, or line of dialogue, and make it smaller. Tone it down; understate it; make it quieter, more internal, more personal, more ironic, more offhand, less impassioned, barely noticeable. *Make the change in your manuscript.*

_____

_____

> **!**
> **NOTE:**
> Did you ever think of the perfect thing to say about an hour after a conversation has ended? Have your protagonist let loose the perfect zinger at just the right moment. How to do that: Take your time. Work at it. When you get it just right, slot it into place. To the reader, it will seem to pop out of nowhere. No one will know that you spent hours on it. The same thing goes for smaller-then-life gestures, such as throwaways, dismissive gestures, calculated disinterest, faint disgust, and indifference.
>
> Dialogue zingers are what most authors dream up most readily, but don't forget to craft larger-than-life actions, thoughts, insights, decisions, and turnabouts. Place them where they will have maximum effect. Don't worry about making your protagonist seem exaggerated. The protagonists in most manuscript that I read are too ordinary and predictable. It is hard to overdo larger-than-life qualities.

Follow-up work: Select twenty-four more points in the story where you can heighten or diminish something that your protagonist does, says, or thinks.

_____

_____

Conclusion: Larger-than-life characters powerfully attract us. Why? They are surprising, vital, and alive. They do not let life slip by. Every moment counts. Every day has meaning. How can you give that kind of life force to your protagonist? Turn up the volume on what she says, thinks, and does.

6

Character Turnabouts and Surprises

It's too bad that some novelists don't publish their early drafts. Or do they? Anyway, it would be interesting to compare early attempts at a given scene with what later is published.

Generally speaking we don't get that opportunity, but even so one can sometimes see in some novels scenes that do not play the way we would expect them to. The whole thrust is a surprise, or perhaps the scene turns in an unexpected direction, or a character does something that we do not anticipate.

Such effects come from trying different approaches to a scene. In essence, that is what Reversing Motives, the exercise that follows, is about: trying a different approach to see if it works better.

Now, how would you handle the following scene? In an ancient agrarian society, one that is tribal and polygamous, women look out for and support each other. One day, a dissolute and cruel husband gambles away his concubine. The women of the tribe are upset. They want to pay the gambling debt and save her. Lacking funds of their own, they must obtain the debt price from the wealthiest man of their tribe—but how?

What would your approach be? Would the women demand the money? Would they go on strike? Perhaps withhold sex? Would they trick or threaten or bribe the wealthy man in some other way? In Anita Diamant's *The Red Tent* this is the situation faced by the four wives of Jacob (who are also sisters) when their father's much-abused concubine, Ruti, is lost in a game of chance. The appeal to Jacob is headed up by the resourceful first wife, Leah, mother of the novel's narrator:

> Leah's cheeks turned red as she approached her husband. And then she did something extraordinary. Leah got down on her knees and, taking Jacob's hand, kissed his fingers. Watching my mother submit like this was like seeing a sheep hunting a jackal

or a man nursing a baby. My mother, who never wanted for words, nearly stuttered as she spoke.

"Husband, father of my children, beloved friend," she said. "I come to plead a case without merit, for pure pity's sake. Husband," she said, "Jacob," she whispered, "you know I place my life in your keeping only and that my father's name is an abomination to me.

"Even so, I come to ask that you redeem my father's woman from the slavery into which he has sold her."

Leah's simple appeal for mercy works. Jacob pulls together enough goods to barter away the gambling debt. Leah's approach is a reversal of her usual way of working, and so takes us by surprise. Her appeal to her husband's higher instincts elevates both her and him; and, in a way, us as well.

The exercise that follows is one of the most popular in the live Breakout Novel workshops. A majority of participants prefer the scenes yielded from the approach over their original scenes. If you do too, why use it only once? Do the follow-up work and reverse motives in six more scenes. You just might like what happens.

Reversing Motives

Step 1: Pick any scene in your novel that features your protagonist. What is his main action in the scene? What is he trying to accomplish, obtain, or avoid? *Write that down.*

_____

_____

_____

_____

_____

Step 2: Write a complete list of the reasons why your protagonist is doing what she is doing. Write down as many of her motives as you can. *Do not look at the next step until you are done.*

_____

_____

_____

_____

Step 3: Circle the last reason on your list, the last thing that you wrote down.

_____

_____

Step 4: Rewrite your opening of the scene, only this time, send your protagonist into action (or avoidance) foremost and primarily for the reason you circled. *Start writing now.*

_____

_____

_____

_____

! NOTE:
In my workshops, nearly three-quarters of participants find that they prefer the approach to the scene that this exercise yields. Why is that? First choices in writing a scene often are the easiest: the ones that make sense and feel safest. But safe choices make a scene predictable. Reversing motives shakes up a scene. It makes its course less expected, yet no less logical since the action still comes from your character's true, deep motives.

Follow-up work: Reverse motives in six other scenes.

_____

_____

_____

_____

_____

_____

_____

Conclusion: You may wind up retaining the original motivations in many scenes in your novel, but it is likely that some of them will become more engaging after a motive reversal.

Personal Stakes

It is easy to dismiss the protagonist's *personal stakes* as just another way of saying what motivates him. But that is simplistic. Personal stakes are more than just what a hero *wants* to do. They illustrate *why*: Why this goal and the action that must be performed matters in a profound and personal sense. The more it matters to your hero, the more it will matter to yours readers, too.

Mystery writer Harlan Coben grew popular with his first couple of novels featuring sports agent/sleuth Myron Bolitar, but it wasn't until he made the leap to stand-alone novels with *Tell No One* that he broke out big time. His second stand-alone, *Gone for Good*, also reached *The New York Times* best-seller list, and it provides many lessons in the construction of breakout-level fiction.

Gone for Good tells the story of Will Klein, a New York City counselor of runaway children. Will is haunted by the rape and murder of his high school girlfriend, Julie Miller, in her suburban New Jersey home one year after their all-too-typical breakup during their freshman year of college.

A detective haunted by the unsolved murder of his wife or girlfriend is one of the biggest clichés in mystery fiction. However, Coben gives this familiar element an original twist: Julie, it is widely believed, was raped and murdered by Will's older brother Ken, who disappeared that night and has been a fugitive for eleven years. The case was a media sensation and continues to revive with every purported sighting of Ken. Will and his family continue to believe in Ken's innocence—and that he is dead, or "gone for good."

As the story opens, Will learns from his dying mother that Ken is still alive, news that stirs in Will happy memories of his brother, including Ken's reaction to Will's first makeout session with a girl at a space exploration-themed bar mitzvah:

> When Cindi and I stealthily returned to Cape Kennedy's Table Apollo 14, ruffled and in fine post-smooch form (the Herbie Zane Band serenading the crowd with "Fly Me to the Moon"), my brother, Ken, pulled me to the side and demanded details. I, of course, too gladly gave them. He awarded me with a smile

and slapped me five. That night, as we lay on the bunk beds, Ken on the top, me on the bottom, the stereo playing Blue Oyster Cult's "Don't Fear the Reaper" (Ken's favorite), my older brother explained to me the facts of life as seen by a ninth-grader. I'd later learn he was mostly wrong (a little too much emphasis on the breast), but when I think back to that night, I always smile.

With this memory of brotherly bonding, Coben begins to build Will's stakes. He has a lot invested in his image of his brother. Subsequent events will sorely test Will's faith in Ken's innocence, yet Coben keeps Will's conviction level high by frequently reinforcing Will's feelings with positive memories. Will's faith in Ken cannot be shaken.

Meanwhile, Coben also introduces Will's current girlfriend, Sheila Rogers. Coben tips us off immediately that there is something warm and right about their relationship when, after the funeral of Will's mother, Will decides that he needs a breather:

> I got to my feet. Sheila looked up at me with concern. "I'm going to take a walk," I said softly.
> "You want company?"
> "I don't think so."
> Sheila nodded. We had been together nearly a year. I've never had a partner so in sync with my rather odd vibes. She gave my hand another I-love-you squeeze, and the warmth spread through me.

Coben reinforces these loving feelings several times before introducing the first dark note about Sheila: She was a teenage runaway at one time, but that is all that she will say about her past. This hint of doubt colors the next plot development: That night Sheila disappears, leaving only a note that says, "Love you always." Soon afterward, the FBI comes to Will's office looking for information on her whereabouts. Sheila's fingerprints have been found at the site of a double homicide in Albuquerque, New Mexico.

During the course of the novel it will take a lot for Will to maintain his belief in Sheila's innocence, too, but Coben deepens Will's convictions—in effect, raises his personal stakes—at a number of points. The first of these comes as Will holds Sheila's sweatshirt and recalls a homecoming weekend visit to his alma mater, Amherst:

> Late one night Sheila and I walked the campus, hand in hand. We lay on the Hill's soft grass, stared at the pure fall sky, and talked for hours. I remember thinking that I had never known such a sense of peace, of calm and comfort and, yes, joy. Still on our backs, Sheila put her palm on my stomach and then, eyes on the stars, she slipped her hand under the waistband of my pants.

Personal stakes are more than just what a hero wants to do.

I turned just a little and watched her face. When her fingers hit, uh, pay dirt, I saw her wicked grin.

"That's giving it the old college try," she'd said.

And okay, maybe I was turned on as all get-out, but it was at that very moment, on that hill, her hand in my pants, when I first realized, really realized with an almost supernatural certainty, that she was the one, that we would always be together, that the shadow of my first love, my only love before Sheila, the one that haunted me and drove away the others, had finally been banished.

I looked at the sweatshirt for a moment, I could smell the honeysuckle and foliage all over again. I pressed it against me and wondered for the umpteenth time since I'd spoken to Pistillo: Was it all a lie?

No.

You don't fake that. Squares might be right about people's capacity to do violence. But you can't fake a connection like ours.

Nevertheless, ugly truths surface about Sheila Rogers. At one time she was a prostitute. Will and his co-worker Squares track down her one-time, and now bed-ridden, pimp, Louis Castman, who recognizes that Sheila means something special to Will:

"You," he said.

"What about me?"

"Sheila." He smiled. "She means something to you, am I right?"

I didn't reply.

"You *love* her."

He stretched out the word *love*. Mocking me. I kept still.

"Hey, I don't blame you, man. That was some quality tang. And, man, she could suck the—"

I started toward him. Castman laughed. Squares stepped in the way. He looked me straight in the eye and shook his head. I backed off. He was right.

Castman stopped laughing, but his eyes stayed on me. "You want to know how I turned your girl out, lover boy?"

Castman then recounts winning Sheila's trust on her arrival in New York at the Port Authority bus terminal, and how he subsequently kept her cuffed to a bed, shot her full of drugs, raped her, videotaped it, and kept her high until she was addicted and willing to do anything for a fix. This gruesome story would enrage a stone. Coben keeps Will's reaction muted, but it doesn't take much to see that Will, the runaway counselor, will now do anything to find and rescue Sheila. Given who he is, how could he not? Up go the stakes.

Can Sheila matter even more to Will? Sure. After Will learns that Sheila has been murdered, we learn the true depths of his feelings for her:

> I moved over to the desk, bent down, and reached into the back of the bottom drawer. I pulled out the velour box, took a deep breath, and opened it.
> The ring's diamond was one-point-three carats, with G color, VI rating, round cut. The platinum bank was simple with two rectangle baguettes. I'd bought it from a booth in the diamond district on 47th Street two weeks ago.

The story might end here, but soon after this Will learns that the woman he knows as Sheila left a daughter. Up go the stakes yet again. At Sheila's funeral, Will looks into the casket—and the true Sheila Rogers is not his girlfriend. So who is his girlfriend, and where is she? Will needs to find her more than ever.

Will's personal stakes constantly rise, and so does our interest in the outcome of Coben's tense and twisty thriller.

Neo-noir mystery novelist Michael Connelly also has been on *The New York Times* best-seller list, breaking out with the gripping stand-alone novel *The Poet*. For purposes of discussing personal stakes, however, it might be instructive to have a look at how Connelly handles personal stakes vis-à-vis an ongoing series protagonist: Hieronymous (Harry) Bosch. *City of Bones* finds Harry well established as a Los Angeles homicide detective. What possibly can make a new case matter to him more than the many that have come before?

Connelly makes this challenge even more difficult for himself in *City of Bones* when the bones of a boy, buried twenty years ago, are discovered in a shallow hillside grave by a doctor who is out walking his dog. Harry's supervisor, Lieutenant Grace Billets, is none too excited about this discovery:

> "These kind of cases, Harry . . ."
> "What?"
> "They drain the budget, they drain man power . . . and they're the hardest to close, *if* you can close them."
> "Okay, I'll climb back up there and cover the bones up. I'll tell the doctor to keep his dog on a leash."
> "Come on, Harry, you know what I mean."

Harry himself seems detached, but Connelly quickly tips us off that Harry won't remain indifferent for long:

> Child cases haunted you. They hollowed you out and scarred you. There was no bulletproof vest thick enough to stop you from being pierced. Child cases left you knowing the world was full of lost light.

Sure enough, Harry learns that the study of the bones by forensic anthropologist Dr. William Golliher yields a horrifying story:

> "Bones can tell us much about how a person lived and died," Golliher said somberly. "In cases of child abuse, the bones do not lie. The bones become our final evidence." . . .
> "Let me start by saying that we are learning quite a bit from the recovered artifacts," the anthropologist said. "But I have to tell you guys, I've consulted on a lot of cases but this one blows me away. I was looking at these bones and taking notes and I looked down and my notebook was smeared. I was crying, man. I was crying and I didn't even know it at first."
> He looked back at the outstretched bones with a look of tenderness and pity. Bosch knew that the anthropologist saw the person who was once there.
> "This one is bad, guys. Real bad."

Golliher goes on to describe the boy's lifelong skeletal trauma and chronic abuse. The boy spent most of his life healing or being hurt, in constant pain. Some bone breaks went unset. The ribs record the beatings the boy received almost year by year. Harry walks to the restroom:

> Bosch walked to the sink and looked at himself in the mirror. His face was red. He bent down and used his hands to cup cold water against his face and eyes. He thought about baptisms and second chances. Of renewal. He raised his face until he was looking at himself again.
> *I'm going to get this guy.*

Now Harry's personal stakes are set. The case has gotten to him. He cares. Connelly does not stop there, however. Quickly a suspect develops, a pedophile named Nicholas Trent who lived in the neighborhood. When Trent commits suicide the department has an opportunity to close the case. At a departmental meeting, Harry states that it is too soon to pin the murder on Trent and, indeed, he may not have been guilty, since the boy systematically was abused for a long period of time. There is pressure on him, but he resists it:

> Bosch understood that everyone sitting in the room knew that the closing of a case of this nature was the longest of long shots. The case had drawn growing media attention, and Trent with his suicide had now presented them with a way out. Suspicions could be cast on the dead pedophile, and the department could call it a day and move on to the next case—hopefully one with a better chance of being solved.
> Bosch could understand this but not accept it. He had seen

the bones. He had heard Golliher run down the litany of injuries. In that autopsy suite Bosch had resolved to find the killer and close the case. The expediency of department politics and image management would be second to that.

The pressure to sell out plays against Harry's nature and need to find the truth: the *real* truth. Discovering it takes on the proportions of a calling, as we learn when Golliher later challenges Harry on the importance of faith (he means religious faith) in their work. Harry responds in a passage that shows how intensely personal the case has become for him:

> "You're wrong about me. I have faith and I have a mission. Call it blue religion, call it whatever you like. It's the belief that this won't just go by. That those bones came out of the ground for the reason. That they came out of the ground for me to find, and for me to do something about. And that's what holds me together and keeps me going. And it won't show up on any X-ray either. Okay?"

A couple of plot developments further deepen Harry's stakes. First, the female rookie cop whom he has begun seeing is fatally shot during the detention of a witness. Tragic as this is, Harry's breach of police force rules about relationships between supervisors and patrolwomen lands him in career-threatening hot water. Because Harry is a "shit magnet" who has drawn more than his share of controversy over time, it becomes increasingly likely that he will be transferred to a position so tedious that he will be forced to resign.

These setbacks make him only more determined to find out who killed the boy twenty years earlier. And Harry does. Connelly has won the Edgar, Anthony, Macavity and Nero Wolfe awards, and his books sell like mad. No wonder. His readers care passionately about Harry Bosch because Harry Bosch cares passionately about whatever cases are thrown his way.

Men don't have a lock on personal stakes, of course, and in no novel can we see that more clearly than in Anita Diamant's *The Red Tent*, which I discussed earlier. The narrator of Diamant's novel is a minor Old Testament character, Dinah, the daughter of Leah and Jacob. In the novel's opening, we find out why Dinah is so compelled to tell her story:

> My name means nothing to you. My memory is dust.
> This is not your fault, or mine. The chain connecting mother to daughter was broken and the word passed to the keeping of men, who had no way of knowing. That is why I became a foot-note, my story a brief detour between the well-known history of my father, Jacob, and the celebrated chronicle of Joseph, my brother. On those rare occasions when I was remembered, it was as a victim.

Dinah simply wishes to be remembered the way she actually was. There is another reason, too, why she is compelled to tell her story, as we learn when Dinah, an only daughter, explains why her four mothers longed for more girls in a family richly endowed with boys:

> But the other reason women wanted daughters was to keep their memories alive. Sons did not hear their mothers' stories after weaning. So I was the one. My mother and my mother-aunties told me endless stories about themselves. No matter what their hands were doing—holding babies, cooking, spinning, weaving—they filled my ears.
>
> In the ruddy shade of the red tent, the menstrual tent, they ran their fingers through my curls, repeating the escapades of their youths, the sagas of their childbirths. Their stories were like offerings of hope and strength poured out before the Queen of Heaven, only these gifts were not for any god or goddess—but for me.
>
> I can still feel how my mothers loved me.

Dinah wishes for the women in her life to be remembered, too. Those would be sufficient reasons to occasion Dinah's long and layered tale, but Diamant continues to raise the personal stakes as the novel unfolds. Dinah's bonds with the women around her grow, ultimately becoming mystical. In contrast to her father Jacob's god, the women, out of the men's sight, maintain the worship of the earth goddess, as Dinah's mother explains to her during a visit to Dinah's fabled grandmother, Rebecca, wife of Isaac, now an oracle:

> "The great mother whom we call Innana gave a gift to woman that is not known among men, and this is the secret of blood. The flow at the dark of the moon, the healing blood of the moon's birth—to men, this is flux and distemper, bother and pain. They imagine we suffer and consider themselves lucky. We do not disabuse them.
>
> "In the red tent, the truth is known. In the red tent, where days pass like a gentle stream, as the gift of Innana courses through us, cleansing the body of last month's death, preparing the body to receive the new month's life, women give thanks—for repose and restoration, for the knowledge that life comes from between our legs, and that life costs blood."
>
> . . .
>
> My mother saw my confusion. "You cannot understand all of this yet, Dinah," she said. "But soon you will know, and I will make sure that you are welcomed into the woman's life with ceremony and tenderness. Fear not."

Without personal stakes, even the highest-voltage thriller is an empty plot exercise.

Dinah's passage into maturity indeed involves rituals and care that puts the modern era to shame. The world of women, the culture, and the traditions of the red tent shape and define Dinah. Indeed, the company of women ultimately means more to her than the love of men. Telling their story grows in importance. She wants them to be celebrated for their strength, and, in Anita Diamant's richly imagined novel, they are.

What are your protagonist's personal stakes in your current manuscript, and how do they rise? Why does he care? Why might he care *more*? Without personal stakes, even the highest-voltage thriller is an empty plot exercise. Raise the personal stakes and we will all care what happens in your story no matter whether the plot is boiling or not.

Defining Personal Stakes

Step 1: Write down the name of your protagonist.

_____

_____

Step 2: What is her main problem, conflict, goal, need, desire, yearning, or whatever it is driving her through the story? *Write that down.*

_____

_____

_____

_____

_____

Step 3: What could make this problem matter more? Write down as many new reasons as you can think of. *Start writing now.*

_____

_____

_____

_____

_____

Step 4: When you run out of reasons, ask yourself what could make this problem matter even more than that? *Write down even more reasons.*

_____

_____

_____

_____

Step 5: When you run out of steam, ask yourself what could make this problem matter more than life itself? *Write down still more reasons.*

_____

_____

_____

_____

● NOTE:

In my workshops, most participants report that the results of this exercise look to them a lot like a list of additional plot complications. That is good. A hero who does not have many reasons to solve a problem gradually will become uninteresting. As the story grinds on, the reader will wonder, *why go through all that grief if you don't have to? Let someone else handle it.* You don't want that. You want your reader to hope hard or even cheer for your protagonist's success, right?

Raising personal stakes is especially crucial in character-driven stories. In a pure romance novel, there are no genuine stakes other than the yearning of the hero and heroine for one another. It is similar in coming-of-age novels (yearning for growth), journey stories (yearning for change), and relationship novels (yearning for connection). In such stories, adding stronger reasons for a protagonist to care is the only true way to raise stakes. Raising the stakes—the *inner* stakes—will deepen the reader's concern about the outcome.

Follow-up work: For all the ways to deepen the personal stakes that you created above, work out how to incorporate each into your novel. Include at least six. *Make notes now.*

_____

_____

_____

_____

Conclusion: Every protagonist has a primary motive for doing what he must do. It would not be much of a story without that. Outward motives are easy to devise from plot circumstances, but inner motives most powerfully drive a character forward. Don't just look at all the possibilities, here. *Use* all of them. That is exactly what raising personal stakes is all about. It is extra work, for sure, but the result will be a more gripping novel.

8

Ultimate Stakes

Why do we do what we do? Get up in the morning? Scan the paper? Struggle through rush hour? Placate the boss? Mow the lawn? Save for vacation? Help the kids with their homework? Send birthday cards? Bring a tuna casserole to the reception after the funeral? We have our reasons. We may not think about them all the time, but if pressed we could explain what they are.

We care. We feel that what we do matters, however small it may be. We must. No one can live for long feeling that life is futile, without purpose. If we did, at the very least we would stay in bed in the morning. At worst, after living too long without any reason we probably would check out.

When life tests us to the utmost, our motives grow exponentially greater. Our deepest convictions rise close to the surface. We care still more. We become more determined than ever to make a difference, to persist, to overcome all problems and obstacles. At the moment of ultimate testing we summon our deepest beliefs and swear that nothing, *nothing*, will stop us.

The hero of your novel also will be tested to the limit of his convictions— at least, I hope so! (If not, are there enough obstacles in the way of your protagonist?) How does she respond at this supreme moment? The way that you or I would, let's hope, but even more strongly.

The hero of Dennis Lehane's mystery novel *Mystic River* is homicide detective Sean Devine. At the outset of the novel, his convictions are at low ebb. He has returned from a suspension following an on-the-job "incident" that put his partner on medical leave. At the scene of the murder of Katie Marcus, nineteen-year-old daughter of Sean's one-time friend Jimmy, Sean's boss, Detective Lieutenant Martin Friel, is wary of Sean. Is he up to the investigation that lies ahead? He searches Sean for motivation:

> "Trooper," Friel said, "you know what I like even less than ten-year-old black boys getting shot by bullshit gang-war crossfire?"
>
> Sean knew the answer, but he didn't say anything.

"Nineteen-year-old white girls getting murdered in my parks. People don't say 'Oh, the vagaries of economics' then. They don't feel a wistful sense of the tragic. The feel pissed and they want somebody to be led onto the six o'clock in shackles." Friel nudged Sean. "I mean, right?"

"Right."

"That's what they want, because they're us and that's what we want." Friel grasped Sean's shoulder so he'd look at him.

"Yes, sir," Sean said, because Friel had that weird light in his eyes like he believed what he was saying the way some people believed in God or NASDAQ or the Internet-as-global-village. Friel was Born Again all the way, although what the Again had been Sean couldn't say, just that Fried had found something through his work that Sean could barely recognize, something that gave him solace, maybe even belief, a certainty underfoot. Times, to be truthful, Sean thought his boss was an idiot, spouting bullshit platitudes about life and death and the ways to make it all right, cure the cancers and become one collective heart, if only everyone would listen.

Other times, though, Friel reminded Sean of his father, building his birdhouses in the basement where no birds ever flew, and Sean loved the *idea* of him.

Sean's dedication to the case is, as yet, weak. But he gropes for belief and conviction, and borrows it, albeit abstractly, from Fried.

Later, the murdered girl's father searches Sean, too, for his commitment to the case. In the morgue to identify Katie's body, Jimmy Marcus recalls the crucial childhood event that he and Sean have in common: While planning to steal a car one day on the street with a third tag-along friend, Dave Boyle, two men in a car took Dave, who was missing for four mysterious, presumably horrible, days. Survivor guilt plagues both men, and Sean feels it now:

He met Jimmy's plaintive glare. He wanted to say something. He wanted to tell him that he had also thought about what would have happened if they'd climbed in that car. That the thought of what could have been his life sometimes haunted him, hovered around approaching corners, rode the breeze like the echo of a name called from a window. He wanted to tell Jimmy that he occasionally sweated through his old dream, the one in which the street gripped his feet and slid him toward that open door. He wanted to tell him he hadn't truly known what to make of his life since that day, that he was a man who often felt light with his own weightlessness, the insubstantial nature of his character.

But they were in a morgue with Jimmy's daughter lying on a steel table in between them and Whitey's pen poised over paper, so all Sean said to the plea in Jimmy's face was: "Come on, Jim. Let's go get that coffee."

Sean again comes up short. Later, we learn the more immediate cause of his adult malaise: His stage manager wife, Lauren, has left him and taken their daughter with her. (See Low Tension Fixes Part II: Delaying Backstory in chapter twenty-three.) As the murder investigation unfolds, the emerging evidence and suspects gradually engage Sean's mind, and then his heart. He seeks to lay to rest the past, and at one point visits his father, a retired cop with knowledge of the arrest and jail cell suicide of one of the men who kidnapped Dave. His father sees no good in stirring up memories, and the encounter leaves Sean still unsatisfied:

> Sean used the remote to unlock the car, and he was reaching for the door handle when he heard his father say, "Hey."
>
> "Yeah?" He looked back and saw his father standing by the front door, his upper half dissolved in darkness.
>
> "You were right not to get in that car that day. Remember that."
>
> Sean leaned against his car, his palms on the roof, and tried to make out his father's face in the dark.
>
> "We should have protected Dave, though."
>
> "You were kids," his father said. "You couldn't have known. And even if you could have, Sean . . ."
>
> Sean let that sink in. He drummed his hands on the roof and peered into the dark for his father's eyes. "That's what I tell myself."
>
> "Well?"
>
> He shrugged. "I still think we *should* have known. Somehow. Don't you think?"

In reality, Sean is moving closer to the heart of his motivation. It is the guilt of not protecting his friend that drives him and has made him a detective. He *should* have known how to protect Dave back then, but because he didn't act, *now* he sure as hell is going to find out who killed Katie Marcus.

At the end of the novel he learns that it was none of the developed suspects but other kids who killed Katie: the younger brother of the boy she planned to run away with and his friends. Surprising them at home, Sean finds himself in a standoff: A kid named O'Shea has a gun pointed at Sean, and Sean's partner has a gun pointed at O'Shea. Facing death, recognizing that O'Shea's soul is empty enough for him to fire, Sean discovers why he truly cares:

> Sean had seen this before. Back when he was in uniform and sent as crowd control on a bank robbery gone bad, the guy inside gradually growing stronger for a two-hour period, feeling the power of the gun in his hand and the effect it had, Sean watching

him rant and rave over the monitor hooked up to the bank cameras. At the start, the guy had been terrified, but he'd gotten over that. Fell in love with that gun.

And for one moment, Sean saw Lauren looking over at him from the pillow, one hand pressed to the side of her head. He saw his dream daughter, smelled her, and thought what a shitty thing it would be to die without meeting her or seeing Lauren again.

A minute later Sean talks the gun out of the kid's hand. It turns out that Sean cares for the same reasons that all of us get up, fight the traffic and all the rest: Because he loves his family. It is a simple discovery, really, a fundamental commitment that is obvious to almost everyone.

Yet the unfolding of this primary motivation and its revelation to Sean himself at the moment of his ultimate testing gives it a force that not only carries Dave to the finish, but also resolves the conflicts at the heart of the novel's two secondary plot layers. Lehane deftly fuses the layers together and brings Sean's inner journey to a climax all at once. Sean has to live not only to enact justice, but also to put to rest the past and truly love in the present. He searches for, and finds, his irrevocable commitment.

Is there such a moment of ultimate stakes in your current manuscript? If not, fix it on the page. Your hero's testing and eventual commitment will be fixed in your readers' minds for a long time to come.

Capturing the Irrevocable Commitment

Step 1: Identify the moment in your story when your protagonist's stakes hit home—when she realizes that there is no turning back. This is the moment of irrevocable commitment.

_____

_____

_____

_____

_____

Step 2: Write out that moment in one paragraph. *Start writing now.*

_____

_____

_____

_____

_____

_____

_____

_____

Step 3: Look at the paragraph you have written. Notice its shape, feel its effect. *Now imagine that this is the first paragraph of your novel.*

_____

_____

_____

_____

_____

!

● **NOTE:**
Probably it would be difficult to place that paragraph at the top of page one. Very likely the moment you have chosen occurs late in the novel, probably at the climax. Put that first and you would wind up with a tale told in flashback. Even so, it is tantalizing to think that your protagonist could have that kind of commitment—and your novel that kind of emotional power—right from the opening moment, isn't it? Well, why not? I do not mean dumping a mountain of commitment on your protagonist immediately. Yet can't your protagonist care passionately about *something* at the beginning? Emotionally speaking, why open the novel in low gear?

Follow-up work: The moment of commitment that you just created has an opposite: a moment of irresolution, a healthy aversion, a justified selfishness, or a similar reaction. *Write that down.* Now find a place earlier in your manuscript to slot this in. *Make the change in your manuscript now.*

_____

_____

_____

_____

_____

Conclusion: You may not wind up directly using the paragraphs you create with this exercise; however, let your hero's inner commitment infuse and underlie all his actions. Let him be driven. When resolve weakens, reinforce it. Strong commitment on the part of your protagonist will generate strong commitment on the part of your reader. The same is true, not surprisingly, when you create strong commitment on the part of your antagonist.

Exposition

We all star in our own movie. No one else's life has, for each of us, the immediacy and importance of our own. Nothing is more significant than what is happening to us right now. We are our own most intimate friends. This may sound self-absorbed, but it is a measure of the intensity with which we experience our lives and the importance we attach to what we think, feel, and experience at any given moment of the day.

The protagonist of a novel is no different from us in that respect, or needn't be. Indeed, characters with poorly developed inner lives cannot long sustain reader interest. I am not suggesting writing endless passages of gushy exposition (sometimes called interior monologue), like one finds in low-grade romance novels. Rather, I suggest bringing forward on the page a protagonist's self-regard: that reflection and self-examination that shows us that a character has a compass-true sense of themselves and a grasp of the meaning of what is happening to them at any given moment in the story.

An example of this can be found in Richard Russo's *Empire Falls*, which I discussed earlier. In the book, Miles Roby is the humble proprietor of the local diner, but that doesn't keep him from being self-reflective. Committed to painting the steeple of his parish church despite his fear of heights, Miles frequently procrastinates by talking with his friend Father Mark. One day he finds Father Mark staring up at the steeple:

> "God Himself, a couple of stories up . . . so close."
> "I was just thinking how far *away* it is," Miles admitted. "But then I was contemplating painting it."
> "That does make a difference," Father Mark said.
> "Actually I wasn't contemplating painting so much as falling."
> Interesting, Miles thought. Like himself, Father Mark, as a child, had been reassured by the imagined proximity of God, whereas adults, perhaps because they so often were up to no good, took more comfort from His remoteness. Though Miles

didn't think of himself as a man up to no good, he did prefer the notion of an all-loving God to that of an all-knowing one.

Miles is a man who admits to himself his own discomfort in the presence of God. How can we not admire that? By taking us deep inside Miles, Russo shows us something universal not about Miles's faith but about his humanity.

In Philip Pullman's astonishing fantasy *The Golden Compass*, set in a magical world much like Earth in Edwardian times, the heroine is young Lyra Belacqua, a girl of unusual self-possession and resourcefulness. Pullman enhances her pluck and appeal by taking the opposite approach. Rather than being self-reflective, Lyra is naively self-confident, as in this passage deep in the novel wherein we find Lyra, a practiced liar, captured and in grave danger:

> It wasn't Lyra's way to brood; she was a sanguine and practical child, and besides, she wasn't imaginative. No one with much imagination would have thought seriously that it was possible to come all this way and rescue her friend Roger; or, having thought it, an imaginative child would immediately have come up with several ways in which it was impossible. Being a practical liar doesn't mean you have a powerful imagination at all; it's that which gives their lies such wide-eyed conviction.
>
> So now that she was in the hands of the Oblation Board, Lyra didn't fret herself into terror about what had happened to the gyptians. They were all good fighters, and even though Pantalaimon said he'd seen John Faa shot, he might have been mistaken; or if he wasn't mistaken, John Faa might not have been seriously hurt. It had been bad luck that she'd fallen into the hands of the Samoyeds, but the gyptians would be along soon to rescue her, and if they couldn't manage it, nothing would stop Iorek Byrnison from getting her out; and then they'd fly to Svalbard in Lee Scoresby's balloon and rescue Lord Asriel.

Pullman's passage is written in the objective point-of-view, with the author observing and commenting upon his young protagonist. Yet despite that removal, and his description of Lyra as an unimaginative child, Pullman nevertheless conveys Lyra's view of herself: childishly confident, certain of her allies, trusting of her own ultimate safety. While Lyra may not consciously reflect on these qualities of herself, the author does so for her, and the effect is no less intimate than Richard Russo's passage above.

Recall mystery writer Janet Evanovich's series protagonist, Stephanie Plum, from an earlier chapter. Stephanie is not exactly a deep thinker. The Trenton, New Jersey, bail bond hunter is, rather, a beer swilling, blue-collar ball-buster. But even though the word *philosophy* may not be in her vocabulary, Stephanie nevertheless always has a few wry things to say about herself, as in this early passage in *One for the Money* in which she recounts how, despite maternal warnings to the contrary, neighborhood bad boy Joe Morelli managed to lure her, at age six, into a dilapidated garage to teach her a special "game":

> "What's the name of this game?" I'd asked Joseph Morelli.
>
> "Choo-choo," he said, down on his hands and knees, crawling between my legs, his head trapped under my short pink skirt. "You're the tunnel, and I'm the train."
>
> I suppose this tells you something about my personality. That I'm not especially good at taking advice. Or that I was born with an overload of curiosity. Or maybe it's about rebellion or boredom or fate. At any rate, it was a one-shot deal and darn disappointing, since I'd only gotten to be the tunnel, and I'd really wanted to be the train.

Sooner or later you must bring your reader inside a character's head.

Self-observations like this (never mind Stephanie's scathing and hilarious observations of others) make her enormously appealing. We all wish we could be funny about ourselves, and sometimes we are. But Stephanie is funny on every single page.

In your latest manuscript, how does your protagonist regard himself? What does he see in the mirror? What is the condition of his mind, heart, and soul at any given point in the story?

In life it is difficult, if not impossible, to like someone whom we do not know. But when someone is self-revealing we (usually) are drawn to him. In any event, honesty about oneself is a positive quality. It takes courage to take a hard look inside. Give your protagonist that courage, and you will give your readers a character whose strength they can see and whose inner life is rich and accessible.

Deepening Exposition

Step 1: In your manuscript pick a moment in which a point-of-view character does not react to what is happening, or when in fact nothing is happening and the action of the story is paused or static.

_____

_____

_____

_____

Step 2: Write a paragraph of exposition delineating this character's self-conscious thoughts about her own state of mind, emotional condition, state of being or soul, or perception of the state of the world at this point in time. _Start writing now._

_____

_____

! **NOTE:**
It can be as simple as "He felt lousy" or as complex as "The Hegelian paradigm was shifting." Sooner or later you must bring your reader inside a character's head and show us what is going on there. _Is_ anything going on? Too commonly in manuscripts I meet characters whose inner lives are poorly developed. You yourself have all kinds of ideas, observations, opinions, and gripes, don't you? You reflect. You regard yourself. You perceive how things are in the world around you. How much scope of thought and reflective time do you give your point-of-view characters? Typically there is not enough of that in a manuscript; or, if there is, those passages are not vivid. To make such moments arresting takes work.

Follow-up work: Repeat the above steps at four more points of deep exposition (passages in which we experience a character's thoughts and feelings).

_____

_____

_____

_____

_____

Conclusion: Passages of exposition can be among the most gripping in your novel. Indeed they better be, since nothing is "happening." When nothing overtly is going on, make sure that a great deal is at work beneath the surface. Otherwise you novel will have dead spots that your readers will skip.

10

Creating Secondary Characters

The world is full of people, and so are most novels. But how believable are the secondary characters who fill them out? Too many merely enter, fulfill a function in the story, then exit. They are forgettable, because they are not real. They act in only one way; usually exactly the way we expect.

Secondary characters do not have to be like that. They can engage us as strongly as the primary players do. When that happens it is because the author has bothered to make those characters in some way as multidimensional, conflicted, or surprising as the novel's major characters are. That's tough to do, especially when there is limited space in which to develop them, but it can be done.

Legal thriller writer Phillip Margolin is a lean writer, lavishing attention on the technical details that make credible the cases portrayed in his novels, but otherwise sketching his settings, stories, and characters with efficiency. Even so, he treats his secondary characters as more than props.

In *The Associate*, Margolin spins the story of Daniel Ames, a young associate at Portland, Oregon's most prestigious law firm: Reed, Briggs, Stephens, Stottlemeyer, and Compton. Daniel's background is blue collar, not blue chip. He believes that his hold on success is tenuous. He works late hours.

In the novel's opening Margolin has another young lawyer, Joe Molinari, a good-times sort of guy, amble into Daniel's cubicle one evening to cajole him out for an associates' happy hour at a nearby steakhouse. Daniel declines to stay at work, and Molinari ribs him:

> "Hey, man, you've got to stand up for yourself. Lincoln freed the slaves."
>
> "The Thirteenth Amendment doesn't apply to associates at Reed, Briggs."
>
> "You're hopeless"—Molinari laughed as he levered himself

out of the chair—"but you know where we are if you come to your senses."

That is all that the scene requires, but Margolin goes further, using this opportunity to deepen both Daniel and Molinari:

> Molinari disappeared down the corridor and Daniel sighed. He envied his friend. If the situation had been reversed Joe wouldn't have hesitated to go for a drink. He could afford to give the finger to people like Arthur Briggs and he would never understand that someone in Daniel's position could not.
>
> Molinari's father was a high muck-a-muck in a Los Angeles ad agency. Joe had gone to an elite prep school, an Ivy League college, and had been *Law Review* at Georgetown. With his connections, he could have gotten a job anywhere, but he liked white-water rafting and mountain climbing, so he had condescended to offer his services to Reed, Briggs. Daniel, on the other hand, thanked God every day for his job.

That same evening, Daniel agrees to do a favor for yet another associate, glamorous Susan Webster, who asks him to review late-delivered documents relating to a suit against the firm's client Geller Pharmaceuticals—documents that must be handed to the opposition lawyers the following day in the legal exchange of information called "discovery." Daniel agrees.

Too late, Daniel realizes that the documents are thousands of pages long, occupying five banker's boxes. It's an impossible task. Daniel pulls an all-nighter, but even so must gloss over most of the material. What is worse, buried in the material handed over the next day is a document that Daniel failed to see: an early memo from a Geller researcher expressing fears that the company's pregnancy drug Insufort may, like Thalidomide before it, cause birth defects.

This piece of evidence is devastating to Geller's case, and Daniel takes the blame for letting it slip through unnoticed. He loses his job and, worse, is suspected when his firm's founding partner, Briggs, is murdered. Daniel of course is innocent, and also believes that the incriminating memo was a plant. And so it was. After much effort and danger, Daniel and his love interest prove it.

At the novel's end, Daniel is due an apology and his old job back. Margolin could easily have had Daniel himself demand his due. Instead, he utilizes an unlikely secondary character: Molinari. The associate whom we know as a good-times party animal turns out to have another side, as we see when he confronts the firm's surviving senior partner:

> "Come on in, Joe," J.B. Reed said as his secretary showed Joe Molinari into his corner office. Reed was puzzled by Molinari's visit since he was not working on any of Reed's cases. To be honest, he only remembered Molinari's name because his secretary had told it to him when she buzzed him to say that one of the associates wanted to talk to him.

"What can I do for you?" Reed asked as Molinari sat down. He noticed that Molinari did not seem nervous or deferential the way of the new associates were in his presence.

"Something is going on that you need to know about."

"Oh?"

"Just before he died, Mr. Briggs fired Daniel Ames." Reed's features clouded when Molinari mentioned his friend's murder and accused murderer. "That was wrong."

"I don't see how any of this is your business, Mr. Molinari," Reed snapped.

Molinari met Reed's fierce gaze and returned one of his own.

"It's my business," Joe said forcefully, "because Dan is a friend of mine and someone has to tell you what he's done for this firm and Geller Pharmaceuticals."

*Secondary
shouldn't mean
malnourished.*

Daniel is offered his job back with a raise. (He declines.) By allowing Molinari to stand up for a principle, Margolin gives this minor player an extra dimension. It is a small moment, but one that enriches Margolin's cast and gives his leanly written thriller a touch more texture.

Could there be more dishy fun than in Cecily von Ziegesar's racy *Gossip Girl* series of young adult novels about wealthy New York City private school seventeen-year-olds? Hardly. The series debut, *Gossip Girl*, tells the story of rich and popular Blair Waldorf and her model-gorgeous former friend at the Constance Billard School, the even richer femme fatale Serena van der Woodsen. Serena, away for a year, has returned to New York and Constance Billard School after being kicked out of an even more exclusive private girls' school in Connecticut for showing up three weeks late for the start of the fall semester. (She was having a great summer in France.)

Like, we must pause here to explain the world in which these Platinum card girls live: They are barely supervised by their success-driven parents. Anything goes for them—including sex, drugs, and drinking—as long as they keep up appearances. Are we clear? Fabu. Pay attention now. It gets juicier.

Blair and Serena, once tight, now are estranged but have one thing in common: hunky Nate Archibald. Nate is Blair's boyfriend, but what Blair doesn't know is that a year before Nate had sex with Serena—or, in their private lingo, "parted her Red Sea." (You had to be there.) Nate is a somewhat minor player. He doesn't have much of a role in the story.

He is, however, torn between Blair and Serena. Blair has decided that she is ready to have sex with him, but he is ambivalent. He's really in love with Serena, but when Nate first sees her upon her return, von Ziegesar contrasts their reactions to each other:

"Hey, you," Serena breathed when Nate hugged her. He smelled just like he always smelled. Like the cleanest, most delicious boy alive. Tears came to Serena's eyes and she pressed her face into Nate's chest. Now she was really home.

Nate's cheeks turned pink. *Calm down*, he told himself. But he couldn't calm down. He felt like picking her up and twirling her around and kissing her face over and over. *"I love you!"* he wanted to shout, but he didn't. He couldn't.

Nate was the only son of a navy captain and a French society hostess. His father was a master sailor and extremely handsome, but a little lacking in the hugs department. His mother was the complete opposite, always fawning over Nate and prone to emotional fits during which she would lock herself in her bedroom with a bottle of champagne and call her sister on her yacht in Monaco. Poor Nate was always on the verge of saying how he really felt, but he didn't want to make a scene or say something he might regret later. Instead, he kept quiet and let other people steer the boat, while he laid back and enjoyed the steady rocking of the waves.

He might look like a stud, but he was actually pretty weak.

What is Nate going to do? For most of the novel he does nothing, failing to declare himself for Serena or even to take up Blair's offer of her virginity. He has a strong inner conflict, and, though his indecisiveness relegates him to a minor role, we nevertheless feel for him in his dilemma. *The dork.*

Medical thriller writer Michael Palmer is adept at making complex medical conditions and procedures easy to understand. He puts conflict and tension on every page, relentlessly raises stakes, and keeps his plots humming. His protagonists are highly sympathetic, true heroes and heroines. Palmer could afford to play these strengths and let the fine points go, but he does not. His secondary characters also shine.

In *The Patient*, Palmer tells the story of mechanical engineer and neurosurgeon Jessie Copeland, who has developed a robot, ARTIE, to perform assisted robotic tissue incision and extraction. To the rest of us that means dissolving brain tumors with ultrasound and sucking them out. ARTIE is minimally invasive, a true innovation, but also experimental.

In the novel's tense second scene, Jessie attempts a tumor removal with the help of her longtime surgical nurse, Emily. It would be enough for Emily simply to support Jessie and be a voice for the progress of the procedure, as in "Uh-oh, the robot's going haywire! We have to abort!" But Palmer has more in mind for Emily than that. As the procedure begins, he generously allows her a larger-than-life moment as she reminds Jessie that ARTIE is still unproven:

> Easy does it, Jess," Emily said. "We always expect more from our kids than they can ever deliver—just ask mine."

Snappy larger-than-life zingers like that make Emily a character with whom we bond. She's not in many scenes, but when she is we care.

How much attention have you given your secondary characters? Have you taken the trouble to give them extra dimensions, inner conflict, and larger-than-life qualities? If not, why not give it a try? They will make your cast more lively and engaging. The exercise that follows will help you do it.

Secondary Character Development

Step 1: Pick a secondary character who aids your protagonist. *Write the down the name of that character.*

_____

_____

Step 2: Create an extra dimension: Write down this character's defining quality. Write down the opposite of that. Now create a paragraph in which this character demonstrates the opposite quality that you have identified. *Start writing now.*

_____

_____

_____

_____

_____

Step 3: Create an inner conflict: Write down what this character most wants. Write down the opposite of that. How can this character want both of things simultaneously? How can they be mutually exclusive? *Make notes, starting now.*

_____

_____

Step 4: Create larger-than-life qualities: Write down things that this character would never say, do, or think. Find places where this character can and must say, do, and think those things. *Make notes, starting now.*

_____

_____

_____

_____

_____

> **!**
> **NOTE:**
> Secondary characters can be the most vibrant and active in a manuscript. They can also be lifeless and cardboard—mere prop-ups for the hero. That's a shame. *Secondary* shouldn't mean *malnourished.*

Follow-up work: Follow the steps above for a different minor character who supports your protagonist.

_____

_____

_____

_____

_____

_____

_____

_____

Conclusion: You may wonder whether highly developed secondary characters will over-whelm your protagonist and take over the story. Don't worry. If your secondary folk occupy less page time and do not enact the novel's most significant events, they will add luster to the novel without blinding your readers to your story's true hero.

Antagonists

Antagonists can be fun to write. In fact, villains can be the most memorable characters in a novel. Think Fu Manchu and Hannibal Lecter. Despite that, the antagonists I encounter in many manuscripts are one-dimensional. They do not frighten me, surprise me, or linger in my memory once the story is over.

Developing an antagonist is, in a practical sense, no different than developing a protagonist. It demands the same attention to extra dimensions, inner conflict, larger-than-life qualities, and the rest. When developed well, an antagonist is an equal match, or more, for the protagonist. Not only is there a sense that the antagonist really could win, but that the antagonist has feelings and motives as valid and varied as anyone else's. We believe we understand this character.

Thriller writer Ridley Pearson's novels usually feature Seattle police detective Lou Boldt, but in his stand-alone thriller *Parallel Lies*, Pearson takes a different track to tell the story of disgraced former cop Peter Tyler, who is called by an old friend at the National Transportation Safety Board to help out Northern Union Railroad, whose trains are being sabotaged. Tyler was kicked out of the force when he nearly beat a black man to death; unfortunately, the Northern Union security officer with whom he must work is a black woman who knows his history.

You already can see that Pearson is adept at creating complex characters and inherent conflict. However, it is the train-wrecker in *Parallel Lies*, Umberto Alvarez, who is perhaps this novel's most finely drawn character. Alvarez lost his wife and children when their car stalled at a train crossing and was demolished by a Northern Union locomotive. Now Alvarez is engineering derailments of Northern Union trains. That is as much motive as the plot requires to be effective, but Pearson develops Alvarez more deeply than that.

First, although Alvarez is grief-stricken to a criminal degree, he is not actually homicidal. He arranges derailments so that no one will get hurt. In the novel's opening, Alvarez is living hobo-style in a boxcar and must defend himself when an intruder attacks him. It is the blood-soaked box that finally puts the authorities on his trail. Alvarez, we can see, is a man to whom bad things happen; in other words, he has become the man he is through adverse circumstances.

Pearson next builds sympathy for Alvarez, who sneaks up to a farmhouse in order to steal fresh clothes from the laundry room. Once inside, we learn how much Alvarez misses his wife:

> The kitchen smelled like a home. God, he missed that smell. For a moment it owned him, the poignant feeling carrying him away, and then the distant sound of shower water caught his attention. It was warm in here, the first warmth he'd felt in days. Was she just warming up the shower, or getting in? Each option offered a different scenario. He crossed toward the laundry room. He wanted to stay here; he wanted to move in. He pulled the jeans into his arms, stepped to his left and reached for the flannel shirt in the pile of dry clothes.

This building of sympathy pays off as we follow Alvarez's methodical preparations to destroy Northern Union's new F.A.S.T. bullet train on its maiden run from New York to Washington. What Alvarez plans is horrible, but what has been done to him is horrible, too. He believes that Northern Union was at fault in his wife's death, even though an investigation has cleared the railroad of responsibility. As the novel unfolds, Peter Tyler begins to suspect that Alvarez is right: that the railroad *was* responsible. Although Alvarez is clearly the story's villain, in the end we understand his actions all too well.

Antagonists are not always villains. Cecily von Ziegesar's *Gossip Girl*, discussed in the last chapter, is an ensemble novel about the lives of rich private school girls in Manhattan. Chief among them is Blair Waldorf who pines for (well, truthfully, lusts for) handsome Nate Archibald. What prevents her from carrying out her plan to lose her virginity with Nate? The reappearance of her former best friend, stunning Serena van der Woodsen, at the upscale Constance Billard School.

Serena is Blair's opposition in the novel. She is the antagonist. But Serena is not evil. She is just a girl who is too rich, too beautiful, and too lost to know what she wants. Her junior year abroad in France turned into a journey into dissolution. On returning to New York, she hopes to recapture some of the friendship and fun that she formerly enjoyed with Blair, as we see when she arrives at a dinner party thrown by Blair's parents:

> Serena hugged them happily. These people were home to her, and she'd been gone a long time. She could hardly wait for life to return to the way it used to be. She and Blair would walk to school together, spend Double Photography in Sheep Meadow in Central Park, lying on their backs, taking pictures of pigeons and clouds, smoking and drinking Coke and feeling like hard-core artistes. They would have cocktails at the Star Lounge in the Tribeca Star Hotel again, which always turned into sleepover parties because

they would get too drunk to get home, so they'd spend the night in the suite Chuck Bass's family kept there. They would sit on Blair's four-poster bed and watch Audrey Hepburn movies, wearing vintage lingerie and drinking gin and lime juice. . . .

Serena's memories may not be particularly warm and cozy, but her nostalgia is nonetheless heartfelt. When Blair and her friends snub her and begin spreading vile rumors about why she was kicked out of her last boarding school, Serena is understandably confused. She does not plot revenge, though. Instead she goes her own way, getting involved in student filmmaking and eventually crossing paths with a Riverside Prep scholarship boy who worships her from afar, Dan Humphrey, who to his amazement becomes her love interest.

Blair and Serena have a partial reconciliation at the end of *Gossip Girl*, but remain at odds. Only future novels will tell whether Serena will remain the series antagonist, or whether that role will fall instead to another—possibly even Blair.

The antagonist in a breakout novel can even be invisible. Some mystery novels are like that: The killer is unknown until the detective reveals his identity. Stephen L. Carter's *The Emperor of Ocean Park* is not a murder mystery, as such, since the agent of opposition in the story is dead.

The mystery in *The Emperor of Ocean Park* revolves around the "arrangements" left unfulfilled by Oliver Garland, an African-American judge whose nomination to the Supreme Court was ruined by scandal prior to his death. Garland's son, Talcott, is drawn into an investigation of his father's shady connections. His father's misdoings complicate Talcott's life, which is already encumbered by his wife's own bench nomination, the suspicion of his law school colleagues, and a fake FBI agent who is following him around.

Talcott chases his father's cryptic clues, which are based on chess strategy, and in the end learns the truths of his own life and the dark secrets of the inner workings of Washington, DC. Plenty of people stand in his way, of course, but the person working most against him throughout is his own dead father.

Sometimes the antagonist in a breakout novel is nothing more than life itself. For an example, read Patricia Gaffney's powerful story (also set in Washington, DC) about four women friends who form a support group, *The Saving Graces*. Over the course of several years the friends grapple with infertility, divorce, married lovers, thwarted creativity, terminal cancer, and other challenges. Is there a villain, here? Various characters stand in, but ultimately in *The Saving Graces*, Gaffney makes the antagonist nothing more than the relentless, small, unavoidable domestic tragedies that happen to us all.

As you can see, antagonists come in many shapes and sizes. They can be villains, or they can be life itself. Who, or what, is the antagonist in your novel? How can you develop this opposition for maximum effect? Certainly not by settling for a motive that is nothing more than evil intent.

Evil is more interesting than that. Villains are best when they are complex. Use the exercise that follows to develop those depths. You may wind up with an antagonist that your readers fear or even adore. Hey, why not shoot for both?

Sometimes the antagonist in a breakout novel is nothing more than life itself.

Developing the Antagonist

Step 1: Who is the antagonist in your novel? *Write the down the name of that character.*

_____

_____

Step 2: Create an extra dimension: write down your antagonist's defining quality. Write down the opposite of that. Now create a paragraph in which your antagonist demonstrates the opposite quality that you have identified. *Start writing now.*

_____

_____

_____

_____

_____

_____

_____

_____

Step 3: Create an inner conflict: Write down what your antagonist most wants. Write down the opposite of that. How can this character want both of these things simultaneously? How can they be mutually exclusive? *Make notes, starting now.*

_____

_____

_____

_____

_____

Step 4: Create larger-than-life qualities: Write down things that your antagonist would never say, do, or think. Find places where this character can and must say, do, and think those things. *Make notes, starting now.*

_____

_____

_____

_____

_____

Step 5: Define your antagonist's personal stakes: What is his main problem, conflict, or goal? Next, write down what would make this problem matter more, and then matter more than life itself. *Make notes, starting now.*

_____

_____

_____

_____

_____

> **! NOTE:**
> A well-rounded villain is far more dangerous and interesting than a one-dimensional antagonist. Why is it, then, that so many villains I encounter in manuscripts are cardboard cutouts? Perhaps fiction writers are afraid to touch evil. But you do not need a dark side to create a convincing adversary. Villains are not really so different from the rest of us. They do not believe that they are in the wrong. They can justify everything they do. (Can't you?)

Follow-up work: Follow the steps above for a secondary antagonistic character who supports your villain.

_____

_____

_____

_____

_____

Conclusion: No one is bad all the time. Villains are people, too. Rather than build a villain who is unlike you, use this exercise to build one who resembles you. That might be the most chilling adversary of all.

The Antagonist's Outline

Step 1: What is your antagonist's main problem, conflict, or goal? *Write that down.*

_____

_____

_____

Step 2: What does your antagonist most want? *Write that down.*

_____

_____

_____

Step 3: What is the second plot layer for your antagonist? *Write that down.*

_____

_____

_____

Step 4: What are the five most important steps toward your antagonist's goal, or toward resolving her central problem or conflict? A different way to ask that is: What are the five events, actions, or high points, with respect to your antagonist, that you could not possibly leave out? *Write those down.*

_____

_____

_____

_____

_____

Step 5: What are the three most important steps toward, or away from, your antagonist's greatest need? *Write those down.*

_____

_____

_____

_____

_____

Step 6: Using the material from the above steps, outline the entire novel from the antagonist's point of view.

_____

_____

_____

_____

_____

_____

_____

_____

NOTE:
What if your novel does not have an antagonist? In that case, who or what opposes your protagonist? Is it some external force? If so, who is the human agent who represents it? Is your protagonist his own worst enemy? Can that internal opposition have a life and personality of its own, or be expressed through another character who speaks for your protagonist's dark side?

Follow-up work: Find five new ways in which your antagonist can advance her own interests. Let these be actions that have nothing to do with your hero; stuff that your villain would do anyway. _Note them._

_____

_____

_____

_____

Conclusion: We are not accustomed to thinking of villains as being on an inner journey, but what human being is not? Humanize your villain. Motivate his actions with kindness. Let her be heroic, helpful, and principled. Hannah Ardent wrote of the "banality of evil." For fiction writers, that means creating not passionless cruelty but evil that wears a compassionate face.

Enriching Your Cast

Complexity in a novel generally is a desirable quality, but how do you manage it? Adding plot layers is one way (see Plot Layers in chapter fifteen); enriching your cast of characters is another. One way to achieve that latter effect is not by *adding* new characters but, paradoxically, by *eliminating* them; or more accurately put, by combining them.

Let me explain.

In *Tall, Dark, and Deadly*, by *The New York Times* best-selling author Heather Graham, a Miami criminal defense attorney disappears from her Coconut Grove home. Her fitness therapist neighbor, Samantha Miller, investigates. Sam's story involves some elements that are common to women's fiction, and some that aren't; for instance, the missing neighbor, who is not particularly deserving of help.

Sam sees the good in Marnie Newcastle, but most others do not. Marnie is an ambitious lawyer with no concern for how scuzzy her clients may be, so long as their cases get her where she wants to go. She is also a man-eater. Early on, it is clear that Marnie even has used elegant and graceful Sam as a means to meet men: "Sam could accomplish with a word, the lift of a brow, a simple *look*, something that might take her twenty minutes of flirting to do." Some neighbor!

Graham keeps the elements of her romantic mystery in constant motion, crisscrossing each other in puzzling ways. At the same time, Graham uses characters with combined roles to maintain a sense of narrative cohesion. Marnie leaves behind her buttoned-down assistant, Loretta, who becomes a source of information about Marnie; for instance, that Marnie maintained a financial interest in a strip club, and even stripped there herself once in a while, for kicks.

The strip club, naturally, becomes a focus of investigation. Meanwhile, the reader learns that a serial killer, who enjoys feeding his victims to the alligators in Miami's canals, is targeting new women who are connected to the club. So far, so good. Graham now, wisely, raises the stakes. Why not put a young and innocent exotic dancer in jeopardy? Graham introduces nineteen-year-old Lacey, who is stripping in secret and who hopes to use the money she earns to travel to New York for a legitimate dance audition. It also happens that Lacey is heroine Sam's niece. Graham is raising the stakes and enriching her cast at the same time.

Early in the novel, Lacey learns from a fellow dancer, whose stage name is Tiger Lilly, that she can make even more money by working private parties, which are set up by a mysterious booker. Tiger Lilly also tells Lacey that their part-time profession is honorable work that employs hundreds of thousands of women, giving Lacey courage. It also turns out that Lacey knows Tiger Lilly from her other job: By day Tiger Lilly is Marnie-the-missing-lawyer's assistant, Loretta.

This double-role might sound contrived, but it serves nicely to keep the disparate elements of Graham's story connected. Graham finds other uses for this character, too. Sam's partner in the gym where she does her fitness therapy is muscular Joe Taylor, who has an eye for Loretta. Joe turns out to be the mysterious party booker and serial killer. In the novel's conclusion, Joe traps Sam in his cabin-of-horrors with the still alive-but-drugged Marnie.

Sam has one chance to escape with Marnie, but Graham isn't about to make it easy. Joe has a third drugged victim in the cabin: once again, Loretta. Sam escapes, but only with extreme difficulty thanks to Loretta's now triple function in the story. Any random victim might have served this purpose, but Graham knows that, by combining this bit role with others in the story, she can wring extra tension from it and her keep story elements dancing with each other to the end.

A combined role also can make for a nice reversal and surprise. In an earlier chapter I discussed Barbara Freethy's *Summer Secrets*, in which three grown sisters struggle to keep the dark secret of what happened one stormy night on the round-the-world sailboat race they won as teenagers. The youngest sister, Caroline, is prone to risky behavior, especially vis-à-vis men. Early in the novel we learn that she is involved with a much older man, Mike Stanaway, who has a bad reputation. It is said that he beat his wife, and indeed Caroline turns up with purple bruises on her arm. Her sisters are understandably alarmed.

In the course of the story, Caroline realizes that she has become a drunk like their father. She enters Alcoholics Anonymous, a program in which participants have "sponsors," sobriety mentors. Caroline's sponsor could have been anyone, but Freethy seizes this opportunity to combine roles and work an effective reversal of everyone's expectations:

> "I'm trying to stop drinking," Caroline continued. "Mike is helping me. He's not my boyfriend. He's my sponsor, the person I can call when I'm feeling desperate. Most people don't realize he's been sober for more than a year because of Alcoholics Anonymous. He took me to my first meeting a few weeks ago."

People can change, and Freethy's three sisters all go through many changes before this multilayered novel is finished.

Ann B. Ross's *Miss Julia Speaks Her Mind* is a Southern pecan pie of a novel, rich and hilarious. (What, you don't find pecan pie hilarious?) As illustrated in an earlier excerpt, Miss Julia is Julia Springer, the sixty-ish recent widow of

Abbotsford, North Carolina's upright and civic-minded banker, Wesley Lloyd Springer. In the course of the novel Ross turns Miss Julia's life upside down: Wesley Lloyd Springer had a mistress, trashy Hazel Marie Pucket, who one day dumps her nine-year-old son on Miss Julia's doorstep. The arrival of Lloyd Jr., sets off a landslide of complications for settled and orderly Miss Julia.

First, there are legal ramifications. Ross introduces Miss Julia's easy-going but crafty lawyer Sam Murdoch, who explains to Miss Julia not only her rights but how feared she is in the community. Everyone knew about her husband's affair, but no one had the courage to tell her.

Next, there is consternation in the "session" (governing body) of Miss Julia's local Presbyterian church. It seems that Wesley Lloyd Springer made verbal promises to fund a new family-oriented activities center, and the church was counting on Miss Julia to make good on those promises out of the considerable estate that her husband left her. Now, with a son suddenly in the picture, the church is afraid the money will go to this rival, nine-year-old claimant. They are plotting to sue to have the will set aside. Someone must tip off Miss Julia, but rather than introducing yet another character to do so, Ross appoints Sam Murdoch to the church's session, though as the novel opens he has resigned because of the maneuver that the session is planning.

Now, many protagonists have sidekicks or best friends who stick by them and serve as sounding boards throughout a novel. That is not Sam Murdoch's function in *Miss Julia Speaks Her Mind*. That role is played by Miss Julia's longtime housekeeper, Lillian. Sam is, rather, Miss Julia's sage advisor and troubleshooter—and Miss Julia manages to get herself into quite a lot of trouble before the novel is over.

So it is natural and satisfying when, tying up loose ends at the novel's conclusion, Miss Julia tells us how she resolved her fear of the sinful sickness that her minister Pastor Ledbetter has told her that she suffers, with the help of—who else?—Sam Murdoch:

> "You better turn me loose, Sam" I said, unable to leave him under my own steam. "Pastor Ledbetter and Dr. Fowler said I'm suffering from"—I lowered my voice, hardly daring to say the word but wanting to protect Sam from the consequences—*"nymphomania."*
> "Wha-at?" He started laughing and he laughed so hard, I tried to pull away from him so I could hide in a dark corner somewhere. "Oh, Julia, why didn't you tell me you were suffering from this condition?" He ran a finger down the side of my face and said, "Don't you know I've got the cure for that?"
> And he does, and that's really all I'm going to say on the subject.

I guess Miss Julia doesn't speak her mind about everything. Ann B. Ross does use Sam Murdoch in multiple ways, however, and her novel is warmer for it.

What about your current manuscript? Are there roles that can be combined? It may take less work than you think to accomplish it—and it may add more than you can measure to your novel's sense of complexity.

Give the people in your novel many roles, and your story will be the big beneficiary.

Combining Roles

Step 1: In two columns, list the following: (1) The names of all major, secondary, and minor characters. (2) The purpose of each in the story. (Jot down their purposes in as few words as possible, for example: *supports the protagonist, supports the antagonist, provides special knowledge*, etc.)

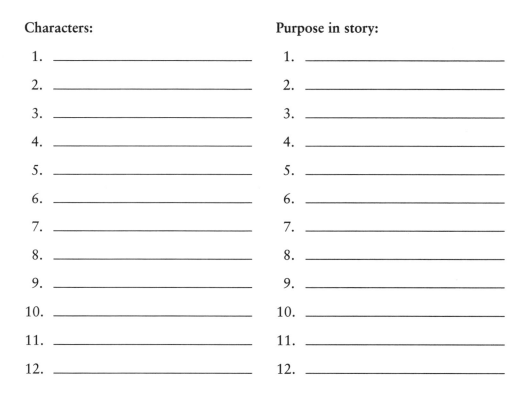

Characters:

1. _____
2. _____
3. _____
4. _____
5. _____
6. _____
7. _____
8. _____
9. _____
10. _____
11. _____
12. _____

Purpose in story:

1. _____
2. _____
3. _____
4. _____
5. _____
6. _____
7. _____
8. _____
9. _____
10. _____
11. _____
12. _____

Step 2: If you have ten or fewer characters, cross out the name of one. Delete him from the story. *Yes, do it.* If you have more than ten characters, cross out the names of two. *Go ahead. It's just an exercise.*

_____

_____

_____

_____

_____

Step 3: Your cast list is now shorter by one or two, but there remain one or two functions to be served in the story. *Assign those functions to one or more of the remaining characters.*

_____

_____

> ● **NOTE:**
> In life, an individual may be only one thing to you, the doorman who hails you a taxi, say. Yet how like life when that same doorman turns up a few nights later playing trumpet in a jazz band. The next time you get a taxi at your building, your perception of that doorman will have changed. How even more interesting it will be, then, when that same doorman shows up at the reading of your rich uncle's will, a beneficiary for once having saved your uncle's life. Give the people in your novel many roles, and your story will be the big beneficiary.

Follow-up work: Are there other characters in your cast who can take on multiple roles? Go down the list and note the possibilities, then put them into practice. Find at least two more roles to combine into one.

_____

_____

_____

_____

_____

Conclusion: Were you able to complete this exercise? Some authors have great difficulty with it. Most, though, find that the number of characters in their cast can be reduced. Furthermore, the remaining characters get more interesting. Why? Because not only do they have more to do, but they have become characters who are capable of more.

Part 2

PLOT DEVELOPMENT

Public Stakes

Things can go wrong in so many different ways, don't you agree? We sometimes think: *It can't get any worse than this.* But it can. That is the essence of raising the outward, or public, stakes: making things worse, showing us that there is more to lose, promising even bigger disasters that will happen if the hero doesn't make matters come out okay.

Raising the public stakes is easy in thrillers, mysteries, action adventure novels, and science fiction and fantasy stories. The action in such novels usually has significance for more than just the characters involved. Public safety and security are issues. But what about sagas, coming of age stories, family dramas, and romances? Whether or not everything turns out well in such stories won't make much difference to the rest of the world, will it? Are there public stakes in these novels and, if so, how do they get raised?

Cowboy romances have become a staple of the genre, and among the best practitioners is Joan Johnston. Her novel *The Cowboy* is the first of a trilogy of novels about two feuding south Texas ranching families, the Blackthornes and the Creeds.

What sets them against each other? The Blackthornes are rich; the Creeds struggle. The Blackthorn ranch, Bitter Creek, completely surrounds the Creed spread, Three Oaks. The Blackthorn patriarch, known as Blackjack, covets the Creed land and, as if that were not enough, also covets the Creed matriarch. (She, it must be said, also still loves him from long ago.)

The feud is nearly overcome by young Trace Blackthorne and Callie Creed when they fall in love as undergraduates at the University of Texas. But then word comes that Callie's younger brother, Sam, has been put in a wheelchair by Trace's younger brother in an accident on the high school football field—or was it an accident?

Callie must return to the ranch to help her family, leaving her college degree and wedding plans with Trace in the dust. Trace, bitter, disappears, not knowing that Callie is carrying his child. Montagues and Capulets? A secret baby? So far we are in familiar romance territory. An uncaring category romance writer might easily churn these simple conflicts for sixty thousand words and tell a story that satisfies her contract, but Johnston has her sights aimed higher. Let us see how she relentlessly raises the public stakes.

Fast-forward eleven years: Callie is a young widow, having married the Three Oaks foreman, who died a year earlier. Times are hard at Three Oaks. They are barely getting by. Callie doesn't need complications. It is, of course, at this moment that Blackjack has a heart attack and Trace returns to help manage Bitter Creek; and, he hopes, to win back Callie.

Blackjack, apparently not much slowed by his heart attack, now covets the Creed land more than ever. Any setback to the Creed clan represents a new opportunity to entice them to sell. But Callie is determined not to do that—and is even more determined to resist her all-too-clear attraction to Trace, who she hates for walking out on her, as she sees it, years before.

Question: Can Callie's twin problems—save the ranch, resist Trace—get worse? Oh, yes, much worse. Is it also possible that her fate can matter to the rest of the world? Are there public stakes here?

Again, yes. By making Callie's problems outward problems—that is, problems imposed on her by outside forces—Johnston slowly but surely makes Callie's story everybody's story. Who has not had a string of multiple disasters, run-ins with enemies, and just plain bad luck? We all have. Anyone can identify with Callie, especially as her problems compound.

As Johnston's novel progresses, calamity piles on calamity for Callie. The Creeds are counting on selling some of their fine quarter horses, but four of them are stolen. On the romantic front, at a dance Trace declares his intention to win her back in brusque cowboy fashion:

> "Look at me, Callie," he commanded.
> Callie tried to jerk free, but Trace tightened his hold. She raised her chin and glared at him. "Whatever we had between us is over and done."
> "Not quite," he said.
> She eyed him warily, her heart thumping crazily. "What is that supposed to mean?"
> "I haven't had my fill of you."
> She snorted derisively. "You make me sound like a bottle of beer you haven't finished swilling."
> His voice was low and seductive. "I was thinking of something utterly soft and incredibly sweet I haven't finished sampling."

Men: Do not try this at home. These are trained romance protagonists. Seriously, Callie does resist Trace, fiercely, though it must be noted that thereafter she does spend a terrific amount of time with the man she hates.

Meanwhile, what about Three Oaks? Things go from bad to worse to horrible. First, Callie's parents are shot out on the range. Her mother is hospitalized, and lack of insurance sets the family back twenty thousand dollars in cash. Her father dies. Callie and her brother Sam, now a wheelchair-bound alcoholic, inherit Three Oaks. Unfortunately, inheritance taxes (a genuine problem for farming and ranching families) make their financial predicament many magnitudes worse. Callie hopes to sell their cattle, but some of the herd comes down with a disease, and the cows are quarantined.

Blackjack presses his offer to buy Three Oaks, but Callie is resolved to hang on. But how can she do that with no money, not enough help, and mouths to feed? To make matters even worse still, Sam poisons himself with alcohol and winds up in the hospital, too.

The only answer seems to be accepting a loan from Trace. The payback? Callie must train his cutting horses. And give him sex:

> "That makes me a pretty expensive whore."
> "If that's the way you want to look at it."
> "There isn't any other way of looking at it," Callie said bluntly. "You're asking me to have sex with you for money."
> His expression hardened as he waited for her answer.
> "How much will I be paid for my services? How many times—?"
> "Till I'm tired of you," he said brusquely.

Those Blackthorne men have a way with women, don't they? Callie accepts his offer. Can her problems get any worse? Certainly. Johnston continues to raise the stakes. Just when Callie has every reason to scrub Trace from her heart for good, he reveals himself as a good man. He turns around Sam's life and wins the love of Callie's two children. He helps Callie in every imaginable way—and isn't too bad in bed, either. For a while it looks like Callie must capitulate.

At the last minute, a final bit of apparent treachery by the Blackthornes almost saves Callie from Trace. Blackjack's foreman is apprehended by Owen and charged with stealing Callie's horses and murdering her father. Blackjack must have been behind the crimes, Callie reasons. But then the ultimate culprit is revealed to be Trace's mother, long jealous of Callie's mother and her hold on Blackjack.

Rats! There's less and less reason for Callie to reject Trace, either on his own terms or because he is a Blackthorne. Finally, Trace rescues Callie's daughter in a mesquite brushfire and lands in the hospital himself. This is too much. Callie must admit defeat: She loves him. Three Oaks is saved with Trace's money, and the feud comes to an end—*or does it?* Only Johnston's two sequels will say for sure.

In a strict sense, how things turn out for Callie Creed doesn't make any difference to the world at large. But Johnston makes Callie's story everybody's story by relentlessly raising the stakes. The worse things get, the more Callie is determined to save her family from disaster, and her ranch from those who would take advantage of their misfortune. In a way, isn't that story universal? Doesn't its outcome matter to us all?

Let's look at another example of public stakes and their escalation in a story that has no immediately obvious public consequences. In Mary Alice

Who has not had a string of multiple disasters, run-ins with enemies, and just plain bad luck?

Monroe's *Skyward*, Ella Majors is a burned-out ER nurse from Vermont. She accepts a position as live-in nanny to a South Carolina preschooler, Marion Henderson, whose single dad, Harris, is overwhelmed and unable to cope with Marion's childhood diabetes.

Quickly, plain-looking Ella falls in love with tall and visionary Harris, the head of a rescue clinic for birds of prey. More slowly, she brings discipline, order, and compassion to both the Henderson household and, later, the clinic itself. Harris gradually discovers the wonder of Ella and falls in love with her, too.

This happiness cannot last, right? Right. Just as the inner obstacles and past hurts that each carries have been overcome, outside obstacles crash down upon them. Ella learns that Harris is married. Marion's mother, Fannie, beautiful and younger than Harris by ten years, is a drug user who has walked out on her family several times for extended periods. Harris has not sought a divorce, however:

> "I've known her since she was a kid, Ella. I've always looked out for her and she's done a lot for me. And for my mother. It's been hard but I'm no saint. I've asked myself, what if she was injured in some accident. Left paralyzed or in a coma. Would I divorce her then? Or what if she was schizophrenic and in a mental institution? Would I leave her then? The answer is always no. The vow says for better or worse."

Ella's newfound happiness is dashed. Still, there is hope. Harris might change his mind about Fannie. Shortly thereafter, Fannie indeed returns.

How would you handle this? It would be easy to show Fannie as a bad mother and drug user. That is what a category romance writer in a rush to meet a deadline might do, perhaps, letting Harris's exaggerated sense of duty drag out a modicum of suspense over the outcome of the marriage. Monroe, however, uses this moment to raise the stakes; that is, to make Ella's problem still worse.

Fannie turns out to be on the wagon and hoping to change her life and regain her family, as she has every right to do. Marion, her child, clings to her. Fannie, however, doesn't know how to manage Marion's diabetes and makes a dangerous mistake with candy, angering Ella, but leading to a turnabout:

> "You know something?" Fannie asked, stopping once more in front of Ella. "I'm mad, too. Not at you, but at me. Because I screwed up. Screwed up good. I hurt the two people I love most in the world. And I hurt myself, too. I've done some pretty horrible things. Things I'm not proud of. But I want to change."
>
> "I've heard that before."
>
> "I do," she repeated. "That's why I came back, see? I haven't used in months. I'm clean. Really I am. And I want a chance to

make it up to Marion. I don't know about Harris. He may never forgive me. But Marion . . . she has so much room for me." . . .

"I want to be a good mother," Fannie said to her, shouting to be heard over the storm.

"Then be one."

"The fact is, I can't do it alone." She released Ella's arm, crossing her own. "I . . . I need to learn to take care of her. I need to learn about this diabetes stuff, her diet and her shots. There's so much I don't know. I've seen you with her. You're good at it. So sure of yourself. Look, I know I'm the last person you want to help, but I have to ask. If not for me, for Marion. Please, Ella, teach me how to take care of my child."

Now Ella is *really* in trouble. Fannie's appeal for help and a second chance, for the sake of her child, is simply too good. Morally, Ella has no choice but to help her.

Can this situation get any worse? Yes, as it turns out, Fannie learns well and turns into a model mother, caring for Marion and conscientiously managing her tests and shots. Now Ella faces the unthinkable—failure, losing out to Fannie. When Fannie appeals to Harris, Ella overhears the result:

She leaned forward to take his hand and hold it tight while her eyes pleaded. "Harris, honey, I'm still your wife. I still love you. And I want to make it up to you. I may not deserve much, but I deserve a chance. It's my place to be here. To care for our child. This is my home," she blurted out before succumbing to tears. . . .

"Sorry," she said when she brought herself back under control. "I've been holding that in for so long I guess it was like the dam just broke." She sniffed and wiped her nose and eyes with the handkerchief. "I'll give this back after I launder it," she said with an attempt at a laugh.

"Mama!"

It was Marion, looking for Fannie.

Fannie laughed, more brightly than before. "That child does flash about. She's going to wear me down. And I love it," she added quickly. She looked up at Harris expectantly, waiting for some answer. "She's our child."

"Marion comes first," he said to her, moving toward an inescapable decision.

"Of course," she replied, her eyes opening wide with anticipation.

"I'll give you this one last chance, Fannie. For Marion's sake."

Defeated, Ella realizes that she must leave Harris and Marion—and she does, taking a new job at an emergency room in Charleston. Monroe raises the stakes—that is, deepens Ella's problems—so far that Ella actually fails. *What? Is that it?* you ask. *Ella loses out. The end?*

Well, let me ask you: How would you pull an ending out of this bleak situation? What resolution would you find for Ella? Is there any hope for her happiness? Of course, though it may not be exactly the form of happiness that we would like her to have.

How does Monroe handle it? Read *Skyward*, and see for yourself. Meanwhile, I think you will agree that Monroe's tale of love, change, forgiveness, and loss is one that anyone can identify with. The birds of prey that are rescued and rehabilitated at Harris's clinic might seem to lend the novel an environmental theme. I would argue that they are, rather, a metaphor for Monroe's injured human beings.

What gives *Skyward* its public stakes? First, as with Johnston's *The Cowboy*, the problems that are imposed on protagonist Ella Majors are from the *outside*: conflicts not inward and circumstances not of her own making. Second, these problems deepen to a degree that finally makes them so big that they attain a universal scale.

Everyday problems presented in an ordinary way, problems that anyone might have on any given day, do not have the power to become universal; that is, to resonate within us and remind us of all humanity and its eternal struggles. But when stakes rise to a high enough order of magnitude, a protagonist's problems will become the problems that we all have. What was personal becomes public.

What about the outward, or public, stakes in your current novel? How far do they rise? How deep do they cut? How bad do they get? Take them higher and deeper. Make them worse; *much* worse. Your novel can only get better.

Raising Public Stakes

Step 1: As briefly as possible, write down your novel's overt and outward central conflict or problem.

_____

_____

_____

_____

Step 2: What would make this problem worse? Write down as many reasons as you can. *Start writing now.*

_____

_____

_____

_____

_____

_____

_____

_____

Step 3: When you have run out of ideas, ask yourself, "What would make this problem even worse than that?" *Write down still more reasons.*

_____

_____

_____

_____

_____

Step 4: When you have run out of steam, ask, "What are the circumstances under which my protagonist(s) would actually fail to solve the problem?" *Write those down.*

_____

_____

_____

_____

_____

Step 5: Have your novel conclude with your protagonist's failure. Can you pull some measure of happiness from this ending? *Make notes.*

_____

_____

_____

_____

_____

> ● **NOTE:**
> Things always can get worse. Yes, they can. Much worse. In fact, there is no end to the misery you can heap on your poor protagonist. Is he in physical danger? Break his arm. Is she uncertain what to do? Take away her wisest friend. Is it raining? Make it flood. Is there a faint ray of hope? Snuff it out.
>
> Alternately, you can raise the stakes by making what might be lost more valuable. Does he stand to lose his wife's love? Have him find out how much more he needs it than he knew. Does she have a noble principle on her side? Show her how that principle works for the good in ways she had never imagined. Will solving the problem make people happy? Show that alternative outcomes will make folks miserable. Oh yes, things can always get worse.

Follow-up work: Incorporate into your story four raisings of the outward (plot) stakes. *Make notes for revision.*

_____

_____

_____

_____

Conclusion: A common failure in novels is that we can see the ending coming. The author signals his preferred outcome, and guess what? That is how things turn out. The only way to keep an ending in doubt is to make failure possible. Even better is to make failure happen. Maybe what's actually at stake isn't what you thought at all.

Complications

Every protagonist has a goal. That means that every protagonist has problems, because no goal is achieved without overcoming obstacles. (If a goal is easily achieved, then it isn't much of a goal, is it?) Those obstacles to a goal are important; indeed, they are the essence of plot.

To put it another way, what is plot if not an account of the many complications thrown in the way of your hero? What kinds of complications might serve? That depends on your story. Complications can be inner, psychological, and private, or they can be external, unprovoked, and public. Or they can be both. It doesn't matter. What matters is that wherever your hero may be going, it isn't easy to get there.

Whether internal or external in origin, it is important that obstacles be believable. If your reader is thinking, *"Oh, come on!"* then your complication isn't going to help your story. Is your hero afraid? Why? Does he face an antagonist? Who? And what makes that antagonist formidable?

Have another look at your favorite novels. You probably will find that a significant number of pages are filled by the business of making the opposition, who or whatever it may be, real and credible. That's as it should be; that is good storytelling.

The simplest-looking way to provide opposition to your protagonist is to create an antagonist; that is, a villain. Actually, villains are the hardest kind of opposition to put across. I know, because most villains I encounter in manuscripts are cardboard cutouts that do not frighten me for a minute.

Why? I suspect it is because most authors are not evil at heart. They are not familiar with the compelling reasons that real-life villains do what they do. Criminals rationalize their crimes. They feel justified. The same goes for anyone who deliberately hurts someone else, whether committing a crime or not: They always have good reasons. Thus, motivating the villain is an essential breakout skill.

Erica Spindler's *Cause for Alarm* is a women's thriller with not one, but two villains. The obvious villain is a deranged CIA hit man, John Powers, who stalks all four of the novel's main players: adoptive New Orleans parents Kate and Richard Ryan, their baby's birth mother, Julianna Starr, and the friend the couple turns to for help, author Luke Dallas.

The less obvious villain—and the more interesting one, to my eye—is the birth mother. Julianna, you see, becomes obsessed with adoptive father Richard, seeing in him the caring man she needs in her life. Indeed, for fulfilling Kate's wish to have a baby, Julianna thinks it is a reasonable trade-off for her to get Richard. So far so good, or bad I suppose, but how does Spindler go about making this obstacle active in a way that is real and believable?

First, Spindler removes potential guilt that might inhibit Julianna from stealing another woman's husband. Riding a streetcar, pregnant Julianna daydreams about how things will fall out with the adoptive parents that she already has picked for her baby:

> Julianna turned to the window and gazed out at the waning afternoon, trying to ignore the greasy smear on the glass. This wasn't forever, she reminded herself. Soon she would have all the things she loved and needed. Soon, she would feel like her old self again.
> *Richard.*
> *And Julianna.*
> She closed her eyes and pictured her future, imagined her days, how she would spend them, what her life would be like. Her life with Richard.
> It would be perfect, everything she ever longed for.
> She smiled to herself. Last night Richard had come to her in her dreams. He had whispered in her ear. That *she* was his everything. His lover and partner. His best friend.
> He told her he couldn't live without her.
> And they had been together. Sexually. Spiritually. Two souls made one, bodies entwined in an act of love so pure, so perfect, it defied the physical plane of existence.
> Kate had come to her as well. She had been smiling. Holding a baby in her arms. Completely content.

This young woman is delusional, obviously, but by reinforcing her delusions Julianna is making them more and more real for herself. At the adoption agency, Julianna sneaks a look at Kate and Richard's address. She watches them, realizing that to win Richard she will have to become like Kate. She visits Kate's coffee café and practices speaking like Kate. After delivering her baby she befriends a lonely secretary in Richard's law office and learns through her of an opening as Richard's assistant. She then gets the job, goes to work on Richard, seeds doubt in his mind about Kate's fidelity, becomes his confidant and, finally, his lover.

Julianna is not a deep psychological study. The sources of her sickness are as obvious as can be: an inadequate mother and her mother's sexually abusive boyfriend (John, the CIA assassin). But what Julianna lacks in subtlety, Spindler makes up for in deliberate, determined, step-by-step seduction. Julianna knows what she wants and goes after it with enough cunning to become a CIA operative herself. As a villain, she becomes formidable by her actions— and Spindler spins a formidable number of scenes making this opposition credible.

What happens after that? Suffice it to say that Richard's problems are only beginning. Julianna's sick abuser, John Powers, is after her and everyone whom he believes is corrupting her. He is a professional killer, too—and sets about proving it. Spindler's complications keep coming.

Is there an antagonist in your current novel? Or is your protagonist her own worst enemy? It does not matter who complicates your protagonist's life, so long as *someone* does it—and does it actively, deliberately, and for solid reasons. Put your people into play, and let them mess things up. Have a ball. The better the complications, the better your story.

If a goal is easily achieved, then it isn't much of a goal, is it?

Making Complications Active

Step 1: What is your novel's main conflict? *Write that down.*

_____

_____

_____

_____

Step 2: What are the main complications that deepen that conflict? (This list should have gotten longer in the last exercise.) *Write those down.*

_____

_____

_____

Step 3: To each complication, assign the name of the character who primarily will enact it. How will he do so? *Make notes, starting now.*

_____

_____

Step 4: Work out the primary motives for each character who introduces a complication. Then list all secondary motives, and underline the last one you wrote down. *Pick a scene involving that character and reverse that character's motives, as you did in the Reversing Motives exercise in chapter six.*

_____

_____

> **!**
>
> **NOTE:**
> Plot complications obviously need to be brought about via the actions of characters, but which characters? The obvious choices may not always be the most effective. For instance, who should let your protagonist know that time is running out? Usually it is someone in authority; for example, the precinct commander who tells your homicide detective that he has until Monday to catch the killer or he's off the case. But what if instead that information comes from the station janitor? ("I saw what happened to the last guy who didn't bring an indictment fast enough to make the boss look good on the six o'clock news. I'd say you have until Monday, boy-o.") That messenger may have even more force than the logical candidate.

Follow-up work: For at least three complications, work out who will be hurt the most when it happens. Incorporate that damage into the story.

_____

_____

_____

_____

_____

_____

_____

_____

Conclusion: Most authors underutilize their secondary characters. Adding complications is a way to get more mileage out of your cast.

15

Plot Layers

In understanding how breakout novels are built, it is crucial to grasp the difference between a subplot and a layer: Subplots are plot lines given to *different* characters; layers are plot lines given to the *same* character. Contemporary breakout fiction makes extensive use of plot layers, which reflect the multitiered complexity that most people feel is the condition of life today.

Think back to our earlier discussion of Dennis Lehane's mystery novel *Mystic River*. In the story, Boston detective Sean Devine's two boyhood friends Jimmy Marcus and Dave Boyle both have subplots: Jimmy struggles with the murder of his teenage daughter and his belief that Dave killed her; Dave struggles to suppress the homicidal urges of The Boy, an alter ego that surfaced in him following his abduction by child molesters years earlier.

What gives the novel its resonance, though, are Sean's own three plot layers we looked at earlier: (1) He is the lead detective in the investigation of the murder of Katie Marcus, and, although he owes his childhood friend Jimmy his utmost efforts, he struggles against a debilitating emotional numbness. (2) His wife has left him, taking with her the baby daughter who may or may not be Sean's, and he doesn't how to get her back.

Then there is the final layer: (3) Because the case reconnects him with Jimmy and Dave, Sean must with them face again what happened to them all one afternoon as they argued about whether or not to steal a car. Another car with two men inside stopped, Dave got in, and his two friends did not. Guilt over this random event haunts Sean powerfully in the present:

> "Like this Dave Boyle stuff," his father said. "What does it matter what happened twenty-five years ago to Dave? You know what happened. He disappeared for four days with two child molesters. What happened was exactly what you'd think would happen. But here you come dredging it back up again because . . ." His father took a drink. "Hell, I don't know why."
>
> His father gave him a befuddled smile and Sean matched it with his own.

"Hey, Dad."

"Yeah."

"You telling me that nothing ever happened in your past that you don't think about, turn over in your head a lot?"

His father sighed. "That's not the point."

"Sure, it is."

"No, it isn't. Bad shit happens to everyone, Sean. Everyone. You ain't special."

Layers are plot lines given to the same character.

But Sean *is* special, and so is the case of the murder of Katie Marcus. It draws together all three of the layers that Lehane has given his hero. Because it is Sean's job to investigate, he cannot avoid revisiting the past he shares with the victim's father, Jimmy, and the prime suspect, Dave. Nor can he avoid the loss of his wife, whose spooky phone calls torment him as much as his survivor's guilt. Sean is a man beset by multiple conflicts, outer and inner. Who cannot identify with that?

In his complex and erotic literary novel *The Sixteen Pleasures*, Robert Hellenga demonstrates a similar flair for laying down plot layers. The novel's opening paragraph nicely reveals the two principle reasons that his heroine, American book conservator Margot Harrington, decides to travel to Florence in 1966:

> I was twenty-nine years old when the Arno flooded its banks on Friday 4 November 1966. According to the Sunday *New York Times*, the damage wasn't extensive, but by Monday it was clear that Florence was a disaster. Twenty feet of water in the cloisters of Santa Croce, the Cimabue crucifix ruined beyond hope of restoration, panels ripped from the Baptistry doors, the basement of the Biblioteca Nazionale completely underwater, hundreds of thousands of volumes waterlogged, the Archivio di Stato in total disarray. On Tuesday I decided to go to Italy, to offer my services as a humble book conservator, to help in any way I could, to save whatever could be saved, including myself.

Thus, Margo embarks on an outer journey (visit Italy, save rare books) and an inner journey, a search for the self that she could not find in America in the mid-sixties:

> Instead of going to Harvard, I went to Edgar Lee Masters College, where Mama had taught art history for twenty years. Instead of going to graduate school I spent two years at the Institute of Paper Technology on Green Bay Avenue; instead of becoming a research chemist I apprenticed myself to a book conservator in Hyde Park and then took a position in the conservation department of the Newberry Library. Instead of getting married and having a daughter of my own, I lived at home and looked after

Mama, who was dying of lung cancer. A year went by, two years, three years, four. Mama died; Papa lost most of his money. My sister Meg got married and moved away; my sister Molly went to California with her boyfriend and then Ann Arbor. The sixties were churning around me, and I couldn't seem to get a footing.

Margot is a woman clearly in need of an awakening, and where better to find it than in Italy? Margot's two layers are strong; all that remains is for Hellenga to weave them together, which he does by means of a masterfully conceived device that becomes the *node of conjunction* between these two journeys—and which I will discuss in the next chapter. Stay tuned.

Best-selling novelist Nora Roberts cut her teeth writing short "category" romances, but has since become expert at building the layers that turn romance stories into breakout-level fiction. Her best-selling novel *Carolina Moon* is the story of a wounded young woman who returns home to face her past, and who finds love in the process.

There's nothing new in that. That story has been told hundreds, maybe thousands, of times. Roberts does not allow her novel to remain that simple, however. She starts with a strong first layer: As a child, heroine Tory Bodeen was regularly and savagely beaten with a leather belt by her fanatic, sharecropper father. Tory longs to face those memories in the town where they happened, open an upscale gift store there, and prove to herself that she can be happy.

Brutal childhood beatings would be plenty to load up any backstory, but Roberts goes further. At age eight, Tory had a special friend in Hope Lavelle, whose family owned the land that Tory's father farmed. One night the two girls planned to sneak out of their homes for a midnight adventure. Hope escapes to their rendezvous in the woods, but Tory is prevented by her father, who chooses that night to administer another beating.

Eight-year-old Hope is raped and murdered. Even in the present day, the murderer remains at large. This second layer of guilt and mystery also might be enough to heap on a heroine, but not for Roberts. To this burden she adds another: Tory has the gift of second sight. She can "see" the minds and memories of others, particularly those who have suffered extreme distress. On the night Hope was murdered, Tory helplessly saw the whole thing happen, sharing the horror of the incident—though not the knowledge of who murdered her best friend.

That makes three layers, by my count. But why stop there?

Tory's gift of sight continues to plague her into the present. She would like to be free of this "gift," but Roberts has other plans: Soon enough, Tory's sight reveals to her the horrific experiences of fresh victims of Hope's long-ago killer. Tory must both cope with the psychological pain of what she witnesses and follow the imperfect trail opened by her visions—for not only is the identity of Hope's killer within reach, that killer now has targeted Tory.

Enough? No way. Roberts has still more in mind. Her heroine is staunchly uninterested in men, having been badly burned by an early love: "I don't intend to be involved again. Once was enough." Naturally, there is a fabulous and caring man waiting for her in her home town of Progress, South Carolina. The identify of this love interest provides one of the powerful nodes of conjunction that connects up the now—Do I have this right?—five layers of Tory's story.

Childhood memories to face down, an unsolved murder, painful-but-persistent visions of violence, a love that she does not want yet cannot avoid . . . there's a lot happening in the life of Tory Bodeen, don't you agree? Is this plot overloaded? I would argue that it is effectively layered: It is the multiplicity of Tory's problems that makes *Carolina Moon* engrossing—and Nora Roberts one of America's best-selling storytellers.

How many layers have you heaped on your protagonist in your current manuscript? Just one? Heck, get busy! As you can see, even two layers may be too few to build a breakout novel.

Building Plot Layers

Step 1: What is the name of your protagonist? *Write that down.*

_____

_____

_____

_____

_____

Step 2: What is the overall problem he must solve? *Write that down.*

_____

_____

_____

_____

_____

_____

_____

_____

Step 3: What additional problems can she face? Not complications to the main problem (we dealt with those in the last exercise) but altogether different problems? *Write those down.*

_____

_____

_____

_____

_____

_____

_____

_____

> **!** **NOTE:**
>
> A plot is *layered* when more than one thing is happening simultaneously to the hero. He has a murder to solve, and at the same time his father is dying of cancer. Why not add a further layer? He is searching for the soul of Mozart's piano concerti. What is it that gives them their power, their drive? He has to know, so along the way he achieves that insight, too. Thus, there are levels of problem to utilize: public problems, personal problems, and secondary problems. Small mysteries, nagging questions, dangling threads—those also can be woven into the plot.

Follow-up work: For each plot layer (or at least for each two) that you have added, work out at least four steps or scenes that you will need to bring this narrative line to its climax and resolution. Make notes for these additional steps or scenes.

_____

_____

_____

_____

_____

_____

_____

_____

Conclusion: Have you ever noticed how everything seems to happen at once? *Good things come in threes. When it rains it pours.* Layers give novels the rich texture of real life. Building them into your story is extra work, but the reward is a rich resonance and complexity.

16

Weaving a Story

Having added layers to your novel, the next step is to get them working together; that is, to connect them. Without links you might as well be writing separate novels (sequels, I suppose) for each layer. Finding reasons for your layers to coexist is what I call weaving them together.

The particular devices you use to make the connections happen are called nodes of conjunction. A setting in your story may recur, serving double duty in different layers. A character who faces his own problem in a subplot may bring relief, or introduce a complication, to your protagonist, who is facing his own conflict. Secondary characters can get dragged into storylines they did not expect to grapple with. These are the ways in which storylines cross.

As we saw earlier, for example, Will Klein, the hero of Harlan Coben's twisty thriller *Gone for Good,* has several big problems. First, his older brother Ken, whom everyone believes murdered Will's one-time girlfriend eleven years before and then disappeared, is innocent—or so Will believes. Several none-too-pleasant people disagree and want to find Ken, who is still alive and at large. Will needs to find him before others do.

Second, Will's girlfriend, Sheila Rogers, has vanished, but not without leaving behind her fingerprints at the scene of a double homicide. Will knows that she, too, is innocent. As if those things were not enough, a shadowy hit man called The Ghost is on Will's trail, as well. But why?

These three layers easily could send Coben's plot careening out of control, but he skillfully weaves them together. Will is a counselor of runaway teens, and two of the most important people in his life have now run away, too. But the FBI sees it in a more sinister light, as is clear when they come to question Will and his co-worker Squares about Sheila's disappearance:

> "Are you aware," Fisher said, "of Ms. Rogers's criminal record?"
>
> I tried to keep a straight face, but even Squares reacted to that one.

Fisher started reading from the sheet of paper. "Shoplifting. Prostitution. Possession with intent to sell."

Squares made a scoffing noise. "Amateur hour."

"Armed robbery."

"Better," Squares said with a nod. He looked up at Fisher. "No conviction on that one, right?"

"That's correct."

"So maybe she didn't do it."

Fisher frowned again.

I plucked at my lower lip.

"Mr. Klein?"

"Can't help you," I said.

"Can't or won't."

I still plucked. "Semantics."

"This must all seem a little déjà vu, Mr. Klein."

"What the hell is that supposed to mean?"

"Covering up. First for your brother. Now your lover."

Thus, Coben puts Will on the FBI's bad side on two counts—and also begins to draw these two sides of the story together. A second node of conjunction occurs when The Ghost summons a New York gangster, Philip McGuane, to see him in a graveyard. The Ghost wants something from McGuane:

"You have sources, Philip. Access to information I don't." The Ghost looked at the tombstone, and for a moment McGuane thought he saw something almost human there. "Are you sure he's back?"

"Fairly sure," McGuane said.

"How do you know?"

"Someone with the FBI. The men we sent to Albuquerque were supposed to confirm it."

It quickly becomes clear that The Ghost and McGuane are talking about Will's brother, but alert readers will also pick up that Albuquerque is where Sheila's fingerprints were left at a murder scene. Thus, the runaways in Will's life have crossed somehow. A while later Will finds someone lying in wait for him in his apartment: The Ghost, whom we now find out is someone known to Will from his childhood, violent John Asselta, who is no less scary now:

He tilted his head, and I remembered the way he would simply lash out. John Asselta had been a classmate of Ken's, two years ahead of me at Livingston High School. He captained the wrestling team and was the Essex County lightweight champ two years running. He probably would have won the states, but he got disquali-

fied for purposely dislocating a rival's shoulder. His third violation.
I still remember the way his opponent screamed in pain.

Look again: Now The Ghost is tied to Ken, and the three plot layers are stitched together. Exactly how remains to be seen. Still more connections are forged later in the story. Katy, nineteen-year-old sister of the long-ago murdered Julie, forces her way into Will's investigation. It is Katy who finds the next node of conjunction, this one between her dead sister and Will's runaway girlfriend:

> "I still don't get it, Katy."
> "Sheila Rogers went to Haverton, Will. With Julie. They were in the same sorority."
> I stood, stunned. "That's not possible."
> "I can't believe you don't know. Sheila never told you?"
> I shook my head. "Are you sure?"
> "Sheila Rogers of Mason, Idaho. Majored in communications. It's all in the sorority booklet. I found it in an old trunk in the basement."
> "I don't get it. You remembered her name after all these years?"
> "Yeah."
> "How come? I mean, do you remember the name of everyone in Julie's sorority?"
> "No."
> "So why would you remember Sheila Rogers?"
> "Because," Katy said, "Sheila and Julie were roommates."

The plot, as they say, thickens. Or, to put it another way, Harlan Coben has found yet another clever way to weave his plot layers together. The two loves of Will's life, one murdered eleven years earlier and his current girlfriend, by this point in the story also murdered, knew each other. A trip to Haverford reveals that a third sorority sister was killed by strangulation, too—this time in North Dakota. Much more is going on than Will knew—or than the FBI told his family way back when. They must knowingly have lied to them about the case, Will realizes.

But why? Now the FBI is an additional thread woven in. The investigators are playing a double game, and how they fit into the overall picture is one of the many surprises waiting at the end of Coben's novel. Julie, Sheila, Ken, The Ghost, McGuane, and the FBI are all connected in a seemingly elaborate (but once revealed, fiendishly simple) set of circumstances. Coben skillfully spaces out his nodes of conjunction to keep us guessing—and also to keep his plot layers tightly woven.

In the last chapter I mentioned Robert Hellenga's rich and complex literary novel *The Sixteen Pleasures*, the story of American book conservator Margot Harrington, who travels to Florence to aid in the saving of rare books damaged in the disastrous flooding of the river Arno that year. As important as that mission is, Margot also hopes to find in Italy the self that she somehow missed finding as a young woman back home. Hellenga, winner of many grants and prizes, employs a node of conjunction that in one brilliant stroke brings together Margot's outer and inner journeys.

Here is how the twin layers of Margot's story intersect: Her work brings her to a convent library where she is given an unusual project. Bound inside the covers of an old but ordinary prayer book is a rare copy of Aretino's lost erotic sonnets, *The Sixteen Pleasures*, banned and burned by the Pope of its time, illustrated with highly explicit drawings. It is worth a fortune. The abbess wishes both to preserve it and to keep it out of the hands of her bishop, who almost certainly will use it to finance his own interests instead of the convent's. She asks Margot to restore the volume—and then to arrange for its sale in secret.

For Margot, the volume is both the book conservation challenge of a lifetime and, in its content, an awakening to the sexuality lying dormant inside her. Her sensual side finds release in her affair with an older roguish and charming art scholar, Dottor Alessandro (Sandro) Postiglione, a man with a gift for happiness. As the story unfolds, Hellenga deftly shows us that Margo's act of book conservation and Sandro's awakening of Margot really are much the same thing:

> The more I got to know this man, the more I loved him. I loved him for himself, and for his bald head and for his uncircumcised uccello (his little bird that sang so sweetly in the night); I loved him for his attentiveness; I loved him because he seemed so at home in this world and because at the same time he was so hopelessly unworldly; I loved him because he'd invested half his money in a fast-food restaurant and the other half in a scheme to export low-calorie wine to the United States; I loved to see him crossing the piazza, I loved to find him waiting for me in the station when my train came back from Prato; I loved to come home and find him waiting for me in his old silk robe; and I loved him for the things I learned about him from others, which seemed great and heroic: on the night of the flood, for example, he opened up his apartment to all the people living on the lower floors who had no place to go, and he waded to the Uffizi to help rescue the paintings in the restoration rooms in the basement and the self-portraits in the Vasari Corridor, which was in danger of collapsing into the Arno.
>
> And I loved him for being so good at his work, for being a true craftsman. He was a man who cared about things, who cherished them, who spent his life preserving them.

Possibly Sandro's greatest work of preservation is Margot herself; although, lest the story be too easy, it also gradually emerges that Sandro is not entirely a saint. Indeed, his charm conceals a selfishness and uniquely Catholic surrender to his fate—a fate that leads to heartbreak for Margot.

Also in the last chapter, I mentioned Nora Roberts's very different novel,

A tightly woven novel is one that your readers will be able to wrap around themselves luxuriously.

Carolina Moon. As we know, in this story Roberts creates five plot layers—that is, big problems—for her heroine, gift store owner Tory Bodeen, to overcome: (1) the crippling memory of the brutal beatings her father administered to Tory as a child; (2) the unsolved rape and murder of Tory's childhood friend Hope Lavelle; (3) the second sight that plagues Tory with painful visions of the suffering of others; (4) Hope's killer still at large, killing others, and now after Tory; (5) a love interest who is unwanted by Tory.

How does Roberts weave these plot layers together? Principally by having characters cross from one storyline to another. For instance, Tory's murdered childhood friend had an older brother, Cade Lavelle. Whom do you think falls in love with the adult Tory when she returns to her hometown? Bingo. Cade draws together the murder in Tory's past and the problem of her resistance to men.

A further node of conjunction is that Cade's mother, Margaret, and Hope's surviving twin sister, Faith, are not at all pleased by Tory's return to the town of Progress; indeed, they blame Tory for Hope's death, since it was a nighttime adventure jointly planned by Tory and Hope that drew Hope to the woods where she was murdered. In the present, Faith takes her hatred of Tory so far as to try to sabotage Tory's effort to heal from the beatings her father inflicted (layer one), as we see the first time Faith confronts Tory:

> "You believe in fresh starts and second chances, Tory?"
>
> "Yes, I do."
>
> "I don't. And I'll tell you why." She took a cigarette out of her purse, lighted it. After taking a drag she waved it. "Nobody wants to start over. Those who say they do are liars or delusional, but mostly liars. People just want to pick up where they left off, wherever things went wrong, and start off in a new direction without any of the baggage. Those who manage it are the lucky ones because somehow they're able to shrug off all those pesky weights like guilt and consequences."
>
> She took another drag, giving Tory a contemplative stare. "You don't look that lucky to me."

Yet another node of conjunction occurs when Tory's father, the physical abuser whose memory cripples Tory in the present, returns to Progress and becomes the prime suspect in the murder of Hope—and in the later murders linked to it.

These storyline-crossing characters give Roberts a way to weave together Tory's plot layers. Some might find these connections forced. I say they are effective, giving *Carolina Moon* a rich connectedness that makes the novel feel complex and engrossing. Roberts's legions of fans obviously agree.

Count the nodes of conjunction that weave together the layers in your novel. How many are there? Why not search for more? That is what the exercise in chapter fourteen is there to help you do. A tightly woven novel is one that your readers will be able to wrap around themselves luxuriously as they curl up in their favorite chairs with a cup of tea. (They are trying to relax, but you are keeping them tense on every page, right?)

Weaving Plot Layers Together

Step 1: On a single sheet of paper, make three columns. In the first column list your novel's major and secondary characters. In the middle column, list the principle narrative lines: main problem, extra plot layers, subplots, minor narrative threads, questions to be answered in the course of the story, etc. In the right-hand column, list the novel's principle places; i.e., major settings.

Step 2: With circles and lines, connect a character, a narrative line, and a place. Keep drawing lines and circles at random, making connections. See what develops. When a random connection suddenly makes sense, *make notes*.

_____

_____

_____

_____

_____

_____

_____

_____

! NOTE:
When we undertake this exercise in the Breakout Novel workshops, most participants at first look puzzled. The random connections they make between characters, plotlines, and settings seem pointless. But after a few minutes many participants are making notes. They are discovering connections they did not see before: characters that cross from one storyline to another, settings that host scenes from more than one storyline. These nodes of conjunction give a novel texture, a feeling of being woven together.

Follow-up work: Add to your novel at least six of the nodes of conjunction that you came up with.

_____

_____

_____

_____

_____

_____

_____

_____

Conclusion: Three hundred pages into a manuscript, your story can feel out of control. The elements can swim together in a sea of confusion. This panic is normal. Your novel will come out okay. Trust the process. If you have set a strong central problem, added layers, and found ways to weave them together, then the whole will come together in the end.

Subplots

Plot layers are the several narrative lines experienced by a novel's protagonist; subplots are the narrative lines experienced by other characters. What constitutes a narrative line? Problems that require more than one step to resolve; in other words, that grow more complicated.

Now that we've got our terms straight, what is the best way to go: layers or subplots? Today, the term subplot has an almost old-fashioned ring. It makes us think of sprawling sagas of the type written by Victor Hugo and Charles Dickens. Subplots are found throughout twentieth-century literature, of course, and in contemporary novels, too.

Yet what is striking about recent fiction is its intimacy. Authorial and objective third-person points of view have been almost entirely replaced by first-person, and close or intimate third-person points of view. The rich woven texture of breakout-scale novels comes more often from the tight weaving of plot layers than from the broad canvas sprawl of subplots.

But that is not to say that subplots have no place in breakout novels. Far from it. Examples of extensive use of subplots abound on the best-seller lists. Many of the novels discussed in this workbook employ subplots as well as plot layers.

Even Dickensian sprawl can be found. Michel Faber's Victorian morality tale *The Crimson Petal and the White* was, in fact, compared by reviewers to Dickens, and it is true that Faber's narrative voice is intrusive and authorial in the manner of nineteenth-century novelists. He frequently addresses his readers directly, as we see in this early passage in which Faber takes pity on the reader following a long section detailing the introspection of the novel's main character:

> So there you have it: the thoughts (somewhat pruned of repetition) of William Rackham as he sits on his bench in St. James Park. If you are bored beyond endurance, I can offer only my promise that there will be fucking in the very near future, not to mention madness, abduction, and violent death.

Well okay, then! Faber goes on to spin out a number of subplots. Rackham is under pressure as his annual stipend is slowly reduced in order to coerce him into assuming directorship of his family's business bottling perfumes and toiletries. Longing for artistic expression but burdened with an invalid wife and child, he seeks release with prostitutes, advised by his jolly friends Bodley and Ashwell and their bible, a slim guidebook called *More Sprees in London*. It is this somewhat inaccurate booklet that brings Rackham to Sugar, a high-priced prostitute of unusual beauty, attentiveness, education, and sexual versatility. Sugar is all that he desires. She is even writing a novel; one, we discover, that is mostly about the mutilation of men.

Sugar herself carries a substantial amount of the story. When first we meet her, she is employed by the sour madam Mrs. Castaway, who may or may not be Sugar's mother. Either because he is rich and easy or because she is won by his genuine affection for her, Sugar agrees to become Rackham's exclusive mistress. She moves into a house that he provides for her.

Meanwhile, Rackham's brother, Henry, a minister, haltingly pursues a charitable widow, Mrs. Emmeline Fox, who runs a Rescue Society for prostitutes. (You can see already that Faber will weave his many subplots together.) Henry's courtship inches forward until consummation, after which, unfortunately, he perishes in a fire in his paper-cluttered cottage.

At the Rackham home, Rackham's bedridden wife, Agnes, preoccupies their dwindling household staff with her hypochondria. She fears she is going mad (and in fact is). She longs for relief and begs Mrs. Fox to direct her to the "convent" where she may find "eternal life." She buries her diaries in the backyard.

Unable to stand being apart from Sugar, Rackham (at Sugar's suggestion) hires her as a nanny to his bed-wetting daughter, Sophie. Sugar enters the Rackham household, but as soon as she does Rackham begins to grow distant. It slowly emerges that Sugar appeals to him as a prostitute, not as a companion. Sugar, in contrast, is drawn to the stability of domestic life. She befriends Sophie with kindness and cures her of her bed-wetting. She digs up Agnes's diaries and reads them, gaining understanding of Agnes's pain.

The climactic events of all these subplots take 200 pages or so to play out. What a saga! Faber's novel in its U.S. hardcover edition clocks in at 834 pages. It's a novel to wander in, and one feels sorry when it is over.

And yet to achieve the tapestry effect of multiple subplots, it is by no means necessary to write at such length. Cecily von Ziegesar's zingy young adult novel *Gossip Girl*, discussed in earlier chapters of this workbook, has just as many subplots but delivers them in a breezy 199 pages. How does she do it?

Gossip Girl first introduces New York private school girl Blair Waldorf, a too-rich, too-busy, and under-supervised seventeen-year-old who wants to lose her virginity with her boyfriend, Nate Archibald. Her various setbacks away from that goal form the principle plotline in the novel.

The main obstacle to Blair's ambition is her former friend, the stunningly gorgeous but troubled Serena van der Woodsen. Serena's return to New York, her abandonment by her former friends, her failure to fire Nate out of his ambivalence, her discovery of avant-garde art (a blurred picture of her eye—or maybe her belly button or possibly a more intimate body part—appears in ads all over the city), and her discovery of filmmaking and a more interesting boy than Nate, occupies a significant portion of the remaining novel.

But there are other subplots, too. Serena's love interest, Dan Humphrey, finds Serena, loses her, and finds her again. Student filmmaker Vanessa Abrams has a crush on Dan, but finds a more interesting possibility in a Brooklyn bartender. Dan's little sister, Jenny, worships Serena, volunteers to work on a film Serena never even scripts, and, to be near Serena, she even crashes a charity fundraiser called "Kiss on the Lips" that raises money for Central Park falcons. (Why do falcons need money, you ask? No one really knows.) Meanwhile, preppy lecher Chuck Bass hits on every girl in sight, including Serena, and winds up with Jenny, whom he molests in a ladies' room stall at the "Kiss on the Lips" party.

All of these doings are tightly woven together. What accounts for the 600-page length difference between *The Crimson Petal and the White* and *Gossip Girl*? Style. Faber's ambling narration minutely details every scene. Von Ziegesar's writing provides as much character detail, but speeds through the action with frenetic music-video pacing. The racy world of privileged Manhattan private school girls feels no less vast than Faber's tapestry of Victorian sexual politics, though, thanks to von Ziegesar's liberal use of subplots.

Are there subplots that can be developed in your novel? Some writers are afraid to add subplots, for fear their story will run away with them. That fear is unfounded. Subplots may make a novel sprawl, but if carefully woven together with the main layers (see the Follow-up Work in the following exercise), the novel not only will hang together, but will have the rich tapestry feeling of real life.

Can subplots and secondary characters steal the show? Of course.

Adding Subplots

Step 1: Who are your novel's most important secondary characters? *Write down the names of one, two, or three.*

_____

_____

Step 2: What is the main problem, conflict, or goal faced by each of these characters? *Write those down.*

_____

_____

_____

_____

Step 3: For each, what are three main steps leading to the solution to that problem, the resolution of that conflict, or the attainment of that goal? Another way to ask that is, what are three actions, events, or developments—with respect to these secondary characters—that you could not possibly leave out? *Write those down.*

_____

_____

Step 4: Outline each secondary character's story. While your protagonist is at work on the main problem, what is each character doing to solve his own problem? *Make notes, starting now.*

_____

_____

_____

_____

!

• **NOTE:**
What if your novel is not really about your hero, but about another character? That is the point of this exercise: To make secondary characters active, to give them lives and stories of their own. These are true subplots.

Follow-up work: Weave your plot layers together with your subplots using the method in the Building Plot exercise found in chapter sixteen. *Add the nodes of conjunction that you discover to your novel.*

_____

_____

_____

_____

_____

_____

_____

_____

Conclusion: Can subplots and secondary characters steal the show? Of course. If they steal it effectively enough, it is even possible that you have the wrong protagonist. But that would be unusual. Most subplots are underdeveloped or nonexistent. This exercise can help give subplots a vital pulse.

Turning Points

A turning point in a story is point at which things change. It could be the arrival of new information, a shift in the course of events, a reversal, a twist (such as revealing a character's second role), a challenge, or a disaster.

Cooking up turning points is easy enough: All stories have them. Making them as dramatic as possible is a bit more difficult. Heightening takes work. But it is work that pays off in a more active, exciting, and involving novel.

Sometimes a turning point simply involves letting go of an old way of looking at things. An example of this can be found in Jodi Picoult's *Salem Falls*, which was discussed in an earlier chapter. Protagonist Addie Peabody is hung up on her daughter, Chloe, who died ten years earlier. Addie refuses to acknowledge that Chloe is gone. She cooks meals for Chloe that never get eaten and keeps Chloe's room preserved exactly as it was when she died. Addie has not even changed Chloe's bedsheets.

One day, Addie stings her new lover, Jack St. Bride, by telling him that he will never mean more to her than Chloe. Later, Addie awakens in Chloe's room feeling remorse:

> Frustrated, she threw back the covers of the bed and began to pace through the house. At the bottom of the stairs, she automatically touched the small picture of Chloe that hung there, the same way she did every time she came up and down, as if it were a mezuzah. And that was the moment she realized she'd lied.
>
> Jack might never mean more to her than Chloe. But God, he meant just as much. . . .
>
> "I love him," she murmured out loud, the words bright as a handful of new coins. "I *love* him. *I* love him." . . .
>
> In Chloe's room, she stripped the bed. She carried the linens downstairs in a bundle, remembering what it had been like to hold her newborn just like this in her arms and walk her through her colic at night. She threw the sheets and pillowcases into the washing machine, added soap, and turned the dial.

The fresh scent of Tide rose from the bowl of the machine. "Goodbye," Addie whispered.

In this passage, Picoult heightens Addie's inner change with an outer action: Laundering (after ten years!) the sheets that her dead daughter slept on the last night of her life. One might not think of the scent of laundry detergent as a symbol, but Picoult makes it a powerful indicator of change. Really, it is herself that Addie is washing clean.

Recall my earlier examination of Barbara Freethy's romantic novel *Summer Secrets*. Freethy's plot has plenty of turning points, thanks to the (count 'em) three stories of three sisters that she spins out. The oldest sister is bookstore owner Kate McKenna. Kate keeps a tight lid on her feelings, and on her two sisters, because of the horrible secret that they share. An additional difficulty is their alcoholic, restless father, Duncan, who, after a triumphant but tragically marred round-the-world sailboat race eight years earlier, promised Kate that he would never race again. As the novel opens, Duncan breaks that promise and signs on as skipper for an upcoming ocean race. Kate is livid.

Kate's temper uncharacteristically breaks, and the man who happens to catch the heat is a reporter, Tyler Jamison, who is investigating the famous sailing McKenna sisters and their father. Note how Freethy heightens this minor turning point of Kate's with careless words that create a major outburst:

> [Tyler says:] "Not so fast. Tell me what's wrong."
>
> "I've had it," she replied. "I've had it with lies. I've had it with people making promises that they have no intention of keeping. They just say the words they think you want to hear, then they do whatever they want. And no one changes. People say they'll change, but they don't. No matter how hard you try, what you say, you can't make them do what they don't want to do. I give up. I quit. I'm throwing in the towel, putting up the white flag. I just wish I had a handkerchief or something. But you don't have one, because you're not a gentleman, and men don't carry handkerchiefs anymore, and it's all such a mess!"

Phew! We get the point. Freethy heightens with more than forceful prose. She also effectively uses settings to make tense moments more dramatic. During the fateful race eight years earlier, Kate's fiancée, Jeremy, was lost at sea one night in a storm. She has never gotten over her loss. Passion rises between Kate and Tyler, but it cannot get very far until her feelings for Jeremy get out in the open, which early on Kate is not ready to do, as we discover:

> "Are you still in love with Jeremy?"
>
> Her mouth went dry. When had this suddenly become so personal? "My feelings are my own, and they will stay that way. Now I'm going home and you're going somewhere else."

Now, let me ask you: Where would you set this exchange? In Kate's living room? In Tyler's rental car? Freethy sets it in the cemetery where Jeremy is buried, which Kate goes to visit and where Tyler tracks her down. The answer to his question—"Are you still in love with Jeremy?"—seems pretty obvious from this, but that is the point. Kate refuses to answer, but anyone, including Tyler, can readily see the truth.

Major life turning points involve accepting loss, such as the end of a relationship or the end of a life. Earlier I discussed Alice Sebold's *The Lovely Bones*, in which fourteen-year-old Susie Salmon is abducted, raped, and murdered. From heaven, she narrates the stories of those left behind, some of which, of course, involve coming to grips with the permanence of her death. The first is Susie's father, whose grief hits as he examines the ships-in-bottles that Susie helped him to make:

> I watched him as he lined up the ships in bottles on his desk, bringing them over from the shelves where they usually sat. He used an old shirt of my mother's that had been ripped into rags and began dusting the shelves. Under his desk there were empty bottles—rows and rows of them we had collected for our future ship building. In the closet were more ships—the ships he had built with his own father, ships he had built alone, and then those we had made together. Some were perfect, but their sails browned; some had sagged or toppled over after the years. Then there was the one that had burst into flames the week before my death.
>
> He smashed that one first.
>
> My heart seized up. I turned and saw all the others, all the years they marked and the hands that had held them. His dead father's, his dead child's. I watched him as he smashed the rest. He christened the walls and wooden chair with the news of my death, and afterward he stood in the guest room/den surrounded by green glass. The bottles, all of them, lay broken on the floor, the sails and boat bodies among them. He stood in the wreckage.

Notice how Sebold uses these fragile objects as the expression of the father's unbearable rage. Sebold also uses an object, a photograph of Susie, as the focal point in showing the grief of the classmate who loved Susie, an Indian boy named Ray Singh, the only boy who she ever kissed. Ray does not attend her memorial service, but rather grieves alone:

> Ray Singh stayed away. He said goodbye to me in his own way: by looking at a picture—my studio portrait—that I had given him that fall.
>
> He looked into the eyes of that photograph and saw right through them to the backdrop of marbleized suede every kid had to sit in front of under a hot light. What did dead mean, Ray wondered. It meant lost, it meant frozen, it meant gone. He knew

Sometimes a turning point simply involves letting go of an old way of looking at things.

that no one ever really looked the way they did in photos. He knew he didn't look as wild or as frightened as he did in his own. He came to realize something as he stared at my photo—that it was not me. I was in the air around him. I was in the cold mornings he had now with Ruth, I was in the quiet time he spent alone between studying. I was the girl he had chosen to kiss. He wanted, somehow, to set me free. He didn't want to burn my photo or toss it away, but he didn't want to look at me anymore, either. I watched him as he placed the photograph in one of the giant volumes of Indian poetry in which he and his mother had pressed dozens of fragile flowers that were slowly turning to dust.

Pressing a photograph in a volume of poetry might not seem terribly dramatic, but in Sebold's hands this small action heightens the inner turning point that Ray Singh has reached: the time when he must put away his feelings for a girl who is no more.

Take a look at the turning points throughout your manuscript. Are they as dramatic as they possibly can be? No—I guarantee it. Go back to work on them. Use stronger words, handy objects, dramatic gestures, more evocative settings—whatever it takes to wring out of them all that they have to give.

Heightening Turning Points

Step 1: Pick a turning point in your story. It can be a major change of direction in the plot or a small discovery in the course of a scene.

_____

_____

_____

_____

_____

_____

Step 2: *Heighten it.* Change the setting in some way. Make the action bigger. Magnify the dialogue. Make the inner change experienced by your point-of-view character as cataclysmic as an earthquake.

_____

_____

_____

_____

_____

Step 3: *Take the same moment, and underplay it.* Make it quieter. Take away action. Remove dialogue. Make the transition small and internal, a tide just beginning to ebb.

_____

_____

_____

_____

_____

> **!**
>
> **NOTE:**
> Which works better, heightening the turning point or underplaying it? How did you change the setting, or use it differently? How did you make action more dramatic? Did the dialogue get louder, sharper, harder, more cutting? If a realization has taken place, how did it deepen?

Follow-up work: Go through your novel and find the turning points in twenty scenes. Find ways to heighten (or pointedly diminish) them.

_____

_____

_____

_____

_____

Conclusion: Most manuscripts I read do not feel dynamic. The stories do not stride forward in pronounced steps. Many authors are afraid of exaggerating what is happening, of appearing arty. That is a mistake. Stories, like life, are about change. Delineating the changes scene by scene gives a novel a sense of unfolding drama, and gives its characters a feeling of progress over time.

19

The Inner Journey

Plot developments create easy-to-see turning points. Less easy to identify are your protagonist's inner turning points: the moments when self-perception changes. Call it growth, call it exposition, call it whatever you like. It is when we get inside your hero's head and find out who he is right now.

In *City of Bones*, Michael Connelly's protagonist is homicide detective Hieronymous (Harry) Bosch. Harry, as I discussed earlier, is Connelly's series hero, but Connelly does not keep him emotionally frozen. Harry evolves. Toward the end of *City of Bones*, Harry finds himself again in hot water for a serious breach of police department regulations. He expects to be forced to retire. Instead, he is given an unexpected promotion and is moved to the downtown Los Angeles precinct. Although this is so that he can be watched more closely, it nevertheless is an unexpected boon:

> Now it was Bosch who was having the drink and falling asleep in his chair. He sensed he was at a threshold of some sort. He was about to begin a new and clearly defined time in his life. A time of higher danger, higher stakes and higher rewards. It made him smile, now that he knew no one was watching him.

Harry does indeed begin a new phase at the end of the story, though not the expected one. (See chapter twenty.) Paradoxically, because Connelly is so careful to pinpoint his hero's inner turning points along the way, we are never sure where those turnings of heart, soul, and mind will lead. Unchanging characters cannot surprise. Dynamic characters take us on journeys, and journeys necessarily involve surprises. Think about it: When did a lengthy trip in your own life ever go exactly as expected? Not often, I bet.

In *Mystic River*, Dennis Lehane tells the story of three Boston friends, Sean Devine, Jimmy Marcus and Dave Boyle, who, as we know from earlier excerpts, were present together at a childhood tragedy: Dave's abduction by two roving child molesters. In the present day the tragedy assumes Greek proportions as Jimmy slowly becomes convinced that Dave has murdered

Jimmy's teenaged daughter, Katie. He kills Dave, but immediately learns from Sean that he was wrong: Dave has committed a murder, but not Katie's.

Lehane now has the problem of providing a resolution for this instrument of backward justice, which he does in the novel's final pages:

> [Jimmy] left the window and splashed warm water on his face, then covered his cheeks and throat with shaving cream, and it occurred to him as he began to shave that he was evil. No big thing, really, no earth-shattering clang of bells erupting in his heart. Just that—an occurrence, a momentary realization that fell like gently grasping fingers through his chest.
>
> So I am then. . . .

In the paragraphs that follow, Jimmy weighs his past crimes and finds that some of them, in some ways, worked for the good. He decides to commit to his neighborhood and pay attention to some of the kids he knows there.

> He finished shaving, looked one more time at his reflection. He was evil. So be it. He could live with it because he had love in his heart and he had certainty. As trade-offs went, it wasn't half bad.

I am not sure that all killers achieve peace as easily, but in changing Jimmy Marcus's heart Lehane orchestrates an inner turning that allows Jimmy—and us—to go on. Jimmy's mistake is worst than most, needless to say, but, because he can forgive himself, we ultimately can forgive him, as well.

Let's again look at Robert Hellenga's literary novel *The Sixteen Pleasures* and see how the author takes his heroine, book conservator Margot Harrington, through a number of inner turning points. One of the more elegant points occurs early in Margot's affair with Florentine art scholar Sandro Postiglione. It is 1966, and Margot has gone to Florence to help preserve books damaged in the flooding of the river Arno. One day she finds herself in the Lodovici Chapel assisting Dottor Postiglione (or Sandro) in applying solution-soaked bandages to four filmed-over frescoes of the life of Saint Francis. Sandro's practical artistry and his cheerful advice to the abbot to "pray without ceasing" put Margot at ease:

> I've always felt intimidated in the presence of great art. I've always felt that my responses were inadequate. "Just sit quietly and look," was Mama's advice. But sitting quietly and looking always made me nervous. Like many people, I'd rather read about a painting than look at it. Or I'd rather hear someone talk about it. But working with Dottor Postiglione gave me a new perspective. The pressure was off. There was no need to work up an intense spiritual experience. No one was going to quiz me to make sure I'd appreciated them properly. The job wasn't to

appreciate them but to keep preparing the compresses. I saw the frescoes as things, pieces of this world rather than venerable icons pointing the way to some remote metaphysical realm called Art, physical objects that could wear out, like a shirt, and then be mended, and as things I found them easier to like. Like old shirts. Saint Francis dancing before the pope, Innocent III, who has just given him permission to found a religious order. What a wonderful image. I'd seen it a dozen times before, but this was the first time it made me want to dance, too.

Margot's changed outlook on great art mirrors an inner change in her. Through her restoration of a rare book of erotic sonnets, her sexual self is coming alive. What formerly had been remotely passionate, elevated, and intimidating is now becoming a practical possibility. Soon after this Margot is intimately involved with Sandro. In a sense, he applies salve to her spirit. Margot comes to enjoy the physical object that is her body, a piece of this world under heaven. The turning described in the passage above is a small one, but in Hellenga's hands its effect is large.

Take the time to demark the inner turning points in your current novel. We want to know about your characters, particularly how they are changing. Show us. A sense of the rich inner lives unfolding is one of the hallmarks of a breakout novel.

Dynamic characters take us on journeys, and journeys necessarily involve surprises.

Inner Turning Points

Step 1: Choose any turning point in your story other than the climax. Who is the point-of-view character?

_____

_____

Step 2: Wind the clock back ten minutes. How does this character feel about himself at this earlier moment?

_____

_____

_____

_____

_____

_____

_____

_____

Step 3: Write a paragraph in which you delineate this character's state of mind or state of being at this earlier moment. _Start writing now._

_____

_____

_____

_____

_____

_____

Step 4: Now write a paragraph in which you delineate this character's state of mind or state of being ten minutes _after_ the turning point. _Start writing now._

_____

_____

_____

_____

_____

Step 5: Use the material you generated in the steps above to pull together a single paragraph detailing this character's inner transition at this moment. As a starting point, try this framework: *Ten minutes before, she had been . . . but now everything was different. Now she was . . .*

_____

_____

_____

_____

_____

> **! NOTE:**
>
> Has your life ever changed in a moment? Was there an incident, a second in time, after which you felt that things would never be the same again? In that moment your life changed irrevocably. So it is in fiction. Such moments have power, but only when the inner transformation that has taken place is carefully detailed. Bring the same precise focus to feelings as you do to descriptive passages, and the inner lives of your characters will have extra vividness.

Follow-up work: Find six more inner turning points to delineate in your novel, and repeat the steps above for each.

_____

_____

_____

_____

_____

Conclusion: Most fiction writers carefully research such story elements as their novel's settings, their characters' professions, and whatever else makes the world of their novel real. However, few fiction writers do emotional research; that is, finding out how real-life human beings think and feel in the circumstances that occur in the novel. Is your hero shot at? How does that really feel? Ask a cop. Does your heroine get a makeover? Do its effects last? Interview a makeover artist. What does it feel like to be a child? Find out from a five-year-old. Psychology texts are useful, but real experience is best.

20

High Moments

I don't know about you, but I love it when a novel makes me suddenly suck in my breath and go, "Oh!" I shake my head and lower the book for a second, admiring what the author has just made happen. These are the high moments, when the story soars above itself and awes or inspires me in some way.

How are such effects achieved? It is simpler than you might think. Indeed, there are certain types of story events that are, if not guaranteed, at least more likely to produce eye-widening reactions. What are they? Check out some examples.

The morality tales of novelist Jodi Picoult show us the best and worst in contemporary humanity. Notice that I mention the "best." Many fiction writers revel in what is wrong with us; Picoult is generous in showing us also what is right.

In my earlier discussions of *Salem Falls*, I noted that Picoult employs a large cast of point-of-view characters. One major point of view belongs to Addie Peabody, the proprietor of the town lunch counter, Do-Or-Diner. At the novel's outset, Addie has two main problems: her alcoholic father, Roy, and her unwanted wooing by the town sheriff, Wes Courtemanche. These two problems converge one day when Wes locks up Roy for drunken driving: Roy was, Addie learns, motoring a lawn mower to a liquor store.

Picoult uses this incident to demonstrate Addie's forcefulness, Roy's intractableness, and, most important, Wes's wisdom. Addie, who doesn't need the extra problem of Roy's arrest, confronts Wes:

> "I think you've done enough, Wes. I mean, gosh, you arrested a man joyriding on a lawn mower. Surely they'll give you a Purple Heart or something for going to such extremes to ensure public safety."
>
> "Now, just a second. I *was* ensuring safety . . . *Roy's*. What if a truck cut the curve too tight and ran him down? What if he fell asleep at the wheel?"

"Can I just take him home now?"

West regarded her thoughtfully. It made Addie feel like he was sorting through her mind, opening up certain ideas and shuffling aside others. She closed her eyes.

"Sure," Wes said. "Follow me."

In this passage, Picoult is up to more than just painting a warm picture of small-town tolerance in the form of an Andy Taylor-style sheriff. Later in the novel, Wes will be caught in the middle of a relentless witch-hunt aimed at Addie's love interest, Jack St. Bride. Wes's conflict—whether to crush his rival, Jack, or to be true to the principles of justice as evidence of Jack's innocence grows—is beautifully prepared in this early moment of small forgiveness. We now know that Wes is, essentially, a decent man, and, when his actions later become hard and unfair, we will not forget.

Forgiveness, in fiction as in life, is powerfully redemptive, even when, as here, the forgiving act is small and everyday. Acts of forgiveness create high moments because they elevate the characters who forgive—and so elevate us all. There are larger moments of forgiveness to come in Picoult's complex novel. She knows that the human spirit can be as generous as it can be mean, and she shows us that spirit at work.

Salem Falls also contains an example of another type of high moment. The novel's protagonist, ex-convict Jack St. Bride, finds work washing dishes in Addie's diner. One day he finds Addie's father, Roy, drinking in the basement food storage area when he should be manning the cash register. Jack takes pity on Roy and decides not to alert Addie, then takes his protectiveness a step further:

"Have you seen my father?" Addie demanded, hurrying into the kitchen. "We've got a line a mile long at the cash register."

Delilah shrugged. "He's not here or I'd have tripped over him. Jack, you see Roy in the basement?"

Jack shook his head but he didn't meet Addie's eye. Then, with impeccably lousy timing, Roy sauntered through the basement door. His face was glowing, and even from across the room Jack could smell the cheap alcohol on his breath.

Addie's face went bright red. Tension filled the confines of the kitchen, and Jack tried to ignore the fact that someone was going to say something any moment that he or she would regret. Words, he knew, could scar.

So he squeezed the base of the potato he was peeling, then watched it fly in an arc over his shoulder toward the grill. Then, taking a deep breath, he grabbed for it, deliberately pressing his palm to the burning plate of metal.

The distraction that Jack creates with this small, if painful, act of self-sacrifice does indeed distract Addie from the hurtful outburst that she was getting ready to let loose. The moment passes quickly, but the effect of Jack's self-sacrifice lingers through the rest of the novel. It is a high moment made of humble elements: a drunk, a dishwasher, a slippery peeled potato, and a hot grill. Picoult knows that self-sacrifice does not have to be grand to be good.

Creating an effective reversal of direction for a character may be a matter not so much of sending him down a new road, but of convincing the reader that it is a road this character would never go down in the first place. Earlier I mentioned Erica Spindler's *Cause for Alarm*, in which a triangle is set up in the novel's backstory. Kate, Richard, and Luke were good friends in college. Unfortunately, both Richard and Luke loved Kate. Even worse, Kate slept with Luke the night before accepting Richard's proposal of marriage. As you can imagine, Luke is bitter.

Ten years later, Richard is a successful lawyer who is planning to run for public office. Kate owns a New Orleans coffee café on Lake Ponchartrain. They have adopted a daughter. Luke, meanwhile, has become a best-selling author. One day, missing her friendship with Luke, Kate attends Luke's book signing at the Tulane University bookstore. They talk, but the conversation is a disaster. Luke still can't believe Kate accepted Richard's proposal, especially since at the time Richard had recently dropped Kate yet again, for yet another blonde. Kate tries to explain:

> "The next morning, Richard came to see me. The way he always did, tail tucked between his legs. I told him we were through, that I'd had enough. He begged me to forgive him, Luke. Begged me. And he cried. He loved me, he said. He wanted to marry me. He wanted us to be together forever."
>
> "And you crumbled?" Luke snapped his fingers. "Just like that?"
>
> "I love him, had loved him for years. Marrying him was what I'd dreamed of for so long. How could I not forgive him?"
>
> "How?" The word roared past Luke's lips. "By remembering where you'd spent the night before. By remembering the promises you made to me."

The rest of the conversation does not go well; in fact, it ends disastrously. Luke accuses Kate of marrying Richard not because she loved him but because of the cushy future she would have with him, as opposed to an uncertain future with aspiring writer Luke. "I won't trouble you again," Kate tells Luke. In one terrible instant, their friendship is over and done.

But trouble him again she must. Much later, after Richard has an affair with his young blonde assistant and is fatally shot by the man stalking her, Kate herself is stalked by the killer and now has only Luke, a writer of mysteries and thrillers, to turn to for help. Help her he does, and eventually their college passion is rekindled. But is it only the circumstances? In a major reversal of direction for Kate, Spindler opens her up toward the novel's conclusion in a direct parallel to her earlier conversation with Luke:

I love it when a novel makes me suddenly suck in my breath and go, "Oh!"

"Why did you marry him, Kate?"

"Because I loved him." At Luke's expression, she shook her head. "I did, but not for the right reasons. I didn't see it then, but I loved Richard because he made me feel safe. And secure and cared for."

"And I didn't?"

"Not hardly." A smile tugged at her mouth. "You made me feel out of control. Uncertain. Of the future, what it would hold." She turned her gaze to the ceiling, remembering. "You made me feel like I could do anything, if only I'd try. If I would just go for it."

"I always believed in you, Kate. I still do."

Tears flooded her eyes. In all their years together, Richard had never said that to her. "That's just it. It wasn't you, Luke. I believed in you. In your strength and character. In your talent. It was me who I didn't believe in."

He opened his mouth to comment, and she laid her fingers gently against it to stop him. "I wanted to be an artist, but I was afraid. That I'd end up like my parents, scrambling to pay the rent, sacrificing my children's comfort for my art. I went to school wearing other people's castoffs and shoes with cardboard stuffed into the soles to cover the holes. I promised myself I wouldn't do that to my children. Or myself."

"Oh, Kate . . ." He threaded his fingers through her hair, fanned across the pillow.

She caught his hand and brought it to her mouth. "I was scared," she whispered. "Too scared to go after what I wanted."

Well, what do you know? Given their history, it is astonishing to hear these revelations from Kate. Kate and Luke have a future after all, which feels all the more remarkable because Spindler has led us to believe that any further *contact* between Kate and Luke, never mind future, was impossible. It is a gigantic change of direction, and adds a moment of high drama to Spindler's novel.

Now if only real life college girlfriends reversed themselves like that!

In *City of Bones*, as we know from earlier discussions, mystery writer Michael Connelly brings us inside the investigation of the chronic abuse and murder of a boy whose buried bones are unearthed after twenty years. In the course of the novel homicide detective Hieronymous (Harry) Bosch begins a love affair with a rookie cop, Julia Brasher. Julia is older than your average rookie, having entered the academy after fleeing from her father's law firm. When he meets her, she is already cynical but inexperienced enough to still be awed and excited by the job.

Their love affair goes against department rules (Harry is supervisor rank), but there is something undeniable and lovely about their relationship. Harry feels lucky to be with her. It is obvious that he is falling in love with a good woman.

And then she dies, shot while a witness is being detained in a parking lot.

At first we think she will be okay, since she is shot in the shoulder, but the bullet hit a bone—bones again!—and ricocheted inside her body, piercing her heart. Harry's own heart is pierced through, too, as we see at Julia's graveside:

> He grabbed a handful of dirt from the mound and walked over and looked down. A whole bouquet and several single flowers had been dropped on top of the casket. Bosch thought about holding Julia in his bed just two nights before. He wished he had seen what was coming. He wished he had been able to take the hints and put them into a clear picture of what she was doing and where she was going.
>
> Slowly, he raised his hand out and let the dirt slide through his fingers.
>
> "City of bones," he whispered.

This passage not only captures the pathos of a love lost too soon, but sends echoes of the sacrifices it takes to be a cop reverberating through the rest of the novel. In a way, we are not surprised by the decision that Harry makes at the end of the novel when, getting ready to move offices due to a promotion, he ruminates as he is cleaning out his desk drawer:

> When the drawer was almost clear, he pulled out a folded piece of paper and opened it. There was a message on it [written by Julia].
>
> *Where are you, tough guy?*
>
> Bosch studied it for a long time. Soon it made him think about all that had happened since he had pulled his car to a stop on Wonderland Avenue just thirteen days before. It made him think about what he was doing and where he was going. It made him think of Trent and Stokes and most of all Arthur Delacroix and Julia Brasher. It made him think about what Golliher had said while studying the bones of the murder victims from millenniums ago. And it made him know the answer to the question on the piece of paper.
>
> "Nowhere," he said out loud.

Harry puts his badge and gun in the desk drawer, locks it, and walks out, Code 7, done with police work. It is impossible to be unaffected by the death of a lover, and Harry is no exception. Connelly does not duck out on the consequences of the high moment he created in Julia's fatal shooting. He brings those consequences down full force on his detective—and on us.

There you have it, story events that create high moments: forgiveness, self-sacrifice, reversals of direction, moral choices, and death. Do any of these occur in your current manuscript? If not, is there a place for them?

Creating High Moments

Step 1: In your novel is there one character who can be forgiven by another? What is being forgiven? When? Why? *Write out the passage in which that happens.*

_____

_____

_____

_____

_____

Step 2: In your novel is there a character who can sacrifice herself, or something dearly loved, in some way? Who is it? What does he sacrifice? *Note it now.*

_____

_____

_____

_____

_____

Step 3: In your novel is there a character who can change direction? Who is it? What causes the turnabout? When does it happen? *Note it now.*

_____

_____

_____

_____

_____

Step 4: In your novel is there a character who faces a moral choice? Who? What choice? How can that choice become more difficult? *Make notes.*

_____

_____

_____

_____

_____

Step 5: In your novel is there a character whom we do not expect to die, but who can nevertheless perish? *Kill that character.*

_____

_____

_____

_____

_____

NOTE:
What are the most memorable moments in a novel? The high moments, of course, but what precisely do we mean by that? High moments can be many things, but often we are talking about instances of reconciliation, self-sacrifice, transformation, tests of character, or death. You would be amazed at how many manuscripts I read in which none of those things occur.

Follow-up work: Using the notes you made above, incorporate each of those high moments into your novel.

_____

_____

_____

_____

_____

Conclusion: For a novel to feel big, big things must happen: irrevocable changes, hearts opening, hearts breaking, saying farewell to one well loved whom we will never meet again. Create these moments. Use them. They are the high moments that make a novel highly dramatic.

21

Bridging Conflict

Did you ever arrive early for a party? It's awkward, isn't it? The music isn't yet playing. Your host and hostess make hurried conversation with you while they set out the chips and dip. You offer to help, but there's nothing you can do. You feel dumb for getting there too soon.

That's how I feel when I read the opening pages of many manuscripts. Pieces of the story are being assembled, but nothing is happening just yet, and often the guest of honor, the protagonist, hasn't arrived. In fact, no one I like has shown up yet. Later on the story will be in full swing, but for now I wonder why I bothered to accept this invitation.

Bridging conflict is a story element that takes care of that. It is the temporary conflict or mini-problem or interim worry that makes opening material matter. There are thousands of ways to create it. Even the anticipation of change is a kind of conflict that can make us lean forward and wonder, *What is going to happen?*

Brian Moore is one of our more reliable novelists, having brought us *The Statement*, *The Emperor of Ice-Cream*, and *The Lonely Passion of Judith Hearne*, among many others. In *The Magician's Wife*, Moore spins the story of Emmeline Lambert, who in Second Empire France is married to a stage magician and inventor, Henri, who is recruited by the government to so dazzle an Algerian marabout (living saint) with his illusions that, outclassed, the marabout will be unable to wage a holy war. That, anyway, is the plan.

However, Emmeline does not immediately know that. Her husband tells her only that they have been invited by the Emperor to attend a weeklong *séries*, a lavish royal house party. Emmeline, who is from a modest middle-class background, is terrified by the prospect and raises objections: "A week? What are we going to wear? We don't belong in that world."

She also worries that Henri is being asked in order to perform, that she has no ladies maid and he no valet. Her husband overrules all her objections, stating that it is an honor to be invited, that they can afford the clothes, and in any event the Emperor has summoned him on a matter of national importance. This simple argument nicely supplies the tension that holds our attention until the next stage of the game.

I hate most prologues. Typically, they are "grabber" scenes intended to hook the reader's attention with sudden violence or a shocking surprise. Mostly they do neither, not because they lack action but because the action is happening to characters about whom I know little; indeed, it is common in prologues for novelists not to name the players. When a nameless victim is killed by a faceless sicko . . . well, honestly, why should I care? I can see that twenty times a night on television.

And then there are prologues like that in Steve Martini's courtroom thriller *The Jury*, which opens with the introduction of a beautiful and ambitious ex-model turned molecular electronics researcher (yeah, I know) in San Diego named Kalista Jordan. As she relaxes one evening in a hot tub at her apartment complex, she hears unusual sounds in the courtyard around her. A killer is creeping up on her.

Many authors would be content with the low-grade suspense that generates, but Martini doesn't leave it at that. He adds tension by taking us inside Kalista's head to reveal the difficulties she is having at her research lab:

> This evening she'd had another argument with David. This time he'd actually put his hands on her, in front of witnesses. He'd never done that before. It was a sign of his frustration. She was winning and she knew it. She would call the lawyer and tell him in the morning. Physical touching was one of the legal litmus tests of harassment. While she was sure she was more than a match for David when it came to academic politics, the tension took its toll. The hot tub helped to ease it. Enveloped in the indolent warmth of the foaming waters, she thought about her next move.

It emerges that Kalista seeks to be the director of the lab and its twenty-million-dollar annual budget. To reach her goal, she has undercut her boss's authority on part of the funding and has developed allies in the chancellor's office.

What will be the downfall of Dr. David Crone (the David mentioned above), though, is his complete lack of tact. When Kalista is murdered, the police seize on him as the suspect with the best motive. Crone does himself no favors with his poor social grace. It is up to Martini's crack attorney, Paul Madriani, to clear the name of this difficult client. The first chapter picks up the trial midstream, but meanwhile Martini has held our attention and simultaneously has won sympathy for the defendant by showing us the victim's true colors while she was alive.

One of the most sustained examples of bridging conflict in recent fiction can be found in Daniel Mason's tour-de-force debut novel *The Piano Tuner*. This historical tale tells of a London piano tuner, Edgar Drake, who specializes in rare Erard grand pianos. Drake is recruited to journey to upper Burma to tune an Erard that was transported to the far jungle at the insistence of an eccentric army Surgeon-General and naturalist, Anthony Carroll, whose whims are tolerated by the army only because he is able to keep the peace among the local tribes. Drake is intrigued by Carroll's reputation and the challenge of getting there.

He sets off, but it is almost two hundred pages before Drake reaches Carroll. The trip from London, across the Mediterranean by steamship, over the Red Sea, though India by train, by ship to Rangoon, then on to Mandalay, there to languish for many days due to bureaucratic delays, should, by rights, be nothing but boring travelogue. Mason, however, fills the journey with bridging tension of every type.

There is Drake's longing for his wife, and his long letters home telling of his maladjustments to the strange conditions he meets. He meets strangers with mysterious stories, embarks on a tragic tiger hunt, and encounters friction in the barracks. His adventures escalate tales of Carroll—from both those who hate him and those who venerate him—and at last, in Mandalay, he meets Khin Myo, the mysterious Burmese woman who becomes his guide and with whom he becomes—tragically, it turns out—infatuated.

Even the anticipation of change is a kind of conflict that can make us lean forward and wonder, What is going to happen?

Mason does not indulge in mere travelogue; instead, he turns Drake's journey into a series of mini-stories. The dread and fascination Drake feels about meeting Carroll gradually builds, too, making the trip itself one that I, for one, thought could only end in a sense of anti-climax. I was wrong. Carroll proves to be every bit as large as anticipated.

How do you bridge from your opening page to your novel's main events? Do you just get us there, filling space with arrival, setup, and backstory? Or do you use the preliminary pages of your manuscript to build tension of a different sort?

Developing Bridging Conflict

Step 1: Does your novel include a prologue that does not involve your protagonist, or one or more opening chapters in which your hero does not appear? Move your hero's first scene to page one. *Yes, really do it. See how it feels.*

_____

_____

Step 2: Once your protagonist arrives on stage, what business do you feel must be included before the first big change, conflict, problem, or plot development arrives? *Write down those steps.*

_____

_____

_____

_____

Step 3: What is the bridging conflict that carries us through those opening steps to the first big change, conflict, problem, or plot development? *Write it down.*

_____

_____

_____

_____

Step 4: Open your manuscript to page one. How can you make that bridging conflict stronger at this point? *Make a change that makes the conflict more immediate and palpable.*

_____

_____

_____

_____

Step 5: Turn to page two. *Repeat the previous step. Continue until you reach the first big change, conflict, problem, or plot development.*

_____

_____

_____

_____

> **! NOTE:**
> The number one reason my agency rejects manuscripts is insufficient tension or conflict, especially in the opening pages. When little is happening, why keep reading? I don't, and neither do most readers. Think about yourself as you browse novels in a bookstore. How many times have you returned a novel to the shelf after reading just one page? That is the way book consumers are going to treat *your* novel, too.

Follow-up work: Find four places in your novel, ones that fall between plot developments or scenes, in which the problem does not immediately arrive. *Add bridging conflict.*

_____

_____

_____

_____

_____

Conclusion: To maintain high tension it isn't necessary to keep your novel's central conflict squarely front and center. Bridging conflicts adds contrast and variety, and makes even peripheral action matter. It is what keeps your readers' eyes glued always to the page, even when your main plot is taking a break.

Low Tension Part I: The Problem With Tea

The most controversial part of my Writing the Breakout Novel workshop is this exercise, in which I direct authors to cut scenes set in kitchens or living rooms or cars driving from one place to another, or that involve drinking tea or coffee or taking showers or baths, particularly in a novel's first fifty pages. Participants looked dismayed when they hear this directive, and in writer's chat rooms on the Web it is debated in tones of alarm. No one wants to cut such material.

Best-selling author Jennifer Crusie even tracked me down at a writers retreat in Kentucky to debate the point about kitchens. She argued that kitchens are the hearth and heart of family, the anchoring point where what is normal is demonstrated and what is abnormal is discussed. Without kitchen scenes, she argued, how can you tell a family story?

Indeed. It's hard to find a novel, even a novel discussed in this workbook, that does not have scenes set in kitchens, cars, showers, or what have you. Tea and coffee frequently are served. And they work. So how do these breakout authors get away with it when in 99.9 percent of manuscripts that I read such scenes invite me to skim (which I do)?

The reason is that in careless hands such scenes lack tension. They do not add new information. They do not subtract allies, deepen conflict, or open new dimensions of character.

Typically, scenes like these relax tension, review what already has happened, and in general take a breather. They are a pause, a marking of time, if not a waste of time. They do not *do* anything. They do not *take* us anywhere. They do not raise questions or make us tense or worried. No wonder they do not hold my attention. Am I being harsh? If you go by the novels I have cited as examples in this workbook, it might seem so. Hey, these novels are best sellers, critical successes, and award winners.

But these are breakout novels. Yes, they work, even when tea is being served.

The manuscripts that I am complaining about . . . well, frankly, most of them never see print. And for good reasons. Let's take a look at some breakout novels and see how their authors make potentially low-tension scenes work.

Is there anything necessary about driving a hero across Paris from his hotel to a murder scene? No, not really. Suppose that scene tells us nothing new about the murder? Worse, suppose it involves a catalog of Paris monuments and sights? Worse still, suppose the author takes up an entire chapter with this drive. Does that sound dynamic? Certainly not.

However, in the hands of Dan Brown in his massive best-seller *The Da Vinci Code*, which I discussed earlier, that is exactly what occupies the third chapter. Brown's protagonist, American symbologist Robert Langdon, is driven from the Hotel Ritz to the Paris Louvre museum in a police car. He is not driven at top speed. No one's life is at stake. Langdon takes in the sights as they go. But Brown takes this mundane act of traveling from here to there and invests it with subtle tension:

> Outside, the city was just now winding down—street vendors wheeling cars of candied amandes, waiters carrying bags of garbage to the curb, a pair of late night lovers cuddling to stay warm in a breeze scented with jasmine blossom. The Citroen navigated the chaos with authority, it's dissonant two-tone siren parting the traffic like a knife.
>
> "*Le capitaine* was pleased to discover you were still in Paris tonight," the agent said, speaking for the first time since they'd left the hotel. "A fortunate coincidence."
>
> Langdon was feeling anything but fortunate, and coincidence was a concept he did not entirely trust. As someone who had spent his life exploring the hidden interconnectivity of disparate emblems and ideologies, Langdon viewed the world as a web of profoundly intertwined histories and events. *The connections may be invisible*, he often preached to his symbology classes at Harvard, *but they are always there, buried just beneath the surface*.

Notice how Brown uses the contrast of the late-night city winding down with the car's siren cutting traffic "like a knife" to create a mood of unease. The driver's casual, offhand comments are too studied. They feel menacing, somehow. Langdon himself is uneasy. Nothing is an accident, he believes; everything is connected. He is in this police car for a reason he cannot yet see, and is connected to events and mysteries that have not yet been revealed.

That is indeed the case, as we soon learn, but even in this preliminary moment Brown is working to create a sense of foreboding. He keeps Langdon, and us, off balance. And what of the sights? Brown uses even these, working from Langdon's unique point of view, to show us that things are not always what they seem:

When they reached the intersection of Rue de Rivoli, the traffic light was red, but the Citroen didn't slow. The agent gunned the sedan across the junction and sped onto a wooded section of Rue Castiglione, which served as the northern entrance to the famed Tuileries Gardens—Paris's own version of Central Park. Most tourists mistranslated Jardins des Tuileries as relating to the thousands of tulips that bloomed here, but *Tuileries* was actually a literal reference to something far less romantic. This park had once been an enormous, polluted excavation pit from which Parisian contractors mined clay to manufacture the city's famous red roofing tiles—or *tuiles*.

It's hard to find a novel that does not have scenes set in kitchens, cars, or showers.

The Jardins des Tuileries was once a polluted pit? Yikes! But that's nothing. The Paris Louvre is shortly to be revealed as anything but a serene temple to art; rather, in Brown's novel, it is a cesspool of suspicion, secrets, codes, and murder. There is tension on every page of Brown's novel. Even when nothing big appears to be happening, small anxieties keep us on edge. This thriller thrills all the way.

Karen Joy Fowler's literary novel *Sister Noon*, which I also discussed earlier, tells the story of a conventional, turn-of-the-twentieth-century San Francisco spinster, Lizzie Hayes, who falls under the influence of the colorful and questionable Mrs. Pleasant, a woman who is nominally a housekeeper for Thomas and Teresa Bell, but whose actual occupation is somewhere between society benefactress and voodoo queen. Lizzie has questions for Mrs. Pleasant and visits the Bell's "House of Mystery" where Mrs. Pleasant holds sway. Lizzie hopes to get Mrs. Pleasant alone, but the social ritual of serving tea gets in the way:

> Mrs. Pleasant entered the room. "Teresa," she said. She spoke quickly as she moved. "You've met Miss Hayes, then. I'm delighted. She's a woman of good works." She didn't look delighted. She didn't look surprised. Her face was gracious, but this could have been an illusion created by age, the texture of her skin, like a crumpled handkerchief. Her hair was white about her face, but still, even now, when she was in her seventies, mostly black. She's gathered it into a knot with bits curled tightly around her temples. Her eyes were sharp; they seemed to take much in while giving nothing away.
>
> "Really?" said Mrs. Bell. "Now, she didn't say. I'm rather a creature of ideals, myself."
>
> "Would you like a cup of tea?" [Mrs. Pleasant asks.]
>
> Lizzie did not want to stay long enough to drink a cup of tea. She didn't wish to make a social call. She didn't wish to conduct her business in front of the peculiar Mrs. Bell. She couldn't think of a courteous way to send Mrs. Bell from her own drawing room. "Tea would be lovely," she said. "Aren't you kind."

She took a seat on the couch. Mrs. Pleasant vanished. . . .

"Don't eat or drink nothing," Mrs. Bell warned Lizzie.

Is the tea poisoned? Oh, dear. Do you see how Fowler creates strong undercurrents of tension in this outwardly gracious social situation? Read the passage again. Notice the ambivalence in Mrs. Pleasant, and in Lizzie. Notice Mrs. Pleasant's eyes, which are "sharp" and "take much in while giving nothing away." Then there is that warning from Mrs. Bell. Is anybody in this scene relaxed? No. Tension in this scene is as thick as clotted cream on a scone.

Consequently, we can't wait to see how it comes out. This is in striking contrast to most tea scenes I see in manuscripts, which generally are an excuse to slack *off* tension, rather than build it. Coffee scenes aren't much better, by and large, despite the bigger caffeine jolt. Cigarettes are disappearing from novels, just as they are disappearing from offices and restaurants, but they, too, have big tension killing potential. They should come with a warning from the Editor General: Can Be Hazardous to Your Scene.

As I noted in chapter three, Alice Sebold's literary novel *The Lovely Bones* is a story that, objectively speaking, has no outward tension. The tension that infuses the novel is the inner conflict experienced by Susie Salmon, the murdered fourteen-year-old who narrates the novel from heaven, who is dead but wishes to be alive so that she can grow up.

But that is not to say that Sebold ignores the need for plot developments or tension within a scene. Early in the novel, Susie's father goes to visit the boy who had a crush on Susie, Ray Singh; however, when Susie's father arrives at the Singh home he encounters Ray's beautiful, icy, and hostile mother. She is outwardly cordial, but her protectiveness of her son is readily apparent:

A little while later, as my father was thinking of how tired he was and how he had promised my mother to pick up some long-held dry cleaning, Mrs. Singh returned with tea on a tray and put it down on the carpet in front of him.

"We don't have much furniture, I'm afraid. Dr. Singh is still looking for tenure."

She went into an adjoining room and brought back a purpose floor pillow for herself, which she placed on the floor to face him.

"Dr. Singh is a professor?" my father asked, though he knew this already, knew more than he was comfortable with about this beautiful woman and her sparsely furnished home.

"Yes," she said, and poured the tea. It was quiet. She held out a cup to him, and as he took it she said, "Ray was with him the day your daughter was killed."

He wanted to fall over into her.

"That must be why you've come," she continued.

"Yes," he said. "I want to talk to him."

"He's at school right now," she said. "You know that." Her legs in the gold pants were tucked to her side. The nails on her toes were long and unpolished, their surface gnarled from years of dancing.

"I wanted to come by and assure you I mean him no harm," my father said. I watched him. I had never seen him like this before. The words fell out of him like burdens he was delivering, back-logged verbs and nouns, but he was watching her feet curl against the dun-colored rug and the way the small pool of numbered light from the curtains touched her right cheek.

"He did nothing wrong and loved your little girl. A schoolboy crush, but still."

Here is another scene involving tea, and set in a living room to boot, but do you notice much cream-or-sugar-no-thank-you-isn't-it-lovely-weather dialogue going on here? No. The tension between Susie's father and Ray's mother is under the surface, but not far and not for long. It makes this scene matter.

Put your tension meter on its most sensitive setting. When your fingers begin to type any scene set in a kitchen, living room, or car going from one place to another, or that involves tea, coffee, cigarettes, a bath, or reviewing prior action, I hope your tension meter will sink into the red zone and set off a screaming alarm in your brain. *Low tension alert!*

If that doesn't work, take another look at your novel the next time it comes back from an agent or editor. Does it have enough tension to make every scene, even every paragraph, matter? Have a cup of tea and think it over. Maybe not.

EXERCISE

Brewing Tension

Step 1: Find a scene that involves your hero taking a shower or bath, drinking tea or coffee, smoking a cigarette or reviewing prior action. *Look especially in the first fifty pages.*

_____

_____

_____

_____

_____

Step 2: *Cut the scene.*

_____

_____

Step 3: If you cannot cut the scene, add tension.

_____

_____

_____

_____

_____

Step 4: Find a scene set in a kitchen, living room, office, or in a car that your hero is driving from one place to another. *Look especially in the first fifty pages.*

_____

_____

Step 5: *Cut the scene.*

_____

_____

Step 6: If you cannot cut the scene, add tension.

_____

_____

_____

_____

NOTE:
The above exercise usually provokes anxiety in workshop participants. "But I need that tea scene!" one writer cried. "It's how I find out what my heroine is feeling!" Maybe. The fact is, when reading manuscripts my eyes jump over such material. It is so often lapses into pointless review: rehashing what already has happened. Another trap is telling us how your hero reaches a decision. Why bother? Instead, show us what happens as a result.

Follow-up work: Find ten more low-tension scenes to cut or to juice up with more tension.

_____

_____

_____

_____

_____

_____

_____

_____

Conclusion: Ninety-nine percent of scenes involving tea, coffee, showers, baths, and cigarettes are by nature inactive. Same thing goes for kitchen, living room, office, and driving scenes. Cut them. They usually are filler. You think you need them, but probably you don't.

Low Tension Part II: Burdensome Backstory

One of the most common ways that inexperienced and even practiced novelists bog down their openings is with unnecessary backstory. *Now hold on,* you may be thinking, *what do you mean "unnecessary"? Backstory tells us who a character is, where he came from, how he got to be the way he is. How can his actions make sense unless we know that stuff?*

I do not dispute that backstory can deepen our understanding of a character. That still does not make it necessary. Perhaps it is desirable to learn about a protagonist's past, at times, but when? That is where most novelists run into trouble: They presume that we, the readers, need to learn that history right away. But that is not so.

Again and again in manuscripts I find my eyes skimming over backstory passages in chapters one, two, and even three. Backstory doesn't engage me, because it doesn't *tell* a story. It does not have tension to it, usually, or complicate problems. However, once problems have been introduced, backstory can be artfully deployed to deepen them. It can be particularly useful in developing inner conflicts.

In Dennis Lehane's *Mystic River*, Boston detective Sean Devine is in a bad state. As we know from earlier excerpts, he feels empty, devoid of care, unable even to summon interest in the murder of the teenage daughter of a long-ago childhood friend:

> He wondered if this was what clinical depression felt like, a total numbness, a weary lack of hope.
>
> Katie Marcus was dead, yes. A tragedy. He understood that intellectually, but he couldn't feel it. She was just another body, just another broken light.

The case itself is a public sensation and a profound puzzle. As the investigation twists and turns, we begin to wonder why Sean is so distant from it.

Lehane withholds an explanation for nearly half the book, building Sean's inner mystery until one evening, alone in his apartment, when Sean can no longer avoid himself and the truth of what is bugging him:

> And his marriage, too, what was that if not shattered glass? Jesus Christ, he loved her, but they were as opposite as two people could get and still be considered part of the same species. Lauren was into theater and books and films Sean couldn't understand whether they had subtitles or not. She was chatty and emotional and loved to string words together in dizzying tiers that climbed and climbed toward some tower of language that lost Sean somewhere on the third floor.

Lehane recounts the course of Sean's marriage and his wife Lauren's progression from college actress to black box director to stage manager for touring shows. But it isn't her travel that wears their marriage down:

> . . . Hell, Sean still wasn't sure what had done it, though he suspected it had something to do with him and his silences, the gradual dawn of contempt every cop grew into—a contempt for people, really, and inability to believe in higher motives and altruism.
>
> Her friends, who had once seemed fascinating to him, began to seem childish, covered in a real-world retardant of artistic theory and impractical philosophies. Sean would be spending his nights out in the blue concrete arenas where people raped and stole and killed for no other reason but the itch to do so, and then he'd suffer through some weekend cocktail party in which ponytailed heads argued through the night (his wife included) over the motivations behind human sin. The motivation was easy—people were stupid. Chimps. But worse, because chimps didn't kill one another over scratch tickets.
>
> She told him he was becoming hard, intractable, reductive in his thinking. And he didn't respond because there was nothing else to argue. The question wasn't whether he'd become those things, but whether the becoming was a positive or a negative.

I don't know about you, but I ache for this weary young cop and his powerlessness to bridge the widening gulf between him and his vibrant wife. This sympathy is evoked by this sad backstory, however, only because we already are deep into the investigation. The facts of the case mean that Sean should care. He *knows* he should care. He wants to care, but he can't. Over time, his disaffection itself becomes a strong inner conflict that demands a solution. Sean knows that, without genuine zeal, he will be unable to investigate effectively.

Thus, this backstory passage deepens Sean's inner conflict not just by revealing its source, but by showing us how inevitable, unavoidable, and, finally, unsolvable his marriage problems are. With his wife gone, his daughter taken away from him forever, how can Sean possibly regain his thirst for his work? Read it again: Lehane's backstory is not lifeless information; it serves to enhance Sean's inner conflict. But that is only because it comes later in the story.

As I discussed in earlier chapters, the hero of Jodi Picoult's contemporary retelling of *The Crucible*, *Salem Falls*, is a man with a highly tragic backstory. A hint of it arrives on the novel's first page. Jack St. Bride is walking by himself along Route 10 in New Hampshire in the dead of winter, wearing only khaki pants, a white shirt, dress shoes, and a belt:

> He wished he had a winter coat, but you wore out of jail the same outfit you'd worn in. What he did have was forty-three dollars that had been in his wallet on the hot afternoon he was incarcerated, a ring of keys that opened doors to places where Jack no longer was welcome, and a piece of gum.

Perhaps it is desirable to learn about a protagonist's past, at times, but when?

Jail? For what crime was Jack incarcerated? Why has no one come to meet him upon his release? Questions leap unconsciously into our minds. Ninety-nine out of one hundred novelists would rush to answer those questions. Not Picoult. She lets them linger for many pages, adding an underlying tension to Jack's new life in the small town of Salem Falls.

It is only after eighty-nine pages that Jack's employer and lover, Addie Peabody, learns that Jack was an all-girls prep school teacher and soccer coach who plead guilty to the rape of a student. Jack did not rape the girl, but the explanation of how he came to plead guilty is further withheld. Finally, a chapter of backstory halfway through the novel shows Jack in his previous job and his special relationship with a fragile and unstable minister's daughter, teenage Catherine Marsh, who has a dangerous crush on him.

A couple of key incidents set Jack up for a fall: a toga-clad re-creation of the Peloponnesian War places Catherine's bra in his possession. Later, she pleads with him for help: Her boyfriend wants to have sex and she's not prepared. Jack agrees to drive her to a Planned Parenthood clinic in secret. Their close coach-player rapport works against him even further when Catherine turns her inner pain outward and reveals to her father her "affair" with Jack. Unfortunately, Jack now has her bra in his briefcase and undeniably took her to get birth control pills. His goose is cooked.

Picoult easily could have left it at that. However, she understands the magnification effect of backstory. Later in the novel, as support for Jack dwindles, she reinforces the goodness of his character for the reader with several more backstory passages. The birth control pill incident is shown in depth, revealing how deeply Jack cares for his students. His sensitivity is shown again in a trip back to Jack's own high school soccer days and his realization that his jock teammates' way of "seducing" girls (getting them drunk and then passing them around) is hurtful and wrong.

There are even more backstory passages, including a prison sequence that shows Jack's strength, fortitude, and refusal to break. Each passage is strategically placed at low moments to bolster sympathy for Jack, or to contrast his good qualities with the small-minded actions of others. If a piece of Jack's life has no conflict-enhancing value, Picoult leaves it out. For instance, we never find out anything about Jack's father, or why he became a teacher, or how he got hooked on the television game show *Jeopardy*. Why should we? That info contributes nothing to conflict.

In earlier chapters, I discussed *Carolina Moon*, Nora Roberts's novel about the return of a wounded young woman, Tory Bodeen, to her hometown of Progress, South Carolina. At age eighteen Tory fled a physically abusive father and went to New York, where she began working in retail stores and gained the experience that will allow her to open an upscale gift boutique in Progress. Early in the novel, however, Roberts makes us aware that something awful happened to Tory in New York.

A hint of this tragedy arrives unexpectedly when Tory sells the Charleston home in which she is living to raise funds for her fresh start. After the closing her real estate lawyer, Abigail Lawrence, wishes Tory well in her new life, but cannot resist satisfying her curiosity about something:

> "I hope you're happy, Tory."
> "I'll be fine."
> "Fine's one thing." To Tory's surprise, Abigail took her hand, then leaned over and brushed her cheek in a light kiss. "Happy's another. Be happy."
> "I intend to." Tory drew back. There was something in the hand-to-hand connection, something in the concern in Abigail's eyes. "You knew," Tory murmured.
> "Of course I did." Abigail gave Tory's fingers a light squeeze before releasing them. "News from New York winds it way down here, and some of us even pay attention to it now and again. You changed your hair, your name, but I recognized you. I'm good with faces."
> "Why didn't you say anything? Ask me?"
> "You hired me to see to your business, not pry into it."

What is the terrible thing that happened to Tory in New York, so terrible that it caused her to change her name and appearance? Roberts reveals nothing further for almost two hundred pages, letting the unanswered question lend the story underlying tension. Finally, in a confrontation with Margaret Lavelle, mother of Tory's new lover, Cade, we get another hint. Margaret blames Tory for the murder of her daughter and Tory's childhood friend, Hope, and now warns Tory to stay away from Cade:

> "If you go against my wishes in this, I'll ruin you. You'll lose everything, as you did before. When you killed that child in New York."

Tory killed a child? Naturally, we want to find out the details, but Roberts makes us wait until the final quarter of the novel. At last we learn that Tory had put her gift of second sight to work for the New York City Police Department and, along the way, had fallen in love with a police detective. Her life was almost normal until one day she provided information about a child kidnapper, a fired housekeeper with a grudge. The kidnapper wanted only money, she reported, indicating that paying the ransom was the safest course.

Unfortunately, her second sight did not extend to the ex-housekeeper's cohorts who, once they had the money in hand, killed not only the child, but the housekeeper and two pursuing policemen. Tory wound up taking the blame, some of it dished out by the detective who she had thought loved her. The guilt has followed her, never entirely being relieved despite years of therapy and, now, Cade's sympathy.

As guilty secrets go, this is pretty tame compared to *Sophie's Choice*, but that is not the point. The point is that Nora Roberts places this backstory late in the novel and thereby gets from it a double punch: It not only fills in Tory's character history, but deepens the pain she is feeling late in the story over the visions she again has begun to have of the victims of the serial killer who haunts her past and present.

As you can see, it can be quite effective to withhold backstory. Think about doing so in your current novel. You will not want to. That backstory stuff in the first few chapters feels awfully necessary. But it is not. It may be more useful later in the story. If when you get there you find you don't need it after all, then maybe you didn't need it in the first place.

Delaying Backstory

Step 1: In the first fifty pages of your novel, find any scene that establishes the setting, brings the players to the stage, sets up the situation, or that is otherwise backstory.

_____
_____
_____
_____
_____
_____
_____
_____
_____

Step 2: Put brackets around this material, or highlight it in your electronic file.

_____
_____
_____
_____
_____
_____
_____
_____
_____

Step 3: Cut and paste this material into chapter fifteen. *Yes, chapter fifteen.*

_____
_____
_____
_____
_____
_____
_____
_____

! NOTE:

Over and over authors bog down their beginnings with setup and backstory. Why is that? Perhaps it is because while writing the opening chapters the novelist is getting to know his characters. Who are they? How did they get to be that way? The fact is, the *author* needs to know these things, of course, but the reader does not. The reader needs a story to begin.

Follow-up work: Now, look at chapter fifteen. Does the backstory belong here? If not, can it be cut outright? If that is not possible, where is the best place for it to reside *after the mid-point of your novel*?

_____

_____

_____

_____

_____

Conclusion: Backstory is less important than most novelists think. If you must include it at all, place it so that it answers a long-standing question, illuminating some side of a character rather than just setting it up.

Low Tension Part III: Tension on Every Page

O kay, I warned you in my introduction, and here it is: the exercise and follow-up work that everyone knows is necessary, but that no one wants to do. It is a heck of a lot of work. Tension on every page is the secret of great storytelling. Everyone knows that. Practically no one does it.

Do you think you are the exception? Of course you do. Do you want to take that risk that you are wrong? That's a tougher call, isn't it? There's just a shred of doubt in your mind. *Could there be just a wee bit more tension in my manuscript?*

Count on it. There could be much more. Let's see how some breakout novelists get through material that trips up many others.

How interesting is it to hear two people passing the time of day? Usually, not very. Why is it, then, that so much dialogue in manuscripts is of the how-are-you-would-you-like-a-cup-of-coffee variety? Mere talk does not keep us glued to the page. Disagreement does. Friction in dialogue arrests our attention. It begs the unspoken question: Will these people be able to resolve their differences? We slow down and read the next line to find out.

Mystery writer Harlan Coben knows that empty dialogue cannot satisfy. Even when two characters are allies, he sets them against each other, albeit sometimes in friendly fashion. Toward the beginning of *Gone for Good*, Coben's protagonist, Will Klein, goes to his job as a senior director and runaway counselor at New York's Covenant House. There we are introduced to one of the shelter's street workers, a part-time yoga instructor, Squares, so nicknamed for the geometric tattoo on his forehead.

Will and Squares are fast friends, but you might doubt that as Will thanks Squares for bringing flowers to Will's mother's recent, and lightly attended, funeral:

> "Thanks for sending the flowers," I said.
> Squares didn't reply.

"And for showing up," I added. He had brought a group of Covenant House friends in the van. They'd pretty much made up the entire nonfamily funeral brigade.

"Sunny was great people," he said.

"Yeah."

A moment of silence. Then Squares said, "But what a shitty turnout."

"Thanks for pointing that out."

"I mean, Jesus, how many people were there?"

"You're quite the comfort, Squares. Thanks, man."

"You want comfort? Know this: People are assholes."

"Let me get a pen and write that down."

Silence. Squares stopped for a red light and sneaked a glance at me. His eyes were red. He unrolled the cigarette pack from his sleeve. "You want to tell me what's wrong?"

"Uh, well, see, the other day? My mother died."

"Fine," he said, "don't tell me."

The light turned green. The van started up again. The image of my brother in that photograph flashed across my eyes. "Squares?"

"I'm listening."

"I think," I said, "that my brother is still alive."

A less experienced novelist would strive to show the warmth and support between these two friends. Coben knows that tension all the time is more important, and so shows us their friction, letting the friendship under the surface show through.

Janet Evanovich is another mystery writer who understands the importance of tension on every page. In fact, it is her mastery of constant conflict that allows her in *One for the Money*, the debut of her popular series heroine Stephanie Plum, to go against the principle I was pushing in the previous chapter and to open her novel with a lump of backstory.

How does she do it? The backstory concerns the childhood of Stephanie Plum and in particular her seduction (twice) by neighborhood bad boy Joe Morelli. In itself this is not particularly interesting—we all have childhood stories to tell—nor can this piece of backstory be wholly carried off by Stephanie's wickedly ironic first-person narration, either. But look closely, and you will see that Evanovich cleverly sets up conflict in these passages.

Take, for example, the first time Joe seduces Stephanie, when she is six. As I mentioned earlier, he lures her (willingly) into a garage to teach her a dirty game called "choo-choo." Evanovich does not simply relate the incident; instead, she precedes it with a stern, if vague, warning by Stephanie's mother:

When I was a kid I didn't ordinarily play with Joseph Morelli. He lived two blocks over and was two years older. "Stay away from those Morelli boys," my mother had warned me. "They're wild. I hear stories about the things they do to girls when they get them alone."

"What kind of things?" I'd eagerly asked.

"You don't want to know," my mother had answered. "Terrible things. Things that aren't nice."

From that moment on, I viewed Joseph Morelli with a combination of terror and prurient curiosity that bordered on awe.

Did you notice the key words in the passage above? Stephanie didn't just ask her mother for more information about Morelli's rumored bad behavior—she "eagerly asked." When the exact nature of the bad behavior is left unspoken, Stephanie regards Morelli with a "prurient curiosity" that is, to say the least, a bit unusual for a six-year-old. Thus, Evanovich quickly uses what might have been an ordinary scene to set up tension: For good reasons Stephanie's mother wants her to keep her away from Joe Morelli, yet Stephanie is dying of curiosity about him. What will happen? Who will win out, Stephanie or her mom—or Joe Morelli?

Those questions now underlie this piece of backstory, and we eagerly read the next few paragraphs to see how things turn out. Evanovich then immediately uses the same technique in setting up the second seduction of Stephanie by Joe, this time behind a display case filled with éclairs at Tasty Pastry, the bakery where sixteen-year-old Stephanie works after school. Again, Stephanie is warned in advance:

> My best friend, Mary Lou Molnar, said she heard Morelli had a tongue like a lizard.
>
> "Holy cow," I'd answered, "what's that supposed to mean?"
>
> "Just don't let him get you alone or you'll find out. Once he gets you alone . . . that's it. You're done for."
>
> I hadn't seen much of Morelli since the train episode. I supposed he'd enlarged his repertoire of sexual exploitation. I opened my eyes wide and leaned closer to Mary Lou, hoping for the worst. "You aren't talking about rape, are you?"
>
> "I'm talking about lust! If he wants you, you're doomed. The guy is irresistible."

Will Stephanie escape Joe's clutches? Does she even want to? The tension inherent in the unspoken questions that Evanovich now has planted in the reader's mind makes the next couple of paragraphs impossible not to read. When is Stephanie going to encounter Joe next? What will happen when she does?

In any novel, it is difficult to avoid slack moments when nothing overtly is happening. Such a moment occurs early in Eoin Colfer's *Artemis Fowl*, which I discussed earlier. Twelve-year-old criminal mastermind Artemis is bent on capturing a fairy. With his obedient butler, Butler, he has staked out an ancient oak tree by a river bend where he is certain he eventually will observe, and snare, a fairy come to renew its magic under a full moon. But this takes time. Four months pass with Artemis and Butler crouched in a sort of high-tech duck blind:

> It was always the same. They would crouch in their foil-lined blind in complete silence, Butler repeatedly checking his equipment, while Artemis stared unblinking through the eye of the scope. At times like these, nature seemed deafening in their confined space. Butler longed to whistle, to make conversation, anything to break the unnatural silence. But Artemis's concentration was absolute. He would brook on interference or lapse of focus. This was business.

Notice how Colfer introduces tension into a paragraph in which nothing at all is happening; indeed, which portrays inaction. Silence must be maintained during the fairy watch, yet Butler longs to make noise. If he does his employer will be displeased. Nothing happening? Dig deeper. There is plenty of tension to be mined in a slack narrative moment.

Dialogue, backstory, slack moments—these are just three of many low-tension danger spots that breakout novelists make can riveting. It's so simple, really, and yet so many manuscripts that arrive at my office go right back to their authors in their self-addressed stamped envelopes. Why? The number one reason is insufficient tension. Believe it: Tension on every page works. Low tension does not. Make it your mantra.

Adding Tension to Every Page

Step 1: Turn to any page in your manuscript at random. Put your finger on any line at random.

_____

_____

_____

Step 2: Find a way to add tension at this moment. If there is already tension, skip to the next line, and heighten the tension there.

_____

_____

_____

_____

_____

!

● **NOTE:**
Tension can be many things. It can be as obvious as a gun to the temple or as subtle as forlorn hope. Even the mere anticipation of change is a kind of tension. It doesn't matter. Without tension we have no reason to wonder how things will turn out. We have no reason to read the next line. We might at first, but before long we will begin to skim. Sooner or later we will set the novel down.

Follow-up work 1: Pick another page at random, then pick another line. Heighten the tension at _this_ point.

_____

_____

_____

_____

_____

_____

_____

Follow-up work 2: Pick at random a third page and a third line. Heighten the tension at *this* point, too.

_____

_____

_____

Follow-up work 3: Go through all the pages of your novel in random order and raise the tension on each one.

_____

_____

_____

_____

_____

Conclusion: Go back to your favorite novels. Read them with an eye for tension. You will find that your favorite novelists always—*always*—have tension on the page. Tension, in some form or another, on every page is the secret of great storytelling.

Part

3

GENERAL STORY

TECHNIQUES

25

First Lines/Last Lines

No doubt about it, a great first line pulls us immediately into a story. It hooks. It intrigues. It opens a world in which things already are happening, in which discoveries await. Or it can. Sadly, many first lines lie flat on the page doing nothing helpful at all, merely setting a scene or in some other way getting ready for story rather than telling it. Weak first lines greet us like a limp handshake.

What makes first lines effective? Let's try out a few. Listed below are some first lines from recent novels, followed by a rating scale. Read each one and then rate (five being the best) how interested you are in reading the line in the novel that will follow it.

1. *I searched for sleep curled up in my quilt—the one made for me at my birth by my paternal grandmother's own hands.*

    1 2 3 4 5

2. *If half of all marriages end in divorce, how long does the average marriage last?*

    1 2 3 4 5

3. *Mike always teased me about my memory, about how I could go back years and years to what people were wearing on a given occasion, right down to their jewelry or shoes.*

    1 2 3 4 5

4. *When my father finally died, he left the Redskins tickets to my brother, the house on Shepard Street to my sister, and the house on the Vineyard to me.*

    1 2 3 4 5

5. *When the lights went off the accompanist kissed her.*

      1   2   3   4   5

6. *Upon waking this cold, gray morning from a troubled sleep, I realized for the hundredth time, but this time with deep conviction, that my words and behavior towards you were disrespectful, and rude and selfish as well.*

      1   2   3   4   5

7. *Tal stretched out his hand and pulled himself up onto the next out-thrust spike of the Tower.*

      1   2   3   4   5

8. *I was never so frightened as I am now.*

      1   2   3   4   5

9. *Watch your step.*

      1   2   3   4   5

10. *In the fleeting seconds of final memory, the image that will become Burma is the sun and a woman's parasol.*

      1   2   3   4   5

11. *Through my binoculars, I could see this nice forty-something-foot cabin cruiser anchored a few hundred yards offshore.*

      1   2   3   4   5

12. *He plunked two ice cubes into the glass and submerged them with Johnny Walker Black.*

      1   2   3   4   5

1. *Sullivan's Island* by Dorothea Benton Frank
2. *The Saving Graces* by Patricia Gaffney
3. *The Dive from Clausen's Pier* by Ann Packer
4. *The Emperor of Ocean Park* by Stephen L. Carter
5. *Bel Canto* by Ann Patchett
6. *Cloudsplitter* by Russell Banks
7. *The Seventh Tower: The Fall* by Garth Nix
8. *Affinity* by Sarah Waters
9. *The Crimson Petal and the White* by Michel Faber
10. *The Piano Tuner* by Daniel Mason
11. *Plum Island* by Nelson DeMille
12. *Jitter Joint* by Howard Swindle

Which of these first lines worked for you, which didn't, and why? All are taken from successful novels, some huge best sellers, and yet not all of them lead to the next line as effectively as others.

All, however, have their points. Some speak in a narrative voice that engages, talking to us directly as if we are already listening (1, 3, 6). Others have buried in them a little question that is begging to be answered, that makes us wonder, *What does that mean?* (2, 4, 10) Others present a physical situation that is in some way vivid or arresting (5, 7, 8, 9, 10, 11).

Notice that none but one (12) tries to set a mood with flat description. Mood setting is a weak way to go, though this opening to *Jitter Joint* makes sense once you realize that the protagonist is an alcoholic and the plot concerns a murder in a rehab clinic.

However you rated the effectiveness of the first lines cited, each in some way leads us into the world of the novel. Each has a little mystery or intrigue that makes us want to know more. For instance, in *The Emperor of Ocean Park* (4), why did Talcott Garland's father carve up his estate in that particular way? Was the division fair? Does Garland think so?

In that simple but striking opening to *Affinity* (8), what is Margaret Prior afraid of? When soprano Roxanne Coss is kissed by her accompanist in the opening moment of *Bel Canto* (5), what happens next? Is the kiss welcome? Even a detail that is a bit out of the ordinary, such as the spikes "out-thrust" from the Red Tower in *The Seventh Tower: The Fall* (7), can set us wondering why this place is different.

There are many ways to describe this effect, but I call it the intrigue factor. It is the element that makes us wonder—"What does that mean?" or "What happens next?"—and therefore leads us to the next line where we may find the answer.

All this happens so fast that we are unaware of it. In the few seconds it takes to read an opening line, our subconscious minds already are racing ahead. Without us being aware of it, our eyes jump eagerly to the second line. Will that line tell us what we need to know? If not, maybe the third line will.

And so it goes. We are hooked.

Just as surely as an intriguing first line can draw readers into a novel, a stunning exit sentence can propel a reader onward in wonder—wondering, perhaps, when your next novel will be out.

Earlier I discussed the sixth book in Laurel K. Hamilton's series about vampire hunter Anita Blake, *Blue Moon*. Anita, a committed Christian, is deeply unsettled about her work, especially the increasing ease with which she kills. In *Blue Moon* she breaks her own boundaries in still more ways, including sexually and magically. When she finally has rescued the world from the demon that is behind the evil in small town Myerton, Tennessee, Anita absents herself from her home city, St. Louis, for a time to reflect on the changes she has undergone and the remorse she feels.

The last paragraph of *Blue Moon* sums up the irresolvable difference between what Anita Blake is and what she would like to be:

I faced a demon with my faith and prayer. Does that mean God has forgiven me my sins? I don't know. If He has forgiven me, He's more generous than I am.

Do you see the point, here? Anita's story is not over. There is unfinished business, even if it is only the business of forgiving herself. Hamilton's last line opens doors rather than closing them. I, for one, will be reading the next novel in the series to find out what happens next. So, I suspect, will many others.

This same forward-looking quality can be found in the last lines of Kris Nelscott's Edgar Award-nominated first mystery novel, *A Dangerous Road*, the story of a black Beale Street detective, Smokey Dalton. The novel is set in Memphis in February, 1968, the time of a sanitation workers' strike, riots, and the assassination of Smokey's childhood friend Martin Luther King Jr. As the Civil Rights movement marches toward a bloody turning point, Smokey is hired by an alluring white woman from up North, Laura Hathaway, who hires him to investigate a puzzling question: Why has her mother generously remembered Smokey himself in her will?

Smokey's investigation leads him down a dangerous road indeed, to an explanation of how he and Laura are linked and the reason why his parents were lynched. The novel ends with Smokey on the run with a little boy, Jimmy, who saw King's assassination and can identify the man who shot the civil rights leader (and it is definitely *not* James Earl Ray).

Smokey's world has been torn apart by his love affair with Laura, the secrets he has uncovered and the death of his friend. Jimmy represents truth, innocence, witness to the past, and hope for the future. Smokey is determined to safeguard him, to find a place to make a new start. In the novel's closing paragraphs, Nelscott leaves Smokey grappling with the changes that have overcome him—and America—as he and Jimmy run:

> Because once again, my life has changed overnight. If I have learned anything, it is that nothing goes as I plan. I need to adjust, to move, to allow myself to go with whatever happens, however it happens.
>
> I wish I had done that more with Laura.
>
> I think of her sometimes, usually at sunrise, when the light is so golden that it makes the land seem brighter than it can ever be. And, despite myself, I find hope in that light.
>
> It is as Martin said on the last night of his life. Only a man who has seen the darkest night can appreciate the light.
>
> I am just beginning to appreciate it. And for the first time, I am turning toward it, believing it will lead me home.

Admittedly, Hamilton and Nelscott are writing series, so it is perhaps easier for them to write open-ended last lines than for some others. With stand-alone

Weak first lines greet us like a limp handshake.

novels, a last line signals the close of the story. It is the final note of resolution and release, and so a touch of lyricism is called for.

Lisa Wingate's warm and life-affirming literary novel, *Tending Roses*, tells the story of suburban achiever Kate Bowman, who travels with her husband, Ben, and infant son to the family farm in Missouri to face the task of convincing her frail and memory-impaired grandmother to enter a nursing home. It turns out Kate and Ben have bigger problems than Kate's grandmother, though, and it is through reading her grandmother's journal, an account of simpler times, that Kate discovers the secrets of a happy life.

At the end of the novel (get out your hankies) Kate's grandmother dies. Kate, newly pregnant, goes to her grandmother's grave to tend the roses growing there. There in the graveyard at dusk, Kate at last savors the peace and joy in life that she has received from her grandmother's life:

> The light around me dimmed slowly as another day surrendered its grasp on the land. On the hillside, the roses nodded on the breeze, as if inviting the fireflies to come out and dance.

Such a pretty line! Wingate captures a feeling of closure, of peace, of ending, and of beginning all at the same time. The surrender is not the day's, but Kate's; it is a surrender to life itself.

Have you yet reached the last line of your current novel? If you have, go back. If you haven't, pause when you get there. Take the time to get your last line just right. Whether its leads forward or lifts our spirits or softly closes a door, make it a line we will remember—especially when we see your next novel on the bookstore shelves.

Enhancing First and Last Lines

Step 1: What is the intrigue factor in your opening line? What question does it pose, or what puzzle does it present? *Write that down.*

_____

_____

_____

_____

_____

_____

_____

Step 2: If you are not able to answer the question in the first step, try shortening your first line. If that doesn't work, audition your second line for the lead spot. Or combine elements from your first paragraph into one short, super-charged sentence. *Whatever you do, choose or construct a different first line.*

_____

_____

_____

_____

_____

_____

_____

> **! NOTE:**
> In the live Breakout Novel workshops, I ask every participant to read his first line. I then ask the group, "Do you want to hear the next line?" A show of hands immediately tells us how effective a given first line has been. Weather effects, description, and scene setting never get a strong response. Neither does plain action—unless there is something puzzling about it. The best first lines make us lean forward, wondering, *What the heck does* that *mean?* A suggestion of sex is a sure-fire attention getter, but not every story can start that way. The one thing that all good first lines have in common is the intrigue factor.

Follow-up work: Work on your last line until it has wit, a touch of poetry, or a sense of dawning peace. *Try it out on others.*

_____

_____

_____

_____

_____

_____

_____

Conclusion: Whether it is a sigh of satisfaction, a soaring passage of word art, or nothing more than a clever exit line, put the same effort into your last line as went into your first. A book needs front and back covers to hold together; in the same way a novel needs strong brackets to bind it.

26

Moments in Time

There's no doubt that immersing ourselves in another world is one of the pleasures of reading a well-written novel. But as a writer, how can you capture the world of the story, and the lives of its characters, in just the right way? As the exercise in this chapter shows, it is, in part, a matter of selecting individual moments to freeze for the reader.

In Jeanne Ray's *Julie and Romeo*, sixty-ish Boston florist Julie Roseman stirs up her family's longstanding feud with a rival florist family when she falls in love with her sixty-ish counterpart, Romeo Cacciamani. Their first kiss erases all past wrongs and ignores all future conflicts:

> This was the part that no one told me while they discussed the evils of the Cacciamanis. No one said they were such good kissers. I was dreaming, sinking, swimming in a warm dark river of kissing, kissing hands and chins, every kiss soft. I could smell the soap on his skin and the fabric softener in his undershirt. I could smell his hair and taste his mouth, which still tasted like sake and rice. Oh, Romeo, this makes it all worthwhile, all those nights of working late and coming home alone, crying over the books and the roses that came in with brown spots on every petal, the worrying about Sandy and Nora and the children, the anger at Mort, the missing my parents, all of it lifted off of me and was washed back by the sea of tender kissing, maybe not forever but for now, and frankly, what else was there?

Who knew that fabric softener could be so romantic? Ray uses the details at hand along with the drunken, repetitive rush of kissing imagery to suggest a moment suspended in time. She does not describe Julie's emotions, but evokes them by saying what they are not: not loneliness, not sorrow, not worrying, not anger, not missing the departed. Kissing is the opposite of that. We see exactly what she means.

This frozen moment is warm because it captures the out-of-time feeling of kissing. Think about it: When you kiss your partner, do you think about anything else? (Oh? You do? Sorry. Then you are missing the moment. Get into it, why don't you?)

An extremely fine distinction between one place and another is drawn by Dennis Lehane in *Mystic River*. Lehane's story, as we know, concerns three childhood friends in the blue-collar section of Boston known as East Buckingham: Sean Devine, Jimmy Macus, and Dave Boyle. At the outset there might not seem to be much to distinguish one boy from another, but not all of them live on the same *side* of East Buckingham:

> Jimmy and Dave came from the Flats, down by the Penitentiary Channel on the south side of Buckingham Avenue. It was only twelve blocks from Sean's street, but the Devines were north of the Ave., part of the Point, and the Point and the Flats didn't mix much.
>
> It wasn't like the Point glittered with gold streets and silver spoons. It was just the Point, working class, blue collar, Chevys and Fords and Dodges parked in front of simple A-frames and the occasional small Victorian. But people in the Point owned. People in the Flats rented. Point families went to church, stayed together, held signs on street corners during election months. The Flats, though, who knew what they did, living like animals, sometimes, ten to an apartment, trash in their streets—Wellieville, Sean and his friends at Saint Mike's called it, families living on the dole, sending their kids to public schools, divorcing. So while Sean went to Saint Mike's Parochial in black pants, black tie, and blue shirt, Jimmy and Dave went to the Lewis M. Dewey School on Blaxston. Kids at the Looey & Dooey got to wear street clothes, which was cool, but they usually wore the same ones three out of five days, which wasn't. There was an aura of grease to them—greasy hair, greasy skin, greasy collars and cuffs. A lot of the boys had bumpy welts of acne and dropped out early. A few of the girls wore maternity dresses to graduation.
>
> So if it wasn't for their fathers, they probably would never have been friends.

Why does Lehane bother to delineate the differences between the Point and the Flats, a difference of only twelve blocks? Because later in the story these small distinctions will be greatly magnified. Sean becomes a police detective, while Jimmy owns a bar. Their different approaches to enacting justice when Jimmy's eighteen-year-old daughter is murdered is one of many layers of tension in this multi-layered novel. The difference between a private school uniform and street clothes grows up into the difference between a badge and a baseball bat; the difference between the rule of the law and the law of the jungle.

In Alan Furst's finely written and literary-feeling WWII espionage novel *The Polish Officer*, Captain Alexander de Milja finds himself recruited into the Polish resistance and put in charge of smuggling the country's gold reserves out of Warsaw beneath the floorboards of a train. As the train chugs through the countryside south of Warsaw, the passengers are given a choice of disembarking or continuing onward:

> From the last car, de Milja watched the crowd carefully. But the reaction was subdued: a number of family conferences conducted in urgent whispers, and avalanche of questions that God himself, let alone a train conductor, couldn't have answered, and more than a little head shaking and grim smiling at the bizarre twists and turns that life now seemed to take. The Polish people, de Milja realized, had already absorbed the first shock of war and dislocation; now it was a question of survival; ingenuity, improvisation, and the will to live through catastrophe and see the other side of it. So when the train stopped it Pilava, only a few people got off. The farther from Warsaw the better—what consensus there was among the passengers seemed to follow that line of reasoning.

Furst uses this brief pause, occasioned by a piece of incidental detail, to freeze a unique moment in the chronology of Poland's fall to the Nazi's. It is only a few days into the occupation, yet already people have begun to adjust to the new reality. They are newly flexible. Their experience has not yet hardened with long oppression. They are defeated, yet it is the early days.

Indeed, a month later the mood of the Polish public has shifted again:

> Now the war was over, a pleasant autumn.
> Hitler had what he wanted. Maybe he did, after all, have a right to it, a case could be made, you had to accept the reality of politics in central Europe. The days were cool and sunny, the harvest in, a little fog in the morning and geese overhead. Germany had Austria, Czechoslovakia, and Poland, and was, officially, *officially*, at war with England and France. But this was politics; eddies and swirls and tidal shifts in the affairs of diplomats. Slowly the sun warmed the squares and plazas, the boulevards and little winding streets and, by midmorning, all across Europe, it was just right for a coffee on the café terrace.

What a stunning evocation of the ordinariness of a sunny autumn day during wartime! But not just any day: a day in the first autumn of defeat, before rationing, before the restrictions of occupation, before the walling off of Warsaw's ghetto and before the deportations to labor camps. It is a unique moment in Poland's—really, all of Europe's—history, and Furst's eye for detail gives us a snapshot of the minute, the mood, the public shrug of acceptance, the remoteness of far-off politics, the sunny stillness in the cafes and plazas of Warsaw. Once again, this moment in time will quickly pass, but its freezing in this passage gives Furst's story a sense of forward progress, a step along the way.

In her breakout first novel *Sullivan's Island*, South Carolina novelist Dorothea Benton Frank captures a moment that is not so much historical as social and political. Frank's novel tells the layered story of Susan Hayes, who returns to her family's summer home on Sullivan's Island to reinvent herself after the breakup of her marriage. In alternate chapters, Frank flashes back to the 1950s to recount the events leading up to the death of Susan's father at the hands, Susan suspects, of the Klu Klux Klan. It is a time of racial upheaval, a fact that Susan notes as she and her father drive across the island to pick up their new housekeeper, who is the latest in a long string of black housekeepers in their home:

> We lowered the car windows and didn't utter a single syllable about how hot the car was as he backed out of the driveway and started down Middle Street toward the small business district. It was a sticky Saturday in the middle of June and we'd been out of school and shoes for about three weeks as another summer got under way. The United States was in the midst of the Civil Rights movement, which as far as we knew was something happening at lunch counters in Rock Hill, South Carolina, and Montgomery, Alabama. When Medgar Evers was murdered, we thought for a moment how that could happen to our daddy, but he was white and nothing like that ever happened around Charleston. We were frightened, but we were just kids and not focused on it. All the same, violence was everywhere that summer, in the newspapers and in our house.
>
> Because of the high attrition rate of our housekeepers, we hadn't ever had a stretch of time to consider the grave injustices done to the Negro population at a close look. But the world was evolving in front of our eyes and we were changing our minds about a lot of things.

This passage may not be as elegantly written as Furst's, but it nevertheless freezes a moment of American social history and relates it to what is happening to Susan during one childhood summer.

Sullivan's Island was an original paperback that initially shipped, I am told, 450,000 copies and hit *The New York Times* best-seller list for three weeks. Today it has more than 700,000 copies in print. This goes to show that elegant prose isn't the key to success. A great story is, and capturing a story's social context is one way to give it a sense of resonance; ripples that spread outward and lend a story a sense of larger significance.

Whether it is suspending a single moment and isolating its emotional details from all other moments, or whether it is capturing the shifts in the public mood from one week to the next, or whether it is picking up the social nuances that make one place different from the place next door to it, freezing a moment in time is a highly effective way to heighten the reality of the story.

How do you delineate these in your current manuscript? Can you identify six passages in which you go beyond simple scene setting to capture the flavor of a moment in time, the feeling of an historical era of the uniqueness of a place like no other?

If not, is there any reason not to put that stuff in?

Freezing Moments in Time

Step 1: Find in your novel a moment of transition, a pause, a moment of character definition or testing, a place where the action can be momentarily frozen, or the prelude to (or the aftermath of) an important plot event.

_____

_____

_____

_____

_____

Step 2: What are three things that make this minute in time different from any other minute in time? *Write those down.*

_____

_____

_____

_____

_____

Step 3: What are three things that make this place uniquely different from any other place? *Write those down.*

_____

_____

_____

_____

_____

Step 4: What are three things that define the social world of the story at this precise moment? *Write those down.*

_____

_____

_____

_____

_____

Step 5: Use the details generated in any of the steps above to craft a paragraph that freezes for the reader how the world looks and feels to your point of view character at this moment. Pin down the unique feeling of this time, this place, or this social world. *Start writing now.*

_____

_____

_____

_____

_____

> **!**
>
> ● **NOTE:**
> As writers, we mostly want to keep things moving in our novels. Yet for a story to seem real to readers it must happen in time, in space, and in a social context that is credible, detailed, and specific. Using the steps above to create at a given moment a snapshot of the story's time, place of social milieu is a way to bring the world of the story into sharp focus. It heightens the reality of the tale. It aids the reader's suspension of disbelief.

Follow-up work: Choose four other moments in time to freeze in the novel and delineate them using the steps above.

_____

_____

_____

_____

_____

Conclusion: Here is where to apply your powers of observation. You notice things, don't you? You get the world's ironies, appreciate its wonders, and pick up details that others miss, right? Of course you do. You are a writer. Okay, now is the time to use those gifts. Give your protagonist the same awareness of the world that you have, or maybe one that is keener. His observations of time, place, and society will further reveal, delineate, and define this character. How we look at the world is as distinctive as the fingerprints we leave on drinking glass. Make sure that your protagonist has a distinctive take on things, too. He will spring alive in yet new ways for your reader.

Inner Change

We grow and change. We also note the growth and change in others. The moments in breakout novels in which such changes are observed are milestones that measure the journey that is each story. Changes in characters—or rather, characters' perceptions of the changes within themselves and others—may happen within a scene or across long stretches of time. It doesn't matter. Inner changes calibrate a plot, lending it a sense of inexorable progress and pace.

Tim LaHaye and Jerry B. Jenkins's best-selling series Left Behind is a saga of the days following the Rapture foretold in the book of Revelation. The first volume, *Left Behind*, begins with a vivid account of the aftermath of the instant disappearance of millions of faithful people selected for salvation. The novel opens on a full 747 passenger jet flying overnight from Europe to Chicago. In the middle of the night one hundred passengers vanish, their clothing and jewelry remaining behind in their seats. The point-of-view character in this scene is the plane's pilot, Rayford Steele, who at the novel's opening is fantasizing about his senior flight attendant, Hattie Durham, a young and sexy contrast to Rayford's fanatically religious wife:

> Rayford tried to tell himself it was his wife's devotion to a divine suitor that caused his mind to wander. But he knew the real reason was his own libido.
>
> Besides, Hattie Durham was drop-dead gorgeous. No one could argue with that. What he enjoyed most was that she was a toucher. Nothing inappropriate, nothing showy. She simply touched his arm as she brushed past or rested her hand gently on his shoulder when she stood behind his seat in the cockpit.

The simultaneous disappearance of millions of people has caused chaos on the ground. Traffic accidents and airline crashes are the first consequences. Following a harrowing landing at O'Hare, Rayford and his crew find the airport in a state of disarray. Because roads out of the airport are blocked,

Rayford hops a helicopter ride away from the terminal soon after learning that his wife and son probably are among the disappeared. He also finds Hattie Durham in the only available seat in the helicopter—his lap:

> He had been playing around on the edges of his mind with the girl in his lap, though he had never gone so far as touching her, even when she often touched him. Would he want to live if Hattie Durham were the only person he cared about? And why did he care about her? She was beautiful and sexy and smart, but only for her age. They had little in common. Was it only because he was convinced Irene was gone that he now longed to hold his wife?
>
> There was no affection in his embrace of Hattie Durham just now, nor in hers. Both were scared to death, and flirting was the last thing on their minds.

In this passage, LaHaye and Jenkins convey a remorseful change of view on Rayford Steele's part, but at the same time demonstrate the effect of the profound upheaval that is the Rapture. The event blows away temporary desires and petty concerns, and puts old loves into a new perspective. In the face of disaster, what really matters is thrown into sharp relief.

In an earlier chapter I discussed *Empire Falls*, by Richard Russo, in which Janine is the estranged wife of the novel's protagonist, Miles Roby. At the outset of the novel she is planning to marry an obnoxious local entrepreneur, Walt Comeau, owner of a fitness center. Once overweight, she is now in shape and brimming with self-confidence, regret about her marriage to Miles, and admiration for Walt:

> Back when they got married, she hadn't even known who *she* was, her own self, never mind her intended. At least now Janine knew who Janine was, what Janine wanted, and, just as important, what Janine didn't want. She didn't want Miles, or anyone who reminded her of Miles. She didn't want to be fat anymore, either. Never, ever, again. Also, she wanted a real sex life, and she wanted to act young for a change, something she hadn't been able to do when she actually was young. She wanted to dance and have men look at her. She liked the way her body felt after dropping all that weight, and by God she liked to come. For Janine, at forty, orgasms were a new thing and she damn near lost her mind every time she had another. . . .
>
> It was Walt Comeau who'd taught her about herself and her body's needs.

Much later, disillusioned with Walt Comeau (who styles himself The Silver Fox), she reexamines her view of him during a high school football game they attend with her daughter, Tick, and her mother, Bea:

Inner changes
calibrate a plot,
lending it a sense of
inexorable progress
and pace.

Janine was sitting next to her own destiny, of course, and that destiny was itself perched on a damn hemorrhoid cushion. "Oh, leave the child alone, Walt," she heard her mother say, and she then saw through her tears that her husband-to-be had returned, no doubt sneaking down the row behind her just as Tick had done. Apparently he'd given his stepdaughter a kiss on top of the head and been handed his usual rebuff by way of thanks.

"What makes you think a pretty fifteen-year-old girl wants to be kissed in public by an old goat like you?" Bea asked him.

" 'Cause I'm a good-looking old goat," said Walt . . . [He notices that Janine is upset.] . . . The only thing to do was to cheer her up. So he began crooning an apropos lyric of Perry Como's.

"The way that we cheered/Whenever our team/Was scoring a touchdown," he warbled, nudging her, in the idiotic hope of getting her to sing along.

Perfect, Janine thought. At last she finally understood her husband-to-be's infatuation with Perry Como, which had nothing to do with the singer's good looks, charm, or silvery foxiness. The fucker was simply Walt's contemporary.

Notice how Janine's unit of measurement of Walt has shifted from orgasms to hemorrhoids. Russo's strong point-of-view writing enhances this change in one character's view of another.

In Phillip Pullman's complex and compelling fantasy *The Golden Compass*, also discussed in an earlier chapter, orphan Lyra Belacqua is raised by the scholars of Jordan College, Oxford. But she is no ordinary child. She is (or so she is told) the niece of powerful Lord Asriel, heretic and researcher into the mysterious matter of Dust, and (unknown to her) she is a child whose destiny is great and dangerous. One day she is introduced to the elegant Mrs. Coulter, whose ward she will become. At first meeting her at a college dinner, Lyra is awed:

"Are you a female Scholar?" said Lyra. She regarded female Scholars with a proper Jordan disdain: there *were* such people, but, poor things, they could never be taken more seriously than animals dressed up and acting in a play. Mrs. Coulter, on the other hand, was not like any female Scholar Lyra had seen, and certainly not like the two serious elderly ladies who were the other female guests. Lyra had asked the question expecting the answer No, in fact, for Mrs. Coulter had such an air of glamour that Lyra was entranced. She could hardly take her eyes off her.

A day later, Lyra is on her way to London with Mrs. Coulter and their respective daemons, talking animal companions that in Pullman's world are, in effect, the external manifestation of each individual's soul. Lyra's awe deepens:

And now she was on her way to London: sitting next to the window in a zeppelin, no less, with Pantalaimon's sharp little ermine paws digging into her thigh while his front paws rested against the glass he gazed through. On Lyra's other side Mrs. Coulter sat working through some papers, but she soon put them away and talked. Such brilliant talk! Lyra was intoxicated: not about the North this time, but about London, and the restaurants and ballrooms, the soirees at embassies or ministries, the intrigues between White Hall and Westminster. Lyra was almost more fascinated by this than the changing landscape below the airship. What Mrs. Coulter was saying seemed to be accompanied by a scent of grownupness, something disturbing but enticing at the same time: it was the smell of glamour.

Months later, the educated and pampered Lyra learns that Mrs. Coulter is the primary procurer for the General Oblation Board, known among street urchins as the Gobblers because they make children disappear. (Among the missing is Lyra's special friend Roger.) The stolen children are used—hideously, we later learn—in experiments probing the nature of Dust in the arctic North.

Furthermore, Lord Asriel is now captive and being held in the Northern fortress of Svalbard, which is guarded by fearsome armored bears. Lyra runs away. When next she glimpses Mrs. Coulter months later, as a captive among the other kidnapped children in the research facility in the North, her view of her former guardian and her monkey deamon has changed:

> [Lyra] jumped down, pushed back the locker, and whispered to Pantalaimon, "We must pretend to be stupid till she sees us, and then say we were kidnapped. And nothing about the gyptians or Iorek Byrnison especially."
>
> Because Lyra now realized, if she hadn't done so before, that all the fear in her nature was drawn to Mrs. Coulter as a compass needle is drawn to the pole. All the other things she'd seen, and even the hideous cruelty of the intercision, she could cope with; she was strong enough, but the thought of that sweet face and gentle voice, the image of that golden playful monkey, was enough to melt her stomach and make her pale and nauseated.

Lyra's dread is deepened by the knowledge, imparted to her earlier, that, in fact, Lord Asriel is her father and Mrs. Coulter is her mother. Pullman thus deepens the significance, and fearsome power, of Lyra's greatest adult ally and enemy.

How does your protagonist's picture of himself change throughout the course of your novel? How does she view others in the story, and how do those views change? How do others see your protagonist? How do those assessments, in turn, alter? Delineate these shifts in your characters' self-perceptions and perceptions of each other. It is yet another way to tighten the weave of the story.

Measuring Inner Change

Step 1: Find a moment in your manuscript when your hero is speaking with a major secondary character, or when that secondary character carries the point of view while speaking with your hero.

_____

_____

_____

_____

_____

Step 2: Create a paragraph in which your hero assesses this other character; that is, delineates for himself this other character's qualities, mood, or situation in life. Put simply, how does your hero see this character right now? *Start writing now.*

_____

_____

_____

_____

_____

_____

_____

_____

Alternately, have your point of view character regard your hero by the same criteria. How does she view your hero at this particular moment? *Start writing now.*

_____

_____

_____

_____

_____

_____

_____

Step 3: Move forward to a later point in the story when these two characters are again together on the page. Repeat the previous step. How does your hero view this character now?

_____

_____

_____

Alternately, how does that character view your protagonist at this point? *Start writing now.*

_____

_____

_____

_____

> **!**
>
> ● NOTE:
> You grow and change, right? Naturally. Your characters do, too, or at least I hope they do. Indeed, it would be disappointing if they were the same at the end of the novel as they were at the beginning. But how are we to know what has changed unless your stop once in a while to measure the difference?

Follow-up work: Find three points in the story in which to delineate your antagonist's view of your protagonist. *Write a paragraph for each.*

_____

_____

_____

_____

_____

_____

_____

Conclusion: Allowing characters occasional moments to take stock of each other is a powerful way to mark each player's progress through the story. How have events affected each? Possibly one character sees your hero carrying a load of care, while another imagines that she has never looked so alive. Examine your hero from several points of view; later, show us how those views have shifted.

Setting

ow many settings are there in your current novel? From how many points of view is each of them seen? Each outlook on each location is an opportunity to enrich your story. In you novel, how many of those opportunities are you taking?

In Sarah Waters's moody, erotic Victorian novel *Affinity*, fragile Margaret Prior volunteers as a visitor to the female inmates at London's Millbank Prison. Following her first visit, she later recounts her journey through the institution's linked pentagonal buildings in the company of its warden, Mr. Shillitoe:

> I had a plan of Millbank's buildings from Mr. Shillitoe a week ago, and have had it pinned, since then, on the walls beside this desk. The prison, drawn in outline, has a curious kind of charm to it, the pentagons appearing as petals on a geometric flower—or, as I have sometimes thought, they are like the coloured zones on the chequer-boards we used to paint when we were children. Seen close, of course, Millbank is not charming. Its scale is vast, and its lines and angles, when realized in walls and towers of yellow brick and shuttered windows, seem only wrong or perverse. It is as if the prison had been designed by a man in the grip of a nightmare or a madness—or had been made expressly to *drive* its inmates mad. I think it would certainly drive me mad, if I had to work as a warder there.

Waters's choice of words for Miss Prior ("wrong or perverse" and "designed by a man in the grip of a nightmare") not only conveys the frightening and oppressive effect that the prison has upon her narrator, but also foreshadows the variety of madness into which Miss Prior herself will slip as the result of her lesbian affair with an inmate. The psychological effect of the place upon Miss Prior is striking—or is it perhaps more that Miss Prior is projecting her apprehension of her own fearful inclinations upon the place?

A place also can lift spirits as well as sink them, as South Carolina novelist

Dorothea Benton Frank shows in her debut novel *Sullivan's Island*. As I discussed in an earlier chapter, the book tells the story of Charleston real estate executive Susan Hayes, who retreats to her family's summer home on Sullivan's Island following the discovery that her husband is having an affair:

> Coming to the island made me feel younger, a little more reckless, and as I finally went back to my car and closed the door—pausing one moment to lower the audio assault of the radio—I realized the island also made me lighthearted. I was willingly becoming re-addicted. As we arrived on the island, I pointed out the signs of summer's early arrival to Beth, my fourteen-year-old certified volcano.
>
> "Oh, my Lord, look! There's Mrs. Schroeder!" I said. "I can't believe she's still alive." The old woman was draped over her porch swing in her housecoat.
>
> "Who? I mean, like, who cares, Mom? She's an old goat."
>
> "Well, honey, when you're an old goat like her, you will. Look at her, poor old thing with that wet rag, trying to cool her neck. Good Lord. What a life."
>
> "Shuh! Dawg life better, iffin you ask me!"
>
> I smiled at her. Beth's Gullah wasn't great, but we were working on it.

Is it the special qualities of Sullivan's Island working their magic, or would Susan have felt a sense of renewal arriving anywhere other than Charleston? It hardly matters. The beauty of seeing a locale through a particular perspective is that the point-of-view character cannot be separated from the place. The place comes alive, as does the observer of that place, in ways that would not be possible if described using objective point of view.

In alternate chapters, Frank's novel flashes back to the 1950s to relate the series of events that lead to her father's murder, so she later believes, by the Klu Klux Klan. In the first flashback, which we saw part of in an earlier chapter, Susan drives with her father to the rural side of the island to collect the new black housekeeper that the family has hired, the latest in a long string. On this drive young Susan views the island in an entirely different way, thereby giving us a glimpse of a white Southern girl's awareness of race in the 1950s:

> I felt the spirits of freed slaves ambling along the roadside with great baskets on their heads filled with Sweetgrass and palmetto fronds for weaving more baskets to harvest rice or to hold vegetables. I saw small loads of just-picked cotton on the back of a buckboard wagon on the way to market, drawn by the slow clip-clop of a broken-down horse or mule.
>
> When I came out here to Snowden, the hair on my arms stood up from goose bumps. Even though my family never owned a slave in all its history in the Lowcountry, my ancestors had prob-

ably condoned it. Coming here to old plantation country made me uncomfortable having white skin. In the carefree existence of Island living, I never had to think about what slavery must've been, but out here in the country reminders were everywhere.

Each outlook on each location is an opportunity to enrich your story.

When point-of-view writing is done well, place and perception are inextricably entwined. A place is filtered not only through the person, but through the person's age, social station, personality, and where they are in their life's development.

In *The You I Never Knew*, Susan Wiggs made a transition from historical romances to a contemporary setting and broke out. As we saw in an earlier chapter, at the story's outset, Seattle graphic artist Michelle Turner is driving to Montana with her difficult sixteen-year-old son, Cody. She is going there to donate a kidney to her father, a retired movie star from whom she has been estranged for years. As they approach the ranching town of Crystal City, Michelle is reminded why she once was drawn to paint the area:

> The valley slumbered in midwinter splendor, as if the entire landscape was holding its breath waiting for the far-distant springtime.
>
> She read the names on every rural mailbox they passed— Smith, Dodd, Gyenes, Bell, Jacobs. Most people who settled in the area seemed to stay forever. Each farm lay in perfect repose, a picture waiting to be painted: a white house with dark green shutters, a wisp of smoke twisting from the chimney, window-panes glowing at the first touch of twilight.
>
> There was a time when this sight had pierced her in a tender spot. She had painted this very scene long ago. Her brush had given life to the hillocks of untouched snow, to the luminous pink sunset, and to the fading sky behind alpine firs with their shoulders draped in white and icicles dripping from their branches. On a poorly prepared canvas with second rate paints, she managed to convey a sense of soaring wonder at the world around her. It was a good painting. Better than good. But young. Impossibly, naively young as she had never been since the day she left this town in anguish and disgrace.

In contrast to the disquiet that Crystal City stirs in Michelle is the calm that the place inspires in Sam McPhee, a rodeo star turned doctor. Sam is the cowboy who got Michelle pregnant at age eighteen; he is Cody's father, though he does not yet know that as he looks at the same landscape on the same evening that Michelle is driving back into town with his son:

> Sam McPhee stared out the window at the ripples of snow on the hills behind his house. Though it was a familiar sight, he lingered there, watching as the last light of day rode the broken-

backed mountains. The sight was a restful thing for a man to hold in his chest. In his youth, he'd carried the image with him no matter where he went, from Calgary to Cozumel, and when the time came to figure out where home was, he didn't need to look any further than these hills.

Sam's serenity is soon to be shattered, just as Michelle will eventually lose her restlessness and settle in Crystal City, in Sam's arms. They start the novel in opposite states of mind, and Wiggs uses Crystal City itself to illustrate the contrast.

Our perception of place changes as we change. The difference between a town as remembered from long ago and how it seems now is the difference between who we once were and who we are now. The same is true of characters in fiction. Take them anywhere and show us how they feel about the place, or how that places makes them feel, and you will reveal to us volumes about their inner frozenness, or growth.

So get to it.

The Psychology of Place

Step 1: Pick a high moment, turning point, or climax involving your protagonist. Where is it set?

_____

_____

_____

_____

_____

Step 2: Write a paragraph describing how this place makes your character feel, or how your protagonist feels about this place. *Start writing now.*

_____

_____

_____

_____

_____

Step 3: Move forward one week in time or backward one week in time. Return your protagonist to this place. Write a paragraph describing how it makes your character feel now. *Start writing now.*

_____

_____

_____

_____

_____

!

● NOTE:
In the workshop, many participants find that they would like to use the paragraph they wrote in step three. There is something powerful about returning to a place of significant action and discovering how it feels different. Did you ever return to a childhood home and find that it looked smaller to you? Then you know what I am talking about. By the same token, your protagonist will never feel the same way twice about a particular place. Pinning that down is using the *psychology of place*; that is, employing the perception of place as another way to measure change.

Follow-up work: What is the setting that recurs most often in your novel? From whose point of view is it most often seen? Count the number of times that character is in that place. Write a list, and for each return to that place find one way in which that character's perception of it changes.

_____

_____

_____

_____

_____

_____

_____

_____

Conclusion: Bringing to life the world of your novel is more than just describing it using the five senses. A place lives most vividly through the eyes of characters. The unique way in which each one sees what is around him is how the setting itself becomes a character in the story. Think about it: By itself, landscape is unchanging. (Well, mostly.) It takes a person to perceive its differences over time. Delineate those evolving perceptions, and the world of your novel will feel rich, dynamic, and alive.

Point of View

As we have seen, most contemporary novels are written from the point of view of their characters, and this point of view can be quite intimate. (First person is, of course, as intimate as you can get.) There are plenty of alternate points of view to employ, if you like, including the objective and authorial points of view, older approaches now somewhat out of fashion. Whatever your choice, point of view is the perspective you give your readers on the action of the story. It pays to make it strong.

How do parents look at their children? Is there any way to describe them that is not a cliché? Of course there is. In *Skyward*, discussed previously, Mary Alice Monroe finds one by being true to her novel's protagonist, Harris Henderson, head of a South Carolina rescue clinic for birds of prey. Harris's whole life is ospreys, owls, kites, and eagles—so much so that he feels helpless to raise his own pre-schooler, Marion.

This is particularly a problem when Marion, a problem child at the best of times who was abandoned by her mother, develops juvenile diabetes. The finger prick needed for an insulin level check six times a day becomes an occasion for force-ten temper tantrums:

> He looked again at his daughter curled up on the couch watching TV. How sweet and innocent she appeared. And how deceiving it was. He shook his head, took a deep breath and braced himself for what was coming.
>
> "Marion? It's time to do the test."
>
> Instantly, all sweetness fled from her face as she jackknifed her knees to her chest, locking her arms tight around them. "No!" she shouted.
>
> "Come on, honey. You know we've got to do this."
>
> "No!"
>
> Harris released a ragged sigh. So, it was going to be another fight. As he walked toward her, she backed up against the armrest and cowered in the corner of the sofa, her hands up, nails

out, to ward him off. She looked just like one of the wild, terrified birds when he reached to grab them—all glaring eyes and ready to attack.

Under siege himself, Harris reverts to seeing things in a way that is natural to him: in terms of birds of prey. It isn't until the arrival of a nursing-trained nanny, Ella Majors, that Harris finds out how to handle his daughter: as a little human being. Meanwhile, with just a few words Monroe's strong point-of-view writing reveals reams about her novel's protagonist.

Susan Wiggs uses a mother's view of her teenaged son in *The You I Never Knew,* discussed in earlier chapters, in the same way. Her novel's heroine, Michelle Turner, has returned to Crystal City, Montana, to donate a kidney to her father, and has brought along her Seattle-sophisticated son, Cody. When Cody gets interested in a local cowgirl, Michelle is relieved:

> Good, she thought. Maybe he'd finally get over his obsession with Claudia Teller, his girlfriend since the start of the school year. Claudia was a beautiful pale predator who never met Michelle's eyes and who answered her admittedly chirpy questions with monosyllables. Claudia had introduced Cody to cigarettes and Zima, and probably to things Michelle hadn't found out about yet. There was no creature quite so intoxicating as a provocative teenage girl. And no creature quite so malleable as a teenage boy on hormone overload. A girl like Claudia could make Eagle Scouts steal from their grandmothers. She wore makeup with the brand name Urban Decay. She had bottle red hair and kohl-deepened eyes, and she was as seductive as Spanish fly on Cody's defenseless adolescent libido. The most popular girl in school, she wielded her power over him with casual ruthlessness.

Notice the damning details ("Urban Decay") and the hyperbolic language "seductive as Spanish fly" and "casual ruthlessness") that Wiggs uses to convey Michelle's sense of protectiveness toward her "defenseless" teenaged son. As we come to find out, Michelle's protectiveness derives in no small way from her own seduction at age eighteen by a handsome cowboy, Sam McPhee, who got her pregnant with Cody and whom she remeets, with life-changing consequences, in Crystal City.

Young adults have their own view of the world, especially the grown-up realm of work and corporations. They see its shallowness and money-chasing hypocrisy in a way, naturally, that no other generation before has seen. Since the time of Holden Caulfield, youth disaffection has been a staple of fiction. How, then, can a writer capture that disaffection in a way that reflects the discovery and outrage of each new generation?

In her striking debut, *Silk,* a dark urban fantasy, Caitlin R. Kiernan finds an original language with which to express the outsider point of view of the marginal world of goths, post-punks, and the gay/lesbian community of Birmingham, Alabama, in the 1990s. One of the novel's twin protagonists is Daria Parker, songwriter and bassist for the local band Stiff Kitty. As the novel opens, Daria, on her way to rehearsal one early evening, regards Birmingham at quitting time and notes its mix of old and new:

> Tailpipe farts and the gentle rev of engines made in Japan and Germany, the office monkeys calling it a day, reclaiming their cars from the parking garages spaced out along the length of Morris Avenue. Daria closed her eyes, exhaling slow smoke through her nostrils, listening to the bumpity sound of wheels on the polished unevenness of the street. Behind her, behind the offices, the sudden air horn blat and dinosaur herd rumble of a freight train, hurrying along one or another of the six tracks that divided downtown Birmingham into north and south.

Clearly this is not the vocabulary of an insider, of the "office monkeys." Kiernan's language not only anchors Daria's point of view, it also prepares us for a strange and scary tale of dread, dreams, and crawling terrors that may or may not come from the mind of goth/lesbian store owner Spyder Baxter, the novel's other protagonist. The urban underbelly and its horrors once belonged exclusively to novelist Poppy Z. Brite, but with strong point-of-view writing and a fine-tuned feeling for nameless dread that recalls Lovecraft, Bradbury, and King, Kiernan has taken a share of this territory for herself.

What sort of singing voice do you have? Soprano? Alto? Tenor? Bass? What kind of soprano—bright? What kind of tenor—high? Is your voice pop, smooth, operatic, or belting? The type of singing voice you have makes a difference to the sound that comes out of your mouth, correct?

So it is with your "voice" in your novel. What kind of voice is it, exactly? That will in large part be determined by your choice of point of view, but more than that by how you use that point of view. Are the voices of your characters ordinary and generic, or are they highly colored and specific? Heighten point of view throughout your manuscript, and you will strengthen your story's impact.

> *Point of view is the perspective you give your readers on the action of the story.*

EXERCISE

Strengthening Point of View

Step 1: Open your manuscript at random. Through whose point of view are we experiencing this scene? *Write down that character's name.*

_____

_____

_____

_____

_____

_____

_____

Step 2: On this page of the manuscript, select anything that the point-of-view character says, does, or thinks. Heighten it. Change the dialogue. Exaggerate the action. Grow the emotion, thought, or observation to make it even more characteristic of this character.

_____

_____

_____

_____

_____

_____

_____

_____

!

NOTE:
Capturing a character's unique speech and outlook is perhaps easier in a first-person novel, but I find that most manuscripts, whether written in the first or the third person, do not bring us as deeply as they might inside characters' heads. Point of view is more than just a set of eyes looking upon the world. Those eyes come with a mouth and a brain. Those must come into play, too, or your novel will have the chilliness of a movie camera. There may be times when objective point of view is useful, but by and large it is best to use the singular advantage that the novel has over other art forms: the ability to bring us deeply inside a character's experience.

Follow-up work: Turn to another page at random. Whose point of view is it now? Can you heighten anything. *Repeat the steps above once in every scene in your novel.*

_____

_____

_____

_____

_____

_____

_____

Conclusion: What would happen if you actually did the follow-up exercise above, instead of just thinking about it? Your novel would take longer to write, but wouldn't it be stronger? When I pose this question in the workshops there are groans, but also nods of agreement. Weak point of view is a common failing of manuscripts; the cure is painstaking, page-by-page strengthening of point of view. Good news: The next exercise is a tool that might make the job easier.

Character Delineation

Having sharpened the points of view you have chosen for your novel, it is time to take the next step and make sure that your characters sound, act, and think differently from each other. That is the business of character delineation.

The *USA Today* best-seller list is a great place to spot breakout novelists, particularly those whose work appears as original paperbacks. One author who has made it to that list is Barbara Freethy. Novels like *One True Love*, *Some Kind of Wonderful*, and *Love Will Find a Way* established her as a storyteller with a gift for warm, family-oriented stories—usually with a primary romance, a secondary couple, and a long-held secret driving the plot.

In *Summer Secrets*, discussed in earlier chapters, Freethy takes her strengths several steps further. This time there are three women: Sisters, bound together by the secret of what happened on a round-the-world sailboat race that brought them fifteen minutes of fame, a winners' trophy, and a boatload of secrets. Among other things, Freethy faces the task of making these three sisters different from each other, and she does this effectively.

The oldest is Kate, protective, responsible, and understanding; as well as bossy, opinionated, and critical. She watches over their once-magnetic father, Duncan, now a land-locked alcoholic. Formerly a wild adventurer, Kate now is (well, perhaps) a play-it-safe bookstore owner on the island of Castleton in Puget Sound:

> Kate loved her view of the waterfront—loved the one from her house in the hills even better—but more than anything she appreciated the fact that the view didn't change every day. Maybe some would call that boring, but she found it comforting.
>
> The wind lifted the hair off the back of her neck, changing that feeling of comfort to one of uneasiness. Wind in her life had meant change. Her father, Duncan McKenna, a sailing man from the top of his head to the tips of his toes, always relished the wind's arrival. Kate could remember many a time when he had

jumped to his feet at the first hint of a breeze. A smile would spread across his weatherbeaten cheeks as he'd stand on the deck of their boat, pumping his fist triumphantly in the air, his eyes focused on the distant horizon. *The wind's up, Katie girl*, he'd say. *It's time to go.*

And they'd go—wherever the wind took them. They'd sail with it, into it, against it. They'd lash out in anger when it blew too hard, then cry in frustration when it vanished completely. Her life had been formed, shaped, and controlled by the wind. She'd thought of it as a friend; she'd thought of it as a monster. Well, no more.

She had a home now, an address, a mailbox, a garden. She might live by the water, but she didn't live on it.

The middle sister, Ashley, now a photographer, is the most fragile. Since the race eight years earlier she has grown afraid of boats and the ocean, as we learn early in the novel when she tries to board a boat during a Castleton race week to snap a portrait of the crew:

Water splashed over the side of the dock, and she took a hasty step backward. She felt small and vulnerable on this bobbing piece of wood with a storm blowing in. The sea had often made her feel that way. Her father had always told her to look the ocean right in the eye, never back down, never give up, never give in. There was a time when those brave, fighting words had given her courage. Then she'd learned through hard experience that the ocean didn't back down or give in, either. That if it was man or woman against nature, nature would win.

The youngest is Caroline, a reckless young woman who smokes too much, drinks too hard, and flirts too easily. A hair stylist with piercings and a tattoo, she also is impulsive and rebellious. The contrast between the three is pronounced, and nicely summed up in one early moment when the three sisters contemplate whether or not to tell their father that their boat named Moon Dancer, sold years before, has now sailed back into Castleton's harbor—and with it the one man who knows the secret of what happened during the fateful race:

Once again, both sisters looked to Kate for the answer to their problem. They'd played out this scene many times before— Caroline eating chocolate, Ashley biting her fingernails while Kate paced.

The exercise underlying this chapter works toward creating a point-of-view vocabulary that will distinguish one character from another; however, it is not always necessary to be inside characters' heads to accomplish delineation.

In his best-selling literary novel *The Virgin Suicides*, Jeffrey Eugenides has five women to distinguish from one another: five suicidal teenage sisters ranging in age from thirteen to seventeen. Adding to this challenge, Eugenides's novel is narrated by an outside observer, a narrator who speaks with one voice for the whole puzzled Michigan town where the suicidal sisters live and die. Moreover, this narrator's point of view is almost wholly objective.

Eugenides does not slip us inside anyone's head. He achieves his delineations by sheer force of objective observation, as in this early scene when the narrator attends the one and only party that the sisters are allowed to throw. As "we" (as I mentioned, the narrator speaks for an entire Michigan town) enter the downstairs rec room where the party is underway, "we" realize for the first time that the pretty Lisbon girls are all different people:

> We saw at once that Bonnie, who introduced herself now as Bonaventure, had the sallow complexion and sharp nose of a nun. Her eyes watered and she was a foot taller than any of her sisters, mostly because the length of her neck which would one day hang from the end of a rope. Therese Lisbon had a heavier face, the cheeks and eyes of a cow, and she came forward to greet us on two left feet. Mary Lisbon's hair was darker; she had a widow's peak and fuzz above her upper lip that suggested her mother had found her depilatory wax. Lux Lisbon was the only one who accorded with our image of the Lisbon girls. She radiated health and mischief. Her dress fit tightly, and when she came forward to shake our hands, she secretly moved one finger to tickle our palms, giving off at the same time a strange gruff laugh. Cecilia was wearing, as usual, the wedding dress with the short hem. The dress was vintage 1920's. It had sequins on the bust she didn't fill out, and someone, either Cecilia herself or the owner of the used clothing store, had cut off the bottom of the dress with a jagged stroke so that it ended above Cecilia's chafed knees. She sat on a barstool, staring into her punch glass, and the shapeless bag of a dress fell over her. She had colored her lips with red crayon, which gave her face a deranged harlot look, but she acted as though no one were there.

No one is going to mix up the sisters after such sharp, detailed descriptions—especially not Cecelia, who kills herself during the party by throwing herself on the spikes of the fence that surround their yard. Gradually, the narrator's review of later-available evidence, his "interviews" with those who knew the girls, and his close observation of the events of the "year of the suicides" further separates the sisters—and the very different reasons for their deaths.

In a way, you almost cannot pile on too many details that make one character distinct from another. Michael Chabon's third novel, *The Amazing Adventures of Kavalier and Clay*, which won a Pulitzer Prize, tells the story of two cousins who ride the crest of popularity of comic books before, during, and after World

War II. At the novel's opening, Chabon introduces one of them, Sam Klayman, in a passage that piles detail upon detail to bring alive an uniquely Brooklyn adolescent, even before Sam has spoken or done a single thing:

Make sure that your characters sound, act, and think differently from each other.

> Houdini was a hero to little men, city boys and Jews; Samuel Louis Klayman was all three. He was seventeen when the adventures began: bigmouthed, perhaps not quite as quick on his feet as he liked to imagine, and tending to be, like many optimists, a little excitable. He was not, in any conventional way, handsome. His face was an inverted triangle, brow large, chin pointed, with pouting lips and a blunt, quarrelsome nose. He slouched, and wore clothes badly; he always looked as though he had just been jumped for his lunch money. He went forward in the morning with a hairless cheek of innocence itself, but by noon a clean shave was no more than a memory, a hoboish penumbra on the jaw not quite sufficient to make him look tough. He thought of himself as ugly, but this was because he had never seen his face in repose. He had delivered the *Eagle* for most of 1931 in order to afford a set of dumbbells, which he had hefted every morning for the next eight years until his arms, chest and shoulders were ropy and strong; polio had left him with the legs of a delicate boy. He stood, in his socks, five feet five inches tall. Like all of his friends, he considered it a compliment when somebody called him a wiseass. He possessed an incorrect but fervent understanding of the workings of television, atom power, and antigravity, and harbored the ambition—one of a thousand—of ending his days on the warm sunny beaches of the Great Polar Ocean of Venus. An omnivorous reader with a self-improving streak, cozy with Stevenson, London, and Wells, dutiful about Wolfe, Dreiser, and Passos, idolatrous of S.J. Perelman, his self-improvement regime masked the usual guilty appetite. In his case the covert passion—one of them, at any rate—was for those two-bit argosies of blood and wonder, the pulps. He had tracked down and read every biweekly issue of *The Shadow* going back to 1933, and he was well on his way to amassing complete runs of *The Avenger* and *Doc Savage*.

It is as if Chabon filled in several delineation charts and dumped their entire contents into his second paragraph!

How are your characters different from one another? In your mind, I am sure they are all quite different—but how is that specifically conveyed to your readers? Use charts to create separate vocabularies, traits, actions, and more for your characters. You will be surprised how much more individual they become.

Improving Character Delineation

Step 1: In the following chart the columns A, B, and C are for different point-of-view characters in your story. (You can add more columns.) For each character, work down the list of common words on the left and *write in the word that character A, B, or C would use instead.*

	A	B	C
Sofa			
Bureau			
Dress			
Pants			
Shoes			
Auto			
Soda			
Coffee			
Alcohol			
Cash			
"Hello!"			
(Expletive)			
"Cool."			
"Oh well."			
God			
Mother			
Father			
Partner/Spouse			
Man			
Woman			
Attractive			
Unattractive			
Music			
Periodical			

! NOTE:
You can, of course, lengthen the list as much as you want. The point here is to find a unique vocabulary for each character, and to use it when writing from that person's point of view. That distinctive way of "speaking" helps to distinguish, or delineate, one character from another.

Follow-up work: For each point-of-view character list unique gestures, rationalizations, ways of procrastination, peeves, hot buttons, sentimental triggers, principles to live by, superstitions, or anything else that bears upon the way this character speaks or thinks. *Use them in writing from his point of view.*

Conclusion: Have you ever read a novel in which all the characters talk alike and seem alike? That is weak point-of-view writing. Strong point of view is more than just the words a character uses. It is her whole way of feeling, thinking, speaking, acting, and believing. Each will feed into the point of view. One character's cadence and sentence structures will be different from another's. So will his words, so will his thoughts, so will his actions and reactions. Make your characters different from each other, just as are people in life. That way, your novel will have the variety and resonance of real life, too.

Theme

here are so many different ways to discover and develop the themes in your novel. Themes can be motifs, recurring patterns, outlooks, messages, morals—any number of deliberate elements that make your manuscript more than just a story; indeed, that makes it a novel with something to say.

As I discussed in previous chapters, a major secondary character in Mary Alice Monroe's *Skyward* is teenager Brady Simmons. Brady comes from a poor South Carolina low country family. When his father shoots an eagle near the bird of prey rescue clinic that is the focus of the novel's action, Brady takes the rap because the fine will be less for a juvenile. Brady also is sentenced to community service—at the clinic for birds of prey. Angry about everything, he arrives at the clinic vowing to make everyone at this "rehab joint" as miserable as him.

That is not quite how things go. The clinic becomes the vehicle for Brady's salvation. The clinic's head and the novel's protagonist, Harris Henderson, unaware that Brady did not shoot the eagle, grudgingly gives him a chance, but only the slimmest:

> Brady's head shot up. "I thought I was going to be working with the birds."
>
> Harris's eyes flashed. He wanted to tell him hell would freeze over before he'd let him touch his birds. He took a moment to rein in his anger at the kid's arrogance before saying in a level voice, "Let's get this understood right from the start. No one gets to care for the birds without approval. Not any volunteer. And you, Brady Simmons, are not a volunteer. You're going to have to work extra long and extra hard to earn that approval from me. We're all here to serve those birds. It's not the other way around." . . .
>
> Brady shot the man a wary glance.
>
> "You'll start by working with a by-product of birds. See that bottled soap over there? And those scrub brushes? And that

hose? Lijah here's going to show you how to use all that stuff along with some of that muscle power you've got to scrub clean every one of those kennels."

Brady is going to clean out the bird's cages—all for a crime he did not commit. This kid's got problems, not the least of which is his attitude. He needs a break. He needs a friend. He needs a girlfriend. He needs a real father. Most of all, he needs self-respect and a new outlook on the world.

Can he get these things? At first Brady doesn't even know he wants them, but soon enough he yearns for change, though the level of his hope is limited. He'll settle for getting by. Finding a friend is beyond his vision. Getting a girl is pretty much out of the question, given his conviction. His father is a hopeless, violent redneck. As for working directly with the birds of prey—that is too much to hope for.

Here's what happens: Elijah Cooper, a wise old *griot* (African-American oral historian) who works at the clinic, patiently takes Brady under his wing. Slowly, Brady begins to change. He does his work without complaint and earns the respect of the other volunteers and, eventually, even of Harris Henderson.

More than friends, he finds supporters and cheerleaders, among them a brainy and beautiful African-American teenager, Clarice Gaillard, who volunteers at the clinic. Clarice warms to Brady, encourages him, and helps him study. Eventually their relationship even gets a bit physical. Brady's opinion of himself changes, his grades improve, and he begins to think about applying to colleges.

Most of all, Brady begins to discover his affinity for the birds, and to understand the relationship between falcons and humans. His transformation begins one day as he watches Harris retrain a convalescing hawk to hunt. Brady thinks it looks easy; that the hawk is following its instincts, nothing more. Also on hand is a resident bird, Risk, who is not on a tether and yet does not fly away. Brady asks Elijah why:

> "They *choose* to stay."
> When Brady looked back, puzzled, Lijah shook his head. "That's what I mean exactly. Birds of prey ain't the same as the rest of the birds. You can't just train raptors. They ain't like dogs neither. Those animals want to please. Not raptors. They be proud and independent. That being their nature, you can't go demanding obedience from them. Can't do that with a child, neither. All you can do is ask."
> Brady listened, feeling the words take root in his heart. At sixteen years old, he'd had enough of people making him jump when they said jump.
> "That's why," Lijah concluded, "to work with raptors, you first have to be humble."
> "Humble?" he asked, confused.
> "That's the truth," Lijah confirmed with a solemn nod. "And

that be a hard, hard lesson for a man to learn. With a raptor, you're never the master. You're the student. You have to learn the ways of the hawk. To learn the spirit of the hawk."

Having learned the lesson of humility, even Harris recognizes that Brady has something special, and offers to train him as a falconer. This is more than Brady ever dreamed he could get, but even better than winning the chance to work with the birds, for Brady, is the winning the respect of Harris:

> "There was a time when only lords and kings could fly peregrine falcons," he told Brady. "Having one was a sign of status. A privilege. And a great responsibility, not only to the bird but to oneself. When you fly your bird, Brady, you fly with him." . . .
> He saw Brady's shoulders straighten as his chest expanded.

Even Brady's father eventually recognizes the change in his son, and is himself transformed by it, as we see when late in the novel they go fishing together and Brady's father hooks an undersized spot tail, which he refuses to throw back:

> "Aw, no one gives a damn about that, anyway," said Roy, opening the fish bucket on the bottom of the boat.
> Brady shifted his weight on the narrow slat and took a breath. "I do," he said.
> Roy paused, the wiggling fish dangling from his hand. He eyes his son narrowly and considered. "You telling me you care about this puny fish?"
> "Yes, sir."
> His father shook his head and chuckled low in his chest. "If that don't beat all. Those tree huggers really got to you, didn't they?" He held up the fish to look at it up close. "Explain it to me how this one little fish is gonna make one scrap of difference in that big river out there?" . . .
> As he began trying to explain his newfound beliefs to his father, he was amazed when the belligerence on Roy's face slackened and he actually began listening to what his son had to say.
> "See, if everyone went and kept the undersized fish they'd caught, that would be thousands of fish each summer that wouldn't grow to breed. Wouldn't be long before they'd die out and there'd be no fish left for anybody. But if I tossed my undersized fish back in the water, and the next guy did, and so on and so on then we can all come back here and go fishing another day. So the way I figure it, it *does* make a difference if I put that puny fish back in this river. Leastwise, I'd know I did the right thing. A man can live with that."
> His father shook his head and half smiled. But he didn't laugh

At *the heart* of every big issue is a dilemma that has no answer.

at him. To Brady's surprise, he leaned over the edge of the boat and tossed that puny fish back into the river.

It seems that Brady even may have gained a better father. Brady has exceeded his own expectations. By changing, he gains more than he could possibly have hoped for, and what can make a novel more satisfying than that? Throughout *Skyward*, Monroe draws parallels between the healing of wild birds of prey and the healing of humans, and when in the epilogue we see that Brady has become a full-fledged falconer, we know that Monroe theme carries truth: By looking to the natural world around us and observing carefully, we can find the solutions to a sky full of human troubles.

Oh, in case you think that Brady's story wraps up too neatly, I should point out that in the end he doesn't get the girl. When some of Brady's former redneck friends shoot a rooster that Brady has bonded with and insult Clarice as well, Clarice begs him not to seek revenge for her sake, or anyone else's, but to take the high road and succeed for himself alone. This leap is too big for Brady, and the resulting argument results in their breakup:

> "But you got to know how I feel about you."
> She shook her head and said fervently, "Don't go there. Please."
> "You can't deny there's something."
> Clarice took a long, pained breath and dropped her hand. "No, I can't."
> Then just when his heart jumped in hope, she dashed it quickly.
> "But be real, Brady. There'd be so many problems and hassles that I can't even begin to list them. And why even bother? I'm graduating next week and then I'm going straight to California [to Stanford University]. I've got my own life. My own plans. Plans that don't include you."
> "Oh." He stepped back, his face flaming, and stuck his hands in his pockets. "Forget it."
> "Brady, it's not like I don't care."
> He twisted his mouth.
> "Don't do this. Not now. Let's just leave it the way it is."
> "Yeah? And how's that?" . . .
> "Two people who worked together at something they loved. Who had some good times. Friends. I like to think good friends."

Just friends? Ouch. Monroe is a fine enough novelist to know that you can't always get what you want. Except in the case of Clarice, Brady really doesn't have to settle too much. Neither do we. Because Monroe fully plays out her theme through this secondary character, our satisfaction is magnified.

In Ann B. Ross's *Miss Julia Speaks Her Mind*, we already know rich Southern banker's widow Julia Springer is served up a gumbo of problems when her husband's illegitimate nine-year-old son arrives in her life. Among these is the challenge to her husband's will, and later to her own mental competence, that is being mounted by her local Presbyterian church, which is counting on her inheritance from her dead husband to fund a family activities center.

Her pastor's attempts to cause her to doubt her decision-making capability, to seduce her by proxy, and generally to undermine her willpower, are oily and shameful. They also are amplified by a larger denominational problem that surfaces one Sunday morning when Pastor Ledbetter preaches against ordaining women in the Presbyterian Church on the grounds that the practice is not supported by scripture. Miss Julia has a low opinion of this sermon:

> I tried my best to tune him out, tired of church politics that pitted one group of men against another group of men over women's role in the church. I already knew Pastor Ledbetter's position. He held that women's duties consisted of covering their heads, their mouths, and their casserole dishes, and I'd done all three about as long as I wanted to. But when he tied all the woes of the church to women officers, I could've wrung Paul's neck, and Timothy's, too, for giving men like Pastor Ledbetter justification for their prejudices. And don't tell me, as he'd done before, that a woman's submission elevates and ennobles her. I knew all about submission, and all it had gotten me was the humiliation in khaki pants sitting next to me.

Opposition to the ordination of women is a bigger problem than Miss Julia can solve; indeed, than Ross or any of us can solve by ourselves. However, by introducing the issue into the story, Ross ties it (with a bit of a stretch, it must be admitted) to Miss Julia's predicament. The parallel enriches the story, as well as setting its social context.

It doesn't necessarily take much to create the effect of amplifying theme. Heather Graham's *Tall, Dark, and Deadly*, previously discussed vis-à-vis combining roles, is about the disappearance of Miami criminal defense attorney Marnie Newcastle. Her neighbor, Samantha (Sam) Miller, investigates, but the investigation is complicated by the arrival of a new neighbor, the lover who dumped Sam five years earlier, rock star Rowan Dillon.

At one point Rowan's Cuban housekeeper, Adelia, becomes the means for opening further the sense of eternal connection felt by those left behind by the missing, especially when the disappearances in question are unexplained:

> She'd had a husband once, but they had locked him up years and years ago in a Cuban prison, and she didn't even know if he was alive anymore, if she was really a wife or a widow. . . .
> "Your husband may very well be dead, Adelia."
> "I know."
> "But you should know, in case you wish to remarry—"
> "No," Adelia said, turning the wedding band on her finger.

"Mario and I were deeply in love. He would not recognize me now—I am chubby, *si?* But once I was slim, so pretty, and he was so handsome. Proud—he had to say what he believed. So they took him away, but I will always love him. I will just keep praying. Am I silly? A silly old chubby woman?"

"No, Adelia, you're beautiful, and your thoughts are beautiful," Sam told her.

Themes can be motifs, recurring patterns, outlooks, messages, morals—any number of deliberate elements that make your manuscript more than just a story.

This theme—the power that the disappeared have over those left behind—explains why Sam feels compelled to find out what happened to her neighbor Marnie. This theme is further developed when Sam and Rowan's backstory finally is revealed (halfway through the novel, please note!) and with it the reason that Rowan closed the door on Sam five years earlier. Rowan was still married at the time he met Sam, but his wife had disappeared. He was questioned by the police, and then:

"All right. This is the truth, and I swear it, and I don't beg people to believe me, not matter how much I want them to. Dina was self-destructive, and I knew it. When she returned, she was in sorry shape. I had married her. I could never have lived with myself if I hadn't tried to help her."

"You might have said that to me then."

"At the time? Exactly what should I have said? 'Oh, excuse me, thank you, you've been a fabulous lover, but they've found my wife, I didn't do away with her after all, but she's a drug addict and I need to be with her'?"

She swung on him then. "Yes!"

Well, yes, that might have helped, don't you think? Anyway, even more powerful than the effect of a disappearance, Graham is saying, is the effect of a return. Unresolved businesses and unfulfilled commitments that otherwise might be let go are, in the wake of a return, impossible to forget. Breezy and commercial as *Tall, Dark, and Deadly* may be, Graham does not ignore the need to amplify her theme.

In *Empire Falls* by Richard Russo, discussed in previous chapters, protagonist Miles Roby, a man over-educated for his job as proprietor of the local diner, is harried by his nemesis, town sheriff Jimmy Minty. It would have been easy to make Jimmy simply a small-minded, small-town stereotype, but Russo is more expansive. In a late-night confrontation with Miles, Jimmy states his case:

"Thing is, Miles, people in this town like you. A lot of people. You got friends, even some important friends. I admit it. But here's something that might surprise you. People like me too. Something else? I got friends. Might surprise you to hear we even got some of the *same* friends. You're not the only one people like, okay? And I'll tell you something else. What people around here like best about me? They like it that they're more like me than they are like you. They look at me and they see the town they grew up in. They see their first girlfriend. They see the first high school football game they ever went to. You know what they see when they look at you? That they ain't good enough."

For a moment there, we feel that Jimmy Minty has a point. *Empire Falls* has a lot to do with the effect of not fitting in; of feeling like an outsider in your own town. Being part of a place, and what that means, is a major theme in Russo's novel. When Jimmy Minty makes his case, he is touching upon that theme, albeit from a different perspective than Miles.

What are the themes of your current novel, and how are you developing them? Whether you are making your points by creating a backward antagonist, or by giving other characters parallel problems, or by introducing problems that are bigger than your protagonist, or by showing us what your character is aiming for (or at least will settle for), be sure that you have a means to bring out what you want to say. A novel that has nothing to say will have a tough time breaking out.

Alternate Endings

Step 1: With respect to the story as a whole, what does your protagonist want? *Write that down.*

_____

_____

_____

_____

_____

Step 2: If your protagonist cannot get that, what would she take second? *Write that down.*

_____

_____

_____

_____

_____

Step 3: If he can get nothing else, what would he settle for? *Write that down.*

_____

_____

_____

Step 4: Work out alternate endings for the novel based on each of the above answers. How would each ending go? *Make notes.*

_____

_____

_____

_____

_____

_____

_____

_____

● **NOTE:**
The point of this exercise is not necessarily to change the ending of your novel (although it might). It is to use alternate outcomes to understand what it is that your protagonist is really after, and why. Is second-best or the minimum good enough? Then perhaps you need to raise the personal stakes so that those lesser outcomes are in no way acceptable. Buried in the results of this exercise also are clues to what your novel really is about: its theme.

Follow-up work: Again thinking of the story as a whole, what outcome would be more than your protagonist possibly could hope for?

_____

_____

_____

_____

_____

Conclusion: Ah! The answer to that last question may open up even more possible outcomes for the story. Could it be that your protagonist (or you) has her sights set too low? Even if that dream outcome is not practical, how can that vision of greater good be incorporated into the story?

The Larger Problem

Step 1: Thinking about the story as a whole, what is the main problem facing your protagonist? *Write that down.*

_____

_____

_____

_____

_____

Step 2: What is the bigger problem beyond that? *Write down your answer.*

_____

_____

_____

_____

_____

_____

Step 3: What is the problem that your protagonist cannot solve? *Write that down, too.*

_____

_____

_____

_____

_____

Step 4: Find ways to introduce into the story the bigger problem and the problem that cannot be solved. How can that be accomplished? *Make notes.*

_____

_____

_____

_____

_____

> ● **NOTE:**
> What public issues stir you up? Free trade? Energy conservation? Endangered species? Gay rights? If you could change the world, what would you change? While in life it is good to have passionate opinions and to hold high ideals, in your fiction it is bad to impose them from the outside. To keep your theme from feeling heavy-handed and obvious, allow it to emerge not from your own heart but from your protagonist's problems.

Follow-up: What is the main problem in your protagonists second plot layer? *Write it down and follow the steps above to develop a secondary theme.*

_____

_____

_____

_____

_____

Conclusion: Every issue conceals a bigger issue. At the heart of every big issue is a dilemma that has no answer. While it may sound downbeat to introduce these elements into your story, in fact they will amplify the problem at hand. The ripples that they send outward in your readers' minds are, in essence, your novel's deepest issues or, to put it another way, its theme at work.

Same Problem, Other Characters

Step 1: What is the main problem in the novel? *Write that down.*

_____

_____

_____

_____

_____

Step 2: Who else in the story besides your protagonist could have that problem? How would it manifest differently for these other characters? *Write down your answers.*

_____

_____

_____

_____

_____

_____

_____

_____

Step 3: Incorporate the results of the previous step into the story. *Make notes.*

_____

_____

_____

_____

_____

_____

_____

! NOTE:

Theme is not smeared onto your story in the final draft, like frosting on a cake; rather, it emerges from the very substance of the story. To make your theme large and resonant, let it work in your story in more ways than one. It doesn't matter that the central problem is different for other characters. Your variations on the theme will only reinforce the theme itself.

Follow-up work: Who in your story could have the *opposite* problem? *Incorporate that into your novel.*

_____

_____

_____

_____

_____

Conclusion: Just as it is advisable to strengthen your theme, it is also no problem to run counter to it. Does your hero rescue his family from the wilderness, struggling against nature? What about the hermit who helps them? He lives at peace with nature, yes? His struggle may be the opposite: to connect again with his fellow man.

Making the Antagonist's Case

Step 1: What does your antagonist believe in? Why does he feel justified and right? How would the world be better, through his eyes, if things ran the way he would like them to run? *Write down your answers.*

_____

_____

_____

_____

_____

Step 2: Make the antagonist's case stronger. Assume that the antagonist actually is correct: What support for her case can be found in philosophy or religion? On a practical level, how would things really be better? *Explain in writing.*

_____

_____

_____

_____

_____

Step 3: Choose a character who supports your antagonist, and make the antagonist's case from that character's point of view. *Write a paragraph, starting now.*

_____

_____

_____

_____

_____

NOTE:
In most of the manuscripts submitted to my literary agency, most antagonists are cardboard. They are bluntly evil or wrong. One-dimensional villains do not frighten me, or most readers. Far scarier are villains who have a good reason for doing what they do, and who can justify their intents and actions as working for the good. The more sincere your antagonist, the more effective he will be, and the more powerfully you will be forcing your reader to decide what constitutes right and what constitutes wrong. (Which, of course, is more effective than telling your reader your own opinion outright, don't you agree?)

Follow-up work: Find the moment in your story when your protagonist realizes that your antagonist is right, and why. *Write out that moment in a paragraph, starting now.*

_____

_____

_____

_____

_____

Conclusion: Certainly you want your hero to doubt himself at times, don't you? Why not push that all the way and let your hero doubt himself in the extreme? What would be the circumstances? How close to failure does your protagonist come? In that moment, you will be very close to your core values and theme.

32

Symbols

Symbols, which sometimes go by their more academic name, objective correlatives, are another literary device that feels old-fashioned. The very word takes you back to high school English class, doesn't it? Soon we will be discussing stream of consciousness, litotes, parallelism, and syllepsis, eh?

In their simplest form, though, symbols are anything outward that stands in for anything inward or abstract, such as a mood or an idea. A statement like "He was in turmoil" can feel blunt. Instead, we might substitute an image; say, "Outside, the Siberian Elms held their heads in their hands and swayed, wailing like a chorus of Greek women." The image is indirect, but it nevertheless conveys an inner state.

Symbols can be glaringly obvious, of course. Think sunsets and trains rushing into tunnels. At their best, though, they are elegant and evocative. Their effect can be subliminal, barely noticed. A device they may be, but they also can be quite powerful.

One of the most accomplished novels of recent years is Barbara Kingsolver's story of an American missionary family's journey to the Belgian Congo in the 1960s, *The Poisonwood Bible*. This acclaimed saga is itself, among other things, a bible of breakout fiction technique. Kingsolver's rotating narrators are the four daughters of the Price family, and each is an outstanding example of character delineation. The distinctive voices of Rachel, Leah and Adah (twins), and Ruth May are instantly recognizable.

Kingsolver also masterfully sketches a cast of secondary African characters, whose depths are suggested even while their culturally different way of thinking ultimately is unknowable to the Prices. The girls' father, fundamentalist preacher Nathan Price, is a fully developed antagonist, tragically dedicated and unable to grasp the impossibility of his mission. The complications faced by the family steadily escalate as the local villagers' mistrust of Nathan Price grows and the Congolese prepare to wrest their country from the brutal grip of Belgium. The novel's many narrative threads are woven together with impeccable care.

There is so much to admire in *The Poisonwood Bible*, in fact, that fiction writers studying Kingsolver's breakout technique might overlook her deft use of symbols. They can be found all the way through. Even the novel's extended opening image, narrated in flashback by the girls' mother, Orleanna Price, uses the image of a wild okapi stopping to drink in a jungle stream during a family outing. This is a multi-layered symbol for Orleanna's bewilderment at the mystery and beauty of the environment around her, and also for her own essential helplessness:

> She [Orleanna] is inhumanly alone. And then, all at once, she isn't. A beautiful animal stands on the other side of the water. They look up from their lives, woman and animal, amazed to find themselves in the same place. He freezes, inspecting her with his black-tipped ears. His back is purplish-brown in the dim light, sloping downward from the gentle hump of his shoulders. The forest's shadows fall into lines across his white-striped flanks. His stiff forelegs splay out to the sides like stilts, for he's been caught in the act of reaching down for water. Without taking his eyes from her, he twitches a little at the knee, then the shoulder, where a fly devils him. Finally he surrenders his surprise, looks away, and drinks. She can feel the touch of his long, curled tongue on the water's skin, as if he were lapping from her hand. His head bobs gently, nodding small, velvet horns lit white from behind like new leaves.
>
> It lasted just a moment, whatever that is. One held breath? An ant's afternoon? If was brief, I can promise that much, for although it's been many years now since my children ruled my life, a mother recalls the measure of the silences. I never had more than five minutes' peace unbroken. I was that woman on the stream bank, of course. Orleanna Price, Southern Baptist by marriage, mother of children living and dead. That one time and no other the okapi came to the stream, and I was the only one to see it.

Have you ever spent 258 words developing a symbol? Kingsolver does that here, to highly poetic effect. In fact, part of what makes her symbols poetic is that all of them emerge from the natural environment around her characters. Nathan Price's garden provides many of them. Price plants his seeds in a flat rectangle of soil, failing to understand that torrential afternoon downpours will swamp the garden; he should, instead, mound the earth around each plant. Sure enough, the rains make a lake of his Eden patch.

Then, one day early in their stay in the remote village of Kalinga, the Price family finds a nest of baby birds fallen from a hibiscus bush. The baby birds have drowned in the garden. Kingsolver does not belabor the image, but, even so, its effect is felt. Can there be any doubt that Nathan Price's rigid ignorance will have tragic consequences for his children? Later, the poisonwood tree in their yard gives Nathan a hideous, itching rash, and the meaning is the same: Nathan Price is messing with a place he does not understand or respect.

A more amusing symbol is waiting for the Price family upon their arrival: an African gray parrot named Methuselah who was left for them by their predecessor. Unfortunately, Methuselah mimics human speech. The parrot is, consequently, somewhat foul-mouthed. When Nathan Price first hears Methuselah growl "Piss off," he declares, "That is a Catholic bird." Methuselah gets the girls in trouble, and eventually escapes and flies away into the jungle. He would be nothing more than comic relief, but Kingsolver later brings Methuselah back to devil Nathan Price with his uncensored mimicry. The bird becomes a symbol, standing in for the persistence of the jungle, local culture, political reality, and Price's own failure to have an impact on the community that he has come to convert to Christianity.

Are there physical objects or recurring events that might serve as symbols in your novel? The exercise that follows asks you not to impose symbols on your manuscript, but to discover them already there, buried like artifacts that readers can happen upon and enjoy, either consciously or not, for the extra meaning that they add to your story.

Symbols are anything outward that stands in for anything inward or abstract, such as a mood or an idea.

Creating Symbols

Step 1: What is one prominent object, event, or action that appears in your novel? *Write it down.*

_____

_____

_____

_____

_____

_____

Step 2: How can that object, event, or action recur at your novel's end? *Write that down.*

_____

_____

_____

_____

Step 3: Find three other places where this object, event, or action can recur in the course of the story. *Add them to your manuscript.*

_____

_____

_____

_____

NOTE:
Whether it is a gathering hurricane or a pink ribbon from a childhood Christmas package, symbols gain power as they recur. Naturally a hurricane forming in every scene would be a ridiculous run of bad weather, but as the opening and closing framework to a story? That can work. Same thing with rings, ribbons, whopping cranes, green Packard convertibles—any natural or inanimate object that returns at portentous moments. Such objects soak up meaning and then release it.

Follow-up work: What is the opposite of that object, event, or action? Find a place for that to appear or occur too. *Make notes.*

_____

_____

_____

_____

_____

Conclusion: Sometimes called objective correlatives, symbols can be overly obvious, but when cleverly chosen and tactically deployed they can punctuate a story in powerful ways.

33

Brainstorming

Did you ever hear a premise, snap your fingers, and think to yourself, "Now, *that* is a great idea for a story!" Of maybe you thought, "Dang, I wish I had thought of that one myself!"

Some ideas are like that: They immediately engage. They are naturals. Right away the story begins to write itself in your head. You can see what will happen first and exactly how it will go after that. Strangely, although the story already is familiar, so much so that you have begun to appropriate it, your feeling is not "How common," but "How original!"

What causes that reaction? Why is it that although there are no new stories, some ideas nevertheless feel fresh? I believe that there are several qualities that can invoke that feeling.

First is the surprising new twist on an old idea. Take the murder mystery: The essential story is the same every time. Someone is killed, and a detective figures out who did it. So familiar is this formula that it is frequently reduced to "who-dunit." Many mystery manuscripts are pitched to me, and most feel as tired as the formula. They lack spark, meaning they bring nothing new to the genre. But now and again an idea comes along that's got a brand-new twist.

Every detective has a *method* of detection. It started with the ruthless logic of Sherlock Holmes. But logic is not the only way to arrive at a solution. Gut intuition is another, but that, too, has become commonplace. What is left? In Matthew Pearl's *The Dante Club*, set in 1865 in the city of Boston, a killer is dispatching his victims in gristly ways reminiscent of Dante's *Inferno*. Since Dante's work is not yet translated into English in 1865, Boston's scholars fear that they will be suspected. It is understandable, then, when this limited circle (the "Dante Club" of the title) bands together to catch the killer and clear their collective name.

Had Pearl merely assembled, as he does, four famous names of the era (Oliver Wendell Holmes, Henry Wadsworth Longfellow, James Russell Lowell, and publisher J.T. Fields) *The Dante Club* would not have felt original. Historical figures have turned into detectives many times. It is this group's special expertise in Dante and how they employ it to catch a killer that provokes a snap of the fingers. Even better, Pearl uses Dante not only to color the killer, but as a lens to view tensions in the halls of Harvard and in the streets of Boston, where waves of immigration are changing the face of America.

Just as there are methods of detection, there are means of murder, or *modus operandi*. An example can be found in Alice Blanchard's *The Breathtaker*. In this whirlwind thriller, Blanchard spins the story of a small-town police chief, Charlie Grover, who must track a serial killer who strikes only during tornados.

Blanchard told *Publishers Weekly* in an interview that she likes "when a person is confronted with something huge. When someone murders, they rip through someone's life like a tornado will rip through a land and tear everything apart." So it is for Charlie Grover, who in additional plot layers faces the scars left by a childhood fire that killed his mother and sister, and who in the present copes with a sixteen-year-old daughter who is enchanted by a troubled teenage storm chaser.

Wounded detectives and detective dads are nothing new. It is the twisters that stir up *The Breathtaker* and give it originality.

Combining two stories in unexpected ways can be a synthesis that also feels original. Hollywood novels have been written for years. So have novels about diseases and their effects. But putting those together? That is what Elisabeth Robinson does in *The True and Outstanding Adventures of the Hunt Sisters*), the story of struggling Hollywood film producer Olivia Hunt, who chronicles a year during which her sister in Ohio is diagnosed with leukemia. The parallel stories of Olivia's attempt to produce *Don Quixote* and her visits to her dying sister are not obviously compatible, but they work together in ways that they would not if they stood alone. Their combination is original.

Sometimes it is nothing more than the gut emotional appeal of a story that sweeps away comparisons and makes it feel one-of-a-kind. Elizabeth Berg is good at this. She told *The Writer* that her stories start with nothing more than a feeling, a practice that has pulled her into novels about coming to terms with an abusive father (*Durable Goods*), women helping a friend through breast cancer (*Talk Before Sleep*), and a wife's persistence while her husband is in a coma (*Range of Motion*). None of these premises are particularly new, but Berg's ability to get to the emotional heart of these situations has made her a best seller.

Nicholas Sparks also can tug at his readers' heartstrings in ways that make his novels more than run-of-the-mill romantic tragedies. Sparks started his first blockbuster, *The Notebook*, with an ending. Sparks told *Writer's Digest* that he knew it would have to be powerful enough to generate word of mouth. It involves a death (speaking of high moments), but prior to that his story successfully captures the wonder of everlasting love. Who can resist that? Go deep enough, as Sparks does, and readers may feel that they have never before experienced this special bliss.

A reversal of the expected also can feel original. For instance, most single women would not care to become pregnant, right? The results of home pregnancy tests usually are dreaded. But in Lauren Baratz-Logsted's debut novel, *The Thin Pink Line*, named for the telltale line on a pregnancy test strip, London editor

Jane Taylor finds herself pregnant and learns that she likes it. Her lackadaisical boyfriend suddenly seems ready to commit. Friends and strangers treat her well. When it turns out that she is not pregnant after all, Jane fakes it for nine months. Jane's escalating efforts to maintain the ruse are hilarious, and steadily ratchet up the stakes in Baratz-Logsted's most original reversal.

Another lighthearted flip-flop of the familiar can be found in Sherrilyn Kenyon's romance *Fantasy Lover*. Kenyon's heroine is sex therapist Grace Alexander. You would expect that someone in her profession would have a healthy enjoyment of eroticism, but Kenyon neatly upends that expectation. Grace hates sex. Indeed, she has been celibate for four years. Who is the perfect foil for this repression? Who else? A Greek god, and so one is summoned by Grace's friend Selena from the pages of an ancient tome where he is cursed to live until he is called out once in a while to . . . um, lend a hand.

Julian of Macedon, half god, half mortal, fortunately is up to the job of thawing Grace's libido. In yet another switch it turns out that something else needs thawing: Julian's heart, which is frozen thanks to the once-cruel life that cursed him. These two are inwardly conflicted. Kenyon also, by the way, tosses in a cast of secondary characters that includes Julian's family of Greek gods and goddesses. Talk about complications! Retold myths and fairy tales are common in the romance field today, but Kenyon's employment of the power of reversal makes *Fantasy Lover* stand out.

Can a story premise get even more unexpected? If you don't think so, then you have not yet discovered the loopy, inside-out novels of Christopher Moore. In titles like *Bloodsucking Fiends: A Love Story, Island of the Sequined Love Nun,* and *Lamb: The Gospel According to Biff, Christ's Childhood Pal,* Moore more than amply demonstrates his gift for originality. In *Fluke, or, I Know Why the Winged Whale Sings,* Moore introduces Nate Quinn, a researcher of whale squeals.

Nate is swallowed by whale. What is original about that, you ask? Nothing, except that the whale has "Bite Me" scrawled on its fluke, phones a delicatessen to order pastrami on rye, and is part of a huge organism called the Goo. You cannot say you have read that before, can you? With Moore, it is not the basic premise that feels original but its zany and unexpected elaboration.

Every working novelist must come up with ideas, but beyond the premise is its development into a full-fledged plot. The process by which that happens is brainstorming. Step by step, the logic and progression of the story is worked out until something like a novel comes into focus. No one expects an author to stick precisely to the original outline; indeed, some authors cannot work with outlines at all.

It doesn't matter. Whether following a map or making it up as he goes along, every novelist sooner or later spins a basic idea into a full novel. Too often in manuscripts, however, I watch the original inspiration become dissipated. What started out as an original-feeling premise turns into a set of ordinary characters and rote complications.

The key to keeping a novel lively and surprising is remembering the principle of reversal. When mapping out a scene, toss out your first choices and go

Combining two stories in unexpected ways can be a synthesis that also feels original.

the opposite way. Why? Because first choices tend to be the safest choices. We shape action in the ways that we think it ought to go if our novels are going to be accepted by agents, and later by editors. Meaning that they become predictable. Scenes that go in unexpected directions can be more difficult to work out, but they are more engaging to read. (See the Reversing Motives exercise in chapter six.)

The secret of going the opposite way can be seen clearly in the Breakout Novel Workshops when participants and I together brainstorm a story in about fifteen minutes. We start with basic choices about setting, protagonist, and problem, and then riff. Each time it is the less obvious choices for character or plot that engage the group's interest. There is usually one unexpected (read: original) element that requires a lot of discussion. In the end, though, everyone agrees that this path is more interesting to take.

So, when cooking up ideas, look for new twists on old ideas. Combine stories. Go for gut emotional appeal, and reverse the expected. Then work out a full story but not in easy and obvious ways. Remember the power of reversal. Take your first impulses, and go the opposite way. That is the secret of brainstorming.

Will you always be original if you follow this advice? Probably, though sometimes lack of originality cannot be helped: Certain ideas and motifs enter the collective unconscious, and so one year we may find ourselves with a surfeit of novels about, say, coming of age in Eastern Europe. That is what happened in 2002, in fact, when four novels on that subject were published: Arthur Phillips's *Prague*, Gary Shteyngart's *The Russian Debutante's Handbook*, John Beckman's *The Winter Zoo*, and Jonathan Foer's *Everything is Illuminated*. In cases like that there is nothing to do except to make one's novel as original, and tense, as possible. That will almost always put it ahead of the pack.

Mostly, though, originality is within everyone's reach. Practice the techniques of brainstorming: new twists on old ideas, combining stories, gut emotional appeal, and reversing the expected. Those techniques will steer you to some challenging, and definitely interesting, choices for your story.

Developing Brainstorming Skills

Step 1: Pick a time and place. Pick a protagonist. Pick a problem. *Start brainstorming a story.*

_____

_____

_____

_____

_____

Step 2: Every time you write down an idea, reverse it. Go the opposite way. See where it takes you.

_____

_____

_____

_____

_____

> **!**
>
> **NOTE:**
> When brainstorming with a group, when I ask for a villain you would be amazed at how often "a senator" is suggested. It is a default choice: easy, obvious, and safe. Because it is expected, it is also boring.
>
> The best villain is often less obvious; someone who is, say, connected to the hero in a personal way. A better choice than "senator" is almost always, "the hero's mentor." You see? It takes work to make that person a credible antagonist, but the conflict between hero and villain is already more complex because of their prior alliance.

Follow-up work: Go through your folder of story ideas. Put a check mark on those that offer a new twist on an old idea, or that have gut emotional appeal. Try combining ideas. Also try tuning them upside down and inside out. Reverse them. See what happens.

_____

_____

Conclusion: Whatever you do, push your premises and plotlines further. Do not be satisfied with just a good story. Be satisfied only with a story that is original, gut grabbing, unexpected, layered, and complex. In other words, stop working only when your story is great. How will you know? I cannot tell you, but I can say this: It will take longer than you think. Keep pushing.

34

The Pitch

Whether we're aware of it or not, we all pitch stories all the time. Did you see a movie last weekend? Did you tell your co-workers about it at the office on Monday morning? Your quick take on that film is the kind of pitch that either turns on or turns off your co-workers. You are selling it. (Or panning it.)

In the book publishing business everyone must pitch: author to agent, agent to editor, editor to sales rep, sales rep to buyer, bookstore owner to customer. The worst pitchers by far are authors. I know. I get those pitches in the form of query letters: 250 of them per week. The majority of them are ineffective, full of hype and needlessly long plot synopsis. Some rattle on for pages in microscopic fonts, lines crammed together and spread out to the outer edges of the page.

In response, most queries get from us form rejections. A smaller number get a personal response from me, and only a handful (two to six a week) inspire me to request a portion of the manuscript to sample. That is a low ratio of success. Some of the manuscripts on which I pass may be brilliantly written—who knows? The letters pitching them are not.

Why not? I have talked with authors across the country in pitch crafting workshops, and several answers consistently emerge. In pitching their stories authors feel anxious. They do not know the agent to whom they are writing, or the agent's taste. Will their novel appeal? What about it will appeal? What if the crucial detail that would appeal to a particular agent is the detail that is left out?

Then there is the problem of boiling down a 450-page story, say, into four punchy lines. How can one possibly do that? Isn't it better to put in as much of the plot as possible?

From the receiving end of these pitches, I can tell you that it is not. Long plot summary overwhelms the person getting the pitch, and hype has the opposite of the intended effect. Sometimes at writers conferences I sit in rooms where authors are meeting one-on-one with agents and editors. Again and again, I watch my colleagues' eyes glaze over as nervous writers launch into rambling plot summaries or spew empty hype about the impact their novels are certain to have and about the gigantic size of their likely audiences. Query letters along those lines produce the same numbed glaze.

So, what does work in query letters? First, brevity. With 250 queries arriving each week, that is appreciated. Second, writing in a straightforward and businesslike way. This is, after all, a business transaction. Third, just enough about your novel to tell me whether I would like to have a look.

Ah. That's the tough part. What is "just enough"? Think about it: In the office on Monday morning, how much does it take to suggest to you that you might like to go see the movie that opened last weekend? Not much. The same is true in queries. All I need to get hooked on a story is to know its category, the setting, the protagonist, and the main problem. Add to that one unusual detail that makes this story different from any other like it, and you've probably got me.

Start with category. Keep it simple: Mainstream? Literary? Mystery? Thriller? Women's? Romance? Science Fiction? Fantasy? Historical? Western? Horror? Young Adult? You can get more specific than that, I guess, but why bother? The category only locates your novel on a mental map of the publishing business, telling me to which group of editors I might submit it and the section of the bookstore in which it ultimately will live and find its readers.

Setting and protagonist? Those are easy, and again, keep them simple. You can flesh out either one, but only a little coloring is needed. Is there inherent conflict in your setting? Is it a world of clashing values? Fine. Done. Is your protagonist conflicted? Okay. A snippet about that is enough.

What is the main problem? After doing the exercises in this book that should be easier to say simply. Some query writers find a reduction of the central conflict too frightening. They prefer to start with the inciting incident, the moment when the problem begins, and let the story blossom from there. That approach can work, but it is tricky and dangerous. Once cruising down the highway of plot summary it is tempting to stay on it. My advice: Exit immediately.

The detail that makes the story different usually is lacking, even in letters that go on for pages. So many novels sound ordinary and unoriginal, like I have read them before. Probably I have. There are no new stories, after all, just new ways of telling them. And *that* is what I am interested in. What is different about the method of detection in *this* mystery novel? What makes *that* romance heroine's desire more aching than any other's? How about the era portrayed in your historical? What is your new angle on it? What is the twist or turn in your mainstream novel that no one sees coming? Yes, give it away! Why are you saving it?

Can a query letter truly persuade me to request a manuscript based on so little? Yes, and they do. It doesn't take much. The best queries are confident. They put across the essence of the story in one hundred words or less. I have seen it done in forty words and fewer. That is hard to believe, I know, but why would I lie? Take it from a pro.

I must pitch every day. Knowing how little is needed by the editors, subagents, scouts, and producers with whom I work, I keep my pitches short. A certain amount of enthusiasm in my voice can help, and maybe is necessary, but that is because I am an objective third party. From a self-interested author, enthusiasm sounds like hype. It doesn't work.

I usually let the story itself do the work, in fact. If a story is solid, it doesn't take much pushing for savvy editors to see its potential. By way of example, let me show you a couple of pitches that I recently e-mailed to editors.

The first is a smallish but beautifully written literary novel set in contemporary Cuba, full of fine observation of late Castro era Havana and elsewhere. The main character is a dying revolutionary hero who worries that his grandson does not embrace the values that he fought for. Indeed, the grandson does not. He longs for change. In between is a son/father who feels hopeless and stuck in a menial job. There is rich detail and moving incident throughout this novel—far too much to convey in a pitch. So I did not try:

> In Karen Campagna's debut literary novel, *Snowfall on Habana*, three generations of Cuban men—Lazaro, Ruben, and Andres—journey in a beautiful vintage Packard across the length of Cuba with a very dangerous cargo in the trunk. Riding with them is Lazaro's beautiful nurse, Flores, whose presence changes them all in different ways as their journey becomes a metaphor for the past, present, and future of Cuba.

Category, setting, protagonist(s), and problem—the "dangerous cargo" in the trunk. The extra detail is the beautiful nurse who rides with them. As you can see this is a simple pitch, just sixty-seven words, but every editor to whom I sent it asked for the manuscript. I do not know whether or not the novel will sell. That is now up to the novel itself. The pitch, though, did its job: Getting the manuscript into editors' hands.

A more challenging pitch was for a World War II thriller of exceptionally high quality. In this story about the rescue of a train full of Dutch Jews on their way to the camps in Eastern Europe in 1942, the author weaves in many plot layers. The hero begins as an antihero, a hit man for New York Jewish gangster Meyer Lansky.

This amoral thug, nicknamed Mouse, is sent on the rescue mission to watch over Meyer Lansky's money, which is funding this desperate plan. Throughout the course of the story he transforms from amoral crook to proud Jew to true hero. He falls for a girl in the Dutch resistance who teaches him the meaning of love while he teaches her how to kill. A host of secondary characters is included, among them a hot-headed commando who hates Mouse, the commando's beautiful English girlfriend, a Dutch partisan who is desperate to rescue his wife in Amsterdam, the wife who is saved in a heart-stopping act of self-sacrifice, a German SS officer under pressure to round up Jews to meet impossible quotas, a Dutch police officer who is a double agent . . . you get the idea.

Big cast, big story. There is no way to get all that into a pitch, but it wasn't necessary. It was enough merely to suggest the novel's complexity:

In Gregg Keizer's WWII thriller *The Longest Day*, it is 1942. Jewish leaders, aware of the deportation of Western European Jews to the death camps, conceive a bold plan to call the deportations to the attention of Allied leaders. A commando team is ready. The problem? No money. For financing, they turn to New York gangster Meyer Lansky, who sends his cash in the company of an amoral hit man, "Mouse" Weis, who hates the whole idea. Mouse plans to kill the commando team and make off with Lansky's money, but it is not to be.

Through a brave Dutch resistance operative named Reka, Mouse discovers the transforming power of love and the courage to wear a yellow star. Hampered by a commando team wracked by conflict, racing against a German officer who knows in advance their every move, on the longest day of their lives Mouse and Reka together attempt what the SS has declared will be impossible: the diversion of a train full of Dutch Jews to the North Sea coast for rescue.

Even at 173 words, the above leaves out enormous chunks of Keizer's novel. Nevertheless, the above pitch propelled the manuscript into the hands of an editor at G.P. Putnam's Sons. After that, Keizer's superb first novel did the work. Putnam's pre-empted the competition with a six-figure advance.

An even more complex novel that I am currently pitching is an ancient Egyptian saga, a breakout-scale novel by mystery novelist Lynda S. Robinson. Robinson's prior series featured the Chief of State Security for the boy king Tutankhamen, Lord Meren. Robinson here brings Meren back for a gigantic thriller, pitting him against the most deadly adversary Egypt has ever known, his ex-lover and undercover operative Anath, whom Tut has had tortured and executed (so Meren thinks) for treason. With many points of view and a panoramic portrayal of the splendor that was ancient Egypt, Robinson orchestrates a sage of enormous richness and complexity.

How to boil it down? Here's how I did:

In *The Warrior King*, Tutankhamen's powerful empire is beset by outside enemies and torn from within by grasping factions. The son of a heretic, Tut's hold on power is precarious. Only the wise and canny Lord Meren, Tut's spy master, keeps the boy king on his throne. But their father-son relationship, once more important to Meren than life itself, has been ruined by Tut's decision to kill the only woman that Meren has ever truly loved, the traitorous spy Anath. Unknown to both Meren and Tut, Anath has survived her gristly execution and, with the help of the Hittite king Suppiluliumas, has conceived a vast plan to undermine Egypt and wreck hideous revenge on Tut and Meren. Only king and mentor working together can save the empire—yet how can they succeed when their respect and trust has been irrevocably shattered?

Again, tons of action and several huge subplots are left out of brief description. But so what? It is enough merely to suggest something of the sweep and grandeur of the whole.

Use the exercise that follows to hone down the essentials of your story, then trust your premise to excite the agents and editors whom you have targeted. After all, your story is original, isn't it? The world in which it is set is rife with conflict, right? You have invested your story with power and gut emotional appeal? Right, then. You have it all.

Constructing the Pitch

Step 1: Write down your novel's title, category, setting, protagonist, and central problem: the main conflict, goal, need, yearning, or hope.

_____

_____

Step 2: Write down one colorful detail that makes any one of the above elements different.

_____

_____

_____

_____

Step 3: Identify a way in which your story has any one of the following:
- ❑ Credibility *(This could happen to any of us)*
- ❑ Inherent Conflict *(This is a world of conflicting forces.)*
- ❑ Originality *(A reversal of the expected, a new angle on an old subject, or familiar story elements combined in unfamiliar ways.)*
- ❑ Gut Emotional Appeal *(I would hate it if that happened to me!)*

Step 4: Write down these five words: *love, heart, dream, journey, fortune, destiny.*

_____

_____

Step 5: Set a timer for five minutes. *Five minutes only!* In that time, write a one-paragraph pitch for your novel, incorporating the material you wrote down in steps one-three. In your last sentence, use one of the words you wrote down in step four.

_____

_____

_____

_____

_____

NOTE:

Most novelists agonize over pitching their novels, especially in query letters. How to reduce 450 pages to a mere paragraph? It seems impossible, but it is not. In the workshops participants not only boil down their novels, they do so in just five minutes. Impressed? I am not. I pitch novels every day in thirty seconds or less. Sometimes I do not even prepare but improvise on the spot, just for the fun of it. It is easier than you think.

Consider: We summarize movies, TV shows, and books all the time, and rarely take more than thirty seconds to do so. Why is it so much easier to boil down someone else's story than our own? It is because we are afraid: afraid to leave something out. What if we exclude the one crucial detail that would catch someone else's interest? Better to cram in as much as you can, right?

Wrong. Next time you are at a writers conference, listen to someone give a blow-by-blow account of their plot. It is stultifying. Eyes glaze over. People leave, if they can. Actually, all it really takes to interest someone in a story is its beginning: the setting, the protagonist, and the problem. That's it. Fixing the problem and no more leaves your listener wondering what will happen next, rather than wondering when you will ever shut up. The same principle applies in query letters. Get me a little interested in your setting and protagonist (one colorful detail), and set an interesting problem. Probably I will wonder, *so how does it come out?* If I do, and if I ask for some of the manuscript to read, then the query letter has done its job.

Follow-up work: Put away your pitch for a week or more, then re-read it. Shorten it to one hundred words. Put it away for another week. Now shorten it to fifty words.

Conclusion: In pitching, less is more. It is fear that makes us blather on and on about our stories, killing interest in them with every juicy detail that we pile on. Save those for the novel itself. In your pitch, keep it clean and simple. Say less than you want to. Interest in your novel will be that much greater for your restraint.

Appendix A: Outlining Your Novel

Outlines are an essential tool for working novelists, yet even full-time professionals can feel anxiety when faced with writing them. "I'm no good at outlines," many say to me. "How long does it have to be? Can you send me examples?"

This from long-published fiction writers! In a way their anxiety is understandable. There are no courses I know of in outline writing. I can find no books on the subject, no anthologies of successful outlines. It is an arcane art. Even so, every novelist sooner or later must practice it.

Many fiction writers—possibly even half of them, judging from my informal surveys—do not outline their novels in advance. Many simply hate them. They find that plotting ahead of time is obstructive, a brake on creative flow. Such novelists prefer to feel their way through a first draft, counting on subsequent rewrites to fix any problems and shape the final story. There is nothing wrong with that. It is fine to allow the unconscious mind to guide the process.

However, even intuitive, organic writers sooner or later must face up to the necessity of outlines. Agents request them. Publishers may require them when an option novel is proposed. Hollywood executives can demand them, too, for the sake of convenience. Sooner or later, every novelist has to outline.

You might suppose that the process is easier once a novel is complete, and it can be. It is relatively simple to take a manuscript and summarize it chapter by chapter. Authors who do that, however, are missing an opportunity. Outlining can be a creative act either before or after a novel is written.

In fact, I strongly recommend that you let it be so. If you are reading this appendix merely to learn how to format an outline for a novel that already is complete, please reconsider. Use the outlining process to discover new dimensions in your story. There are aspects of your novel that you have not yet discovered, and the outlining process will help you illuminate them. You see untapped potential in others' manuscripts, right? The same probably is true of yours.

If you are planning a story that you have yet to write, the outlining process can be more than drawing a map of what already is in your head. It can expand your mind. There is potential in every premise, and the outline process can develop that. Do not be satisfied merely to sketch your story, or even to flesh it out. Reach for its heights; pull from its depths. The finished outline should surprise you.

Now, some technical points: How long should an outline be? At every writers conference I attend, I get that anxious question. Fiction writers are confused. Some agents say they want two pages, I am told, others ten. What is right?

It amazes me that authors expect consistency in agents' preferences. How can there be consistency? Some agents like short outlines, others like outlines with more detail. What's the big deal? Write both. The process I will lead you through in this appendix will show you how both are done.

There also is no magic number of pages for a detailed outline. *War and Peace* needs more than ten pages, don't you think? Write as long an outline as your novel needs. That said, an outline of less than five pages probably will feel thin, while an outline of more than twenty-five pages probably will feel overburdened. Shoot for ten pages; add more if needed.

Format? Single-spaced or double-spaced is your choice. If you single space, add a line break between paragraphs to make it easier on the eyes. The majority of outlines I see are double-spaced, however, so why not use that format?

For some reason, outlines seem most effective when they are written in the third person and the present tense. Don't ask me why. Perhaps they are more visual, more like film treatments. Who knows? All I can tell you is that professionally written outlines are almost always third person and present tense, regardless of the person and tense of the novel. Stick with that. It reads well and is expected.

For God's sake, include the ending. You wouldn't believe how many authors imagine that they will spoil the story, or fail to entice agents or editors to read the entire manuscript by including it. Rubbish. Agents and editors are pros. They need to know that you can handle the *whole* story.

What sort of tone are you going for? Objective: commenting on the action of the novel, its themes, and so on? Actually, the most effective outlines are those that are like reading the novel in miniature. They bring us inside characters' heads using strong point of view and highlight the story's turning points in various ways. The outline template on the pages that follow will give you a solid plot spine, the extra layers and subplots that add texture, a sense of the characters' inner lives and changes, and ways to highlight key moments. It may even show you your novel in a way that will enrich it with new material.

Whatever you do, whether you are outlining before or after completing your novel, use this as an opportunity to play. A novel is never done, exactly, and this is a fine opportunity to find new ways to build your novel on a breakout scale.

Steps to Creating an Outline

The number in parenthesis after each step tells you the number of paragraphs that each step will yield. If you are able to follow the steps below exactly, you will wind up with fifty paragraphs. If you then average four paragraphs per page, at the end of this process you will have the rough draft of a twelve-and-a-half page outline. Along the way you may also have found some new material for your novel itself.

1. Plot fundamentals.

Write down the following:

1. Where is your novel set, who is your main character, and what is his main problem, conflict, or goal? (1)
2. What does your protagonist most want, and why? (1)
3. What is your protagonist's second plot layer? (1)
4. What is your protagonist's third plot layer? (1)
5. What is the first subplot? (1)
6. What is the second subplot? (1)
7. Who is the most important secondary or supporting character, what is her main problem, conflict, or goal, and what does she most want? (1)
8. Who is the novel's antagonist, what is his main problem, conflict, or goal, and what does he most want? (1)

2. The middle.

Write down the following:

9. What are the five biggest steps toward the solution of your protagonist's main problem? Another way to ask that is: What are the five turning points or events that you positively cannot leave out? (Include your story's climax.) (5)
10. What are the five most important steps toward, or away from, what your protagonist most wants? (5)
11. What are the three most important steps (each) toward, or away from, the resolution of the second and third plot layers? (6)
12. What are the three most important steps (each) toward, or away from, the resolution of your first and second subplots? (6)
13. What are the three most important steps toward, or away from, the resolution of each main problem facing your foremost secondary character and your antagonist? (6)

3. Highlights.

Write down the following:

14. Two moments of strong inner conflict. (2)
15. Three larger-than-life actions. (3)
16. Five places to heighten turning points or high moments.
17. Two moments frozen in time. (2)
18. Two measures of change. (2)
19. The psychology of place with respect to the setting of the novel's climax. (1)
20. Three dialogue snippets. (3)
21. A paragraph of resolution. (1)

4. Putting it together.

Elaborate in a paragraph what you wrote down in each of the steps above.

Appendix B: Follow-up Work Checklist

Here is a checklist of the follow-up work taken from each exercise in this workbook. In the column on the right are the number of steps needed to complete this work. If you truly wish to write a breakout novel, do each piece of work and check it off the list only when you have incorporated the results into your manuscript. There are 591 steps required. The investment of time to complete this work is huge . . . but then your ambition is huge, too, isn't it? I thought so.

Follow-ups	Tasks:
❑ Demonstrate heroic qualities	6
❑ Create extra character dimensions	3
❑ Make goals mutually exclusive	1
❑ Create larger-than-life moments	12
❑ Heighten speech, action, or exposition	24
❑ Reverse motives in additional scenes	6
❑ Incorporate deeper personal stakes	6
❑ Add the opposite of ultimate commitment	1
❑ Deepen passages of exposition	4
❑ Develop an additional secondary character	5
❑ Develop a secondary antagonist	5
❑ Advance antagonist's interests	5
❑ Combine two more roles	1
❑ Incorporate higher stakes into the story	4
❑ Incorporate damage from complications	3
❑ Develop four steps/scenes for two layers	8
❑ Add nodes of conjunction to the story	6
❑ Add subplots, even to a first-person novel	3
❑ Heighten turning points within scenes	20

Follow-ups	Tasks:
❑ Delineate extra turning points	6
❑ Incorporate high moments	5
❑ Add bridging conflict	4
❑ Cut "tea" (inactive or review) scenes	1
❑ Move backstory back in the manuscript	1
❑ Add tension to each page	350 (*approx.*)
❑ Change your first line	1
❑ Change the last line	1
❑ Freeze moments in time	4
❑ Delineate antagonist's changing view of hero	3
❑ Delineate changing view of a place	2
❑ Strengthen point of view	30
❑ Delineate characters' traits	48
❑ Create impossibly good outcome	1
❑ Develop a secondary theme	4
❑ Incorporate related problems	2
❑ Give someone the opposite problem	1
❑ Make the antagonist right	1
❑ Add the opposite symbol	1
❑ Reverse stockpiled story ideas	1
❑ Shorten your pitch	1

TOTAL TASKS: 591

Index

alternate endings
  exercises, 200
antagonists
  commitment in, 55
  creating sympathetic, 72
  developing, 20, 66-68
  exercises, 69-72, 206-207
  motivating, 88-90

backstory
  defined, 141
  exercises, 146-147
  tension and, 141-145, 149-151
  withholding, 141-145
brainstorming, 213-216
  exercises, 217
brevity, in query letter or pitch, 219
bridging conflicts, 129-131
  exercises, 132-133

category, 219
character behavior
  inappropriate, 25-27
  independent, 33-34
  reversal of, 36-37
  uncharacteristic, 31
  unexpected, 33-34
character delineation, 187-190
  exercises, 191-192
  point of view and, 188-190, 192
character development, 7-11
  convictions, testing, 50-53
  exercises, 12-13
  heroic qualities in, 8-10
  revealing new dimensions in, 14-17
  unattractive qualities in, 10-11
character roles, multiple, 73-75
  exercises, 76-77
character transformation, 27-29
  crisis in, 19
  defining qualities, 18
  memorable, 24, 31
characters, larger-than-life, 25-30, 33-34

exercises, 31-32, 35
characters, multidimensional, 14-17
  exercises, 18
  secondary, 60
characters, secondary, see secondary
    characters
complications, 88-90
  exercises, 91-92
conflict, 223, 227, see also inner conflict
  exercises, 202-205
  theme and, 203
credibility, 223

detail that makes your story different, 219

emotional appeal, 223, see also public stakes
endings
  including in outline, 226
  including in pitch, 219
exposition as self-regard, 56-58
  exercises, 59

first lines, 156-158
  exercises, 161-162

heightening turning points, 111-114
heroes, see protagonists
heroic qualities, 8-11
  exercises, 12-13
high moments, 122-126, 227
  exercises, 127-128

inner change, 170-173
  exercises, 174-175
inner conflict, 19-23
  antagonists and, 66
  backstory and, 142
  exercises, 24
inner turning points, 117-119
  exercises, 120-121
interior monologue, 56
intrigue factor, 158

larger-than-life qualities and actions, 25-30,
    33-34, 227